Faith in Poetry

NEW DIRECTIONS IN RELIGION AND LITERATURE

This series aims to showcase new work at the forefront of religion and literature through short studies written by leading and rising scholars in the field. Books will pursue a variety of theoretical approaches as they engage with writing from different religious and literary traditions. Collectively, the series will offer a timely critical intervention to the interdisciplinary crossover between religion and literature, speaking to wider contemporary interests and mapping out new directions for the field in the early twenty-first century.

Also available from Bloomsbury

Beyond the Willing Suspension of Disbelief, Michael Tomko
The Bible in the American Short Story, Lesleigh Cushing Stahlberg and Peter S. Hawkins
Blake. Wordsworth. Religion, Jonathan Roberts
Dante and the Sense of Transgression, William Franke
Do the Gods Wear Capes?, Ben Saunders
England's Secular Scripture, Jo Carruthers
Faith in Poetry, Michael D. Hurley
Forgiveness in Victorian Literature, Richard Hughes Gibson
The Glyph and the Gramophone, Luke Ferretter
The Gospel According to David Foster Wallace, Adam S. Miller
The Gospel According to the Novelist, Magdalena Mączyńska
Jewish Feeling, Richa Dwor
John Cage and Buddhist Ecopoetics, Peter Jaeger
Late Walter Benjamin, John Schad
The New Atheist Novel, Arthur Bradley and Andrew Tate
Pentecostal Modernism, Stephen Shapiro and Philip Barnard
Rewriting the Old Testament in Anglo-Saxon Verse, Samantha Zacher
Victorian Parables, Susan E. Colón

Forthcoming

Romantic Enchantment, Gavin Hopps
Sufism in Western Literature, Art and Thought, Ziad Elmarsafy
Weird Faith in 19th Century Literature, Mark Knight and Emma Mason

Faith in Poetry

Verse Style as a Mode of Religious Belief

MICHAEL D. HURLEY

BLOOMSBURY ACADEMIC
LONDON • NEW YORK • OXFORD • NEW DELHI • SYDNEY

BLOOMSBURY ACADEMIC
Bloomsbury Publishing Plc
50 Bedford Square, London, WC1B 3DP, UK
1385 Broadway, New York, NY 10018, USA

BLOOMSBURY, BLOOMSBURY ACADEMIC and the Diana logo
are trademarks of Bloomsbury Publishing Plc

First published 2018
Paperback edition first published 2019

Cover design: Eleanor Rose
Image shows a detail from *The Dream of the Poet* or, *The Kiss of the Muse*, 1859-60
(oil on canvas), Cezanne, Paul (1839-1906) © Musee Granet, Aix-en-Provence, France /
Bridgeman Images

A catalogue record for this book is available from the British Library.

Library of Congress Cataloging-in-Publication Data
Names: Hurley, Michael D. (Michael Dominic), 1976- author.
Title: Faith in poetry: verse style as a mode of religious belief / Michael D. Hurley.
Description: London; New York: Bloomsbury Academic, 2018. | Series: New directions
in religion and literature | Includes index. Identifiers: LCCN 2017023373|
ISBN 9781474234078 (hardback) | ISBN 9781474234085 (epub) Subjects:
LCSH: English poetry–History and criticism. | Religion and literature–Great Britain. |
Religion in literature. | Theology in literature. | Religious poetry, English–History and criticism.
Classification: LCC PR508.R4 H87 2018 | DDC 821.009/382–dc23 LC record available at
https://lccn.loc.gov/2017023373

ISBN: HB: 978-1-4742-3407-8
PB: 978-1-3501-1163-9
ePDF: 978-1-4742-3409-2
ePub: 978-1-4742-3408-5

Series: New Directions in Religion and Literature

Typeset by Deanta Global Publishing Services, Chennai, India

To find out more about our authors and books visit
www.bloomsbury.com and sign up for our newsletters.

For Jilly

Contents

Acknowledgements

This book was written in a concentrated burst but after a long period of gestation. The debts I owe are therefore pressingly current but also go rather far back, and I cannot register them all here. I should, however, like to pay special thanks to the late Peter Hardwick, formerly of Stonyhurst College, who was the greatest of teachers, and who first inspired my own faith in poetry; he remains 'the reader over my shoulder'. I am immensely grateful to the people who generously (in every sense) read draft chapters, or who took the time to discuss my inchoate ideas: Stephen Blackwood, Thomas Docherty, Martin Dubois, Sarah Haggarty, Jason Harding, Ewan Jones, Robin Kirkpatrick, Raphael Lyne, Anna Nickerson, Marcus Waithe, Phyllis Weliver and Ross Wilson. Mark Knight and Emma Mason, the series editors for Bloomsbury, were good enough to encourage me to write something for them in the first place, and their feedback on my ensuing manuscript was brilliantly insightful, and much appreciated. Over the years, my students have helped me refine my appreciation of the poets covered in this study, and I value especially the MPhil class of 2017 who took my course on 'Faith in Poetry': their lively and incisive contributions were wonderful stimulation in the final stages of writing up. Finally, I must thank the Master and Fellows of St Catharine's College, Cambridge, for supporting my research. This book is dedicated to my fiercely loving and loyal wife, *sine qua non*.

University of Cambridge
Lent 2017

Introduction: Styling Faith

You can refute Hegel but not the Saint or the Song of Sixpence.[1]

Poets profess their faith in poetry by trusting it to say and do things that could not otherwise be said or done. To versify is to believe in verse. Composition is poetry's essential credo, as it is also its best proof, avowing while demonstrating its special status and facility. Why not turn instead to prose, or sculpture, or the medium of dance? If the same or better might be achieved in another way, poetry would have no exclusive value; whereas its presence at the heart of Western culture declares the opposite.[2]

So much is clear, but little else. Poets bear witness to their faith in poetry through their poems, but quite what it is that poetry can achieve, or should do, has yielded diverse and sometimes incompatible verdicts. *The Iliad* and *The Odyssey* are equivocal in the claims they make for poetry's ability to afford, on the one hand, powerfully transporting experiences and, on the other hand, transformative philosophical or moral truths.[3] What is the validity of each of these possibilities, and are they competing or complementary? The ancients had their own answers, prompting further unresolved questions on a vast array of related subjects, from mimesis and genre to sublimity and inspiration; but it is Plato's intervention on poetry (itself intriguingly equivocal, torn between admiration and suspicion) that proves most influential. A. N. Whitehead once claimed that the safest general characterization of the European philosophical tradition is that 'it consists of a series of footnotes to Plato',[4] and something of the same might be said of poetics: Plato's interventions set the terms and frame the debates that follow.

But Christian poets also change the poetic paradigm, by compounding the creative burden. They make their art accountable to the immanent stringencies of the artisan, but also to the transcendent truths of their God. Decanting visions, convictions or dogmas into inapt forms makes poor poetry, and by extension, the religious faith to which it speaks lacks vitality, and perhaps authenticity too. 'Metaphysics snatches at the spiritual in an idea, by the most abstract intellection; poetry reaches it in the flesh, by the very point of the sense sharpened through intelligence':[5] Jacques Maritain captures memorably the incarnational character of verse, its signal capacity to breathe life into thought. But poetry's occulting powers over language are not inevitable; they need to be activated. Religious conviction and a conviction to write is not in itself enough. Faith in poetry demands also an intuitive awareness of its mode, and the artistry to wield it. 'The road to Damascus may offer a pilgrim sudden and miraculous intervention', Dana Gioia allows, 'but faith provides no shortcuts on the road to Parnassus'.[6]

Putting faith in poetry in that double sense – poetic and religious – conjoins aesthetics with metaphysics; if either is forced or faulty, neither succeeds. Or to make the same point positively, exemplars from the Christian tradition evince a profound, creative continuity between their subjects and their styles. Boethius's *De consolatione philosophiae*, for instance, has been described as having had the single most important influence on Christianity of the Middle Ages and early Renaissance,[7] and what sustains that poem's religious faith is a faith in poetry itself. For the 'consolation' it describes and dramatizes – curing the prisoner-protagonist's sickness – is effected through its prosody. Metrical therapy enacts an unfolding of divine simplicity into the movement of time, such that (as Stephen Blackwood has trenchantly observed) the text's psychagogic sounds and rhythms become a sensible meditation of divine eternity, having the quality of a repeated liturgical act.[8]

Almost eight centuries later, when Dante came to write his own *poema sacro*, he was similarly preoccupied with how verse might enable his theological and religious vision, as well as his creedal understanding. I have elsewhere argued for the puissance of Dante's prosody in respect of his faith,[9] but suffice to notice here that he vaunts the poet as craftsman (*fabbro*) as well as visionary, and that while his *Commedia* identifies Boethius as the first of the Scholastics among the doctors in his Paradise, he does not emulate Boethian style. He rejects the august epic of classical antiquity in favour of a self-consciously rough vernacular diction (*De vulgari eloquentia*), and his own metrical innovation of *terza rima* suggests at a macro-level what his micro-choices of individual word, image, rhythm and rhyme reveal throughout. Namely, that while the poem's faith is framed by doctrine, and Dante's theological allegiances are implicated at the deepest level of his verse form (in the Trinitarian associations of *terza rima*, not to mention the wider structural occurrences of threes, nines and thirty-three in the poem), his faith is also experienced dynamically, as a perilously unfolding journey, spurred into life and purpose at the turn of each new rhyme and line.

To take one final example: when, in the turbulent wake of the Reformation, Milton took up his pen to 'justify the ways of God to man', he too was aware that he must first justify the ways of poetry. *Paradise Lost* is governed by a self-consciously re-formed poetics, by strategies that are prosodically as well as doctrinally at odds with Dante's example, seen most conspicuously in his rejection of end-rhyme, which he dismisses as 'bondage', and as part of a regrettable Catholic habit of distracted 'jingling'.[10] When he puts his contradistinctive Protestant faith in poetry, he does so through his own *sui generis* expression of the 'grand style'.[11]

What connects Boethius, Dante and Milton, what makes them exemplars here, is not the plain fact that they were all poets who wrote on religious themes. Collectively, what's instructive about *De consolatione philosophiae*, the *Commedia*, and *Paradise Lost* is the way these great poems – among the greatest in the Christian tradition – explore as well as express the religious truth that is their theme. They form part of an unbroken canon that, while wrangling over ecclesiastical and aesthetic details, invests in verse as a unique mode. Poetry within this tradition is 'religious' not merely for what it illustrates, but for what it is. The pressing challenge for all poets is one of commensurability: to find or found a style adequate to their subjects. But at its height, religious poetry asks more of itself than that its form might find continuity with its content; it aims not simply to delineate theological niceties, but to become itself an efficacious mode of theology. The task is severe, but its importance and possibility are vigorously persistent.

Such confidence, metaphysical and stylistic, does not, however, extend to the present day; it has become frayed at both ends.[12] And that is where this study begins, at the moment when, as David Jones identified it, 'Western Man moved across a rubicon which, if as unseen as the 38th Parallel, seems to have been as definitive as the Styx'.[13] The story of intellectual and social upheaval across the long nineteenth century has often been told in the histories of poetry and religion, but with a tendency towards exaggeration and simplification. Not so long ago, the twin narrative went something like this. For poetry: through the 'organic' prosody of the Romantics and the recherché experimentations of the Victorians (anxiously asserting their wares in a literary marketplace dominated by the novel), poets dissolved the conservative bonds of formal strictness and thereby achieved the imaginative liberty of the 'New Prosody', the blurring of verse with prose, and the radical rupture known as 'free verse'. For religion: under the pressures of scientific advance (in everything from geology to evolutionary biology), as well as from biblical scholarship, historicism and philosophy, not to mention industrialization and urbanization, doctrinal beliefs were progressively undermined and the numinous squeezed out from the world. The long nineteenth century thus endures a loss of faith in both poetry and religion, which poetry itself records with urgent elegance.[14]

Such a summary still has some value. It remains true to say, 'The world was more deeply transformed in the nineteenth century than in any previous millennium.'[15] But over the last couple of decades critics have emphasized continuities across literary movements, the richness of the period's verse theory and craft, and the vaulting claims that were sometimes made for poetry's authority, importance and influence.[16] Historians of religion have likewise shown that while the ways of living and thinking associated with 'modernity' eroded certain kinds of faith (especially as traditionally practised within established institutions), faith was in far ruder health than had previously been imagined, and that in important respects faith evolved and thrived throughout the century.[17] Scholars have also shown the many, and sometimes unexpected, ways in which poetry and poetics shape and are shaped by religion and theology.[18]

This book emerges out of such revisionist studies on the imaginative life of the long nineteenth century, but it does not seek to offer its own overarching literary-religious narrative, by a top-down panoptic. Instead, it works from the bottom up, by assaying the ways in which faith in poetry was conceived and practised in the works of five of the period's finest poets: William Blake, Alfred Tennyson, Christina Rossetti, Gerard Manley Hopkins and T. S. Eliot. These poets have been chosen for three overlapping reasons: because they are self-conscious and consummate verse stylists; because they avow different kinds of Christian faith in different ways; and because, between them, they reach from the disenchanting terror of the French Revolution through to the violet hour of high modernism, and the Continent-consuming violence of the First World War.[19] Suggestive interconnections of style and faith might be drawn out. Between Blake's 'minute particulars' and Hopkins's Scotist *haecceitas*, for instance;[20] or between Tennyson's and Rossetti's close shave with aestheticism, courting while resisting the intransitive self-sufficiency of form for form's sake. Blake's and Eliot's approximations to prose provide another suggestive continuity; Tennyson's, Rossetti's and Eliot's habits of reprise and refrain, another still; to name only a few. Bridgings are also noteworthy: how Rossetti connects Blake to Hopkins, say, by inheriting (among other things) the early sing-song simplicity of the former, while influencing the phrases, metaphors and themes of the latter. But while a number of commonalities are highlighted along the way in the chapters that follow, it is not the object of this study to establish a general conspectus for poetics in this period so much as to refine what's singular in the verse styles of the individual poets under inspection, as they reflect and are inflected by their separate religious faiths.

Focusing on what's original in different poets' responses means taking them on their own terms. 'Willing suspension of disbelief' is indispensable. But Coleridge's well-worn readerly etiquette, which he calls the very definition of 'poetic faith' (and which carries more theological purpose than is usually allowed),[21] often demands more from readers than they are prepared, or perhaps able, to give. Poetry has for some time been read as a secular surrogate for lost religious belief; the idea is already operative in the nineteenth century (as notably articulated in Matthew Arnold's 'The Study of Poetry' (1880)).[22]

The tendency to read religious expression through a secular lens hardened in the twentieth century, however, and can seem irresistible in ours: not only because society at large has become increasingly secular, but also because the hermeneutics of suspicion have been so thoroughly domesticated into our reading practices. Under these conditions, religious devotion is typically interpreted, by default, as a form of repression for the emotionally weak and intellectually purblind, and all tussles of faith as re-expressions of something else, probably sexual. But to lead with such assumptions – disallowing in advance that there may be modalities of faith that are not merely deputizing for other, more vital atavistic needs and desires – is to be awkwardly at odds with the poets under inspection. It is to view them through warped glass.

Another common prejudice imagines that winning styles lack substance, and that sincerity, sophistication and depth expresses itself only through dishevelment.[23] That fallacy is widespread within the period covered by this book (to be called 'musical' is inevitably to be damned with faint praise), but it has become even more entrenched since, following the reactionary poetics of modernist and postmodernist verse, which champions indirection and fragmentariness; and it is abetted also by the exegetical urge of the contemporary, professional literary critic, who typically privileges formal and semantic 'difficulty' as the place where literature's richest 'meaning' is supposed to lie. On both fronts, then, metaphysical as well as aesthetic, religious poetry is subject to significant bias that if not 'suspended' (in Coleridge's sense) will likely end up telling us rather more about our own kinds of faith than those of the poets we are reading.

To put these concerns into context, assuming that 'the poetry that catches our interest is concerned with struggle and loss of faith' renders Rossetti hardly worthy of our time; and historically, she has indeed often been left out of the picture for this reason.[24] The critic's coercive 'our' that prefers vexed faith and formal deformity creates problems in the other direction too. It brings a poet such as Hopkins onto centre stage (whose rhythmic rugosity is never left out of the picture), but in a way that travesties his relationship with his religion and his writing, through the gauche compliment that 'no one with an intellect and an originality such as he possessed' could possibly 'surrender gracefully and easily'.[25] Notions of 'surrender' and 'grace' require more careful handling if we are to understand the paradoxical principle by which both Rossetti and Hopkins submitted to their faith (where discipline and doctrine may be liberating rather than stifling), and the ways they sought expression in verse, such that – this book aims to show – Rossetti's characteristically 'perfect' prosody may complement rather than contrast with Hopkins's stressy measure, which instantiates its own 'affective' grace.[26]

Alexander Pope figured 'modes of faith' as something over which it is best to let 'graceless zealots fight'.[27] But the very notion of grace, both in the sense of virtuosic felicity and also as divine blessing, is an act of faith for which he himself would go into battle, refusing the mechanical notion of correct style as polished poise (where the 'sense' demands it, 'no harshness gives offence'),[28] advancing his poetics in the most compelling way available, through poetry itself. Tennyson is a pressingly relevant figure here too, insofar as his dreamy mellifluence is often said to have been cultivated at the expense of serious thinking about faith (or anything else for that matter). But the chapter on him in this book explores how and why this formulation stages a false dilemma, by obscuring his achievement as one who thinks with and through his sounds and rhythms, as a '*habitus*' and 'virtue' of 'the practical intellect' that aims at 'making'.[29] 'What hope is here for modern rhyme?', posed at the centre and tipping point of *In Memoriam*, is the implacable, sometimes querulous, question haunting all of the poets in this book.[30] To which there is no ready answer, but in which shared pressure of being 'modern' there nonetheless exists persistent 'hope', whereby wagering on verse serves as its own warrant.

What this study attempts, then, is to read afresh the poets it examines, in their particularity: without flatly imposing assumptions that might only generally obtain, either from the period in which they were writing, or from our own moment. To be entirely disinterested is impossible, of course, and not entirely desirable either. All readers are to some extent subject to their own historicity, as well as their own idiosyncrasies, and a certain kind of partiality might be worth hanging on to. But at the very least, this study avoids automatically privileging obliquity and parataxis over directness and pellucidity; as it also attempts to dignify religious faith as something that might just be more than cussed ignorance or pathological redirection. Even where critics are shy of calling Blake a 'mystic', and positively recoil from the possibility that he might have been divinely inspired (as he claimed to be), the chapter with which this book begins takes his claims seriously. Refusing his self-fashioning, it is argued, leaves us little option but to view him as deluded or disingenuous, as a madman or a liar, which in turn makes it much harder to appreciate either the coherence of his faith or the careful intricacy of his verse craft, which is at the same time purposefully destabilized.

Finally, Eliot, who closes this book, comes down to us as a high priest of modernism, and as such he could easily be left stranded at the margins of this five-poet party. Apparently so self-conscious about the literary tradition he inherited that he could only find his voice by undoing the metrical contract on which that tradition had been built.[31] Seemingly so in thrall to intellectual sophistication (those less sympathetic say sophistry) that he mandated a poetics of impersonality, such that he cannot be counted among those who honestly affirm their religion or their strivings with it. But Eliot was as fiercely invested as any poet in questions of artisanal *technê*, and though he started out as a philosopher and made his name as a forbiddingly recondite writer who envisioned contemporary life as cultural ruin and personal anomie, faith blossoms in his verse as a redemptive force that appeals directly to what he called the 'auditory imagination'.[32] It is also fitting (and inspiriting) to end this book's survey with Eliot, whose life and poetry testifies to the truth of Jones's concomitant insight on the fate of 'Western Man'. Even after the rubicon of secularism has been crossed, poets in a society dominated by unbelieving may still, it seems, retain not only the old, 'ineradicable longings for ... the farther shore', but also the verse craft and 'impletive rite' of creation by which faith might yet be forged in poetry.[33]

1

William Blake: Destabilized Particulars

... more than mortal fire
Burns in my soul, and does my song inspire[1]

Some people called William Blake a 'mystic', others called him 'mad'. He preferred to call himself 'inspired'. These are each contested terms, and they may mean different things in different contexts. But they have in common the tendency to distract from, if not to deny in advance, the idea that whatever else Blake might be, he was also a disciplined craftsman. Bluntly put, as George Saintsbury does in his introduction to the poet, Blake's 'curious mental diathesis' – whatever one chooses to call it – 'would certainly not make for what is commonly thought prosodic exactness'.[2]

But Blake himself had little time for what was 'commonly thought'. 'A Spirit and a Vision are not, as the modern philosophy supposes, a cloudy vapour or a nothing: they are organised and minutely articulated beyond all that the mortal and perishing nature can produce' (*E* 541). He makes the point well, and often. Even if the purported clarity of the mystic's vision may be granted in principle, however, it remains to be shown whether that vision is 'minutely articulated' in practice, when it takes expression in verse. Mysticism might refer to the message as much as the medium, to a transcendent insight rather than its translation in concrete terms. Whatever the 'modern philosophy' might suppose about mysticism itself, it is hard to escape the notion that a mystic is after all likely to produce something rather misty. Hence the reluctance of modern scholars to attach the word 'mystic' to Blake at all: that he might be taken seriously as an artist.[3] Mysticism and exacting style are presumed to be exclusive possibilities.

'Inspiration' causes related problems, even where it is not effectively conflated with mysticism or madness. By the time Blake was writing, the idea of afflatus had for some become a mere rhetorical convention, perhaps even a risible one (as per Byron's mock invocation in *Don Juan*, 'Hail, Muse! *et cetera*').[4] But for those who continued to take the idea of inspiration seriously, it was a severe antonym for lucubration, as illustrated by Charles Lamb's wonderfully camp response to viewing the manuscript of *Lycidas*:

> How it staggered me to see the fine things in their ore! interlined, corrected as if their words were mortal, alterable, displaceable at pleasure! As if they might have been otherwise, and just as good![5]

Before that 'evil hour' Lamb had regarded Milton's poem as 'a full-grown beauty – as sprung up with all its parts absolute'. But the manuscript forced him to confront the artist in his workshop, to inspect the incremental and faulting process, 'as if inspiration were made up of parts, and these fluctuating, successive, indifferent!'[6] Quite what inspiration is remains ultimately mysterious, but Lamb is at least clear about what it is not. And Blake appeared to agree, extending Shelley's claim for inspiration as 'interpenetration of a diviner nature through our own', by seemingly evacuating his own agency entirely from the process of poetic composition.[7] He explained that one of his long prophetic poems was written 'from immediate Dictation', 'without Premeditation & even against my Will'; that it happened instantly ('the Time it has taken in writing was thus rendered Non Existent'), and that his 'immense Poem ... which seems to be the Labour of a long Life' was in fact 'all produced without Labour or Study' (*E* 728–9). No will, no study, no labour: Blake's self-styled brand of visioning is for many readers, at the time and since, an embarrassing delusion. In the post-Platonic tradition, the gloriously inspired artist is liberated not merely from his workshop but also from his sanity: 'Beware! Beware! / His flashing eyes, his floating hair!'[8] When Robert

Southey recalled his encounter with Blake he might even have been remembering that very same figure from Coleridge's 'Kubla Khan'. Blake's 'madness' was, Southey thought, 'too evident, too fearful': 'It gave his eyes an expression such as you would expect to see in one who was possessed'.[9]

Not everyone thought Blake mad; surveying contemporary testimonies, Francis Oliver Finch brands him instead as 'perverse and willful'.[10] Blake himself baulked at what he took to be the ignorant and envious ways in which 'the aspersion of Madness' is 'Cast on the Inspired' by what he called 'the tame high finishers of paltry Blots, / Indefinite, or paltry rhymes, or paltry harmonies' (pl. 41.8–10; *E* 142). Here is the crux of the matter. Although certain isolated statements might suggest so, Blake did not wish to venerate inspiration as the single ingredient in art: he aimed instead to explode the false opposition between inspiration and craft. Both are necessary, but neither is itself sufficient (*E* 576):

> I have heard many People say Give me the Ideas. It is no matter what Words you put them into & others say Give me the Design it is no matter for the Execution. These People know <Enough of Artifice but> Nothing Of Art. Ideas cannot be Given but in their minutely Appropriate Words nor Can a Design be made without its minutely Appropriate Execution [.]

Blake's rail against the demystification and naturalization of inspiration as a labour 'earned and learned in time' must thus be read, as Sarah Haggarty has shown, alongside his countervailing conviction that it was 'pernicious to sacrifice the artist's mental and mechanical activity to some abstract, exterior donor'.[11] But Blake does not make it easy or simple to maintain this rounded account of the artist as the beneficiary of inspiration but as also possessing artisanal agency. The diremption he denies continues to assert itself, not least through his own assertions about the exceptionalism of his art, which encourages the suspicion that he, and by his extension his art, was irrational; or at the very least, inscrutable by recognized standards. Announcing himself as a 'prophet', while at the same time denouncing reason as antithetical to creativity, Blake makes claims to truth that are exclusive from the proofs or fruits of intellectual inquiry or experience. Gesturing to the unanchored authorities of 'Poetic Genius' and the

'Imagination' associated with inspiration, he consciously sets himself apart from established aesthetic norms. His interventions were at once counter-cultural but at the same time confirmed the period's generic notions of exceptionalism, as neatly summarized in an article on the subject in 1812, in which 'a person of genius' is said to be 'beyond ordinary criticism', who 'may set rules at defiance', and who should be left to be 'a law to himself'.[12]

Blake certainly was a law to himself, and in the fullest sense, for he was defiant not only about the uniqueness of his vision, as against the skilled imitations of even such celebrated sources as the 'Greek Muses', who were, he thought – for all their distinction – no more than imitators, the 'daughters of Mnemosyne, or Memory' (*E* 531). He was defiant also about the uniqueness of his expression: 'I know my Execution is not like Any Body Else. I do not intend it should be so; none but Blockheads Copy one another'; 'The ignorant Insults of Individuals will not hinder me from doing my duty to my Art' (*E* 527). Cussed self-confidence of that sort might read like defensive conceit, especially given that he was himself routinely estimated as ignorant. When he burst on to the scene with *Poetical Sketches*, his first poems to reach the public – written between the ages of twelve and twenty – were advertised with a heavy accent on their 'originality', and explicitly recommended as 'the production of untutored youth', in which 'irregularities and defects' were to be found 'in almost every page' (*E* 846). His apparent ignorance was the very quality used to promote the aboriginal authenticity of his poems, and to determine their appeal; his roughshod verses were not said to be valuable in spite of their deficiencies, but because of them. Contemporary reviewers inevitably took this cue, and his reputation – as innocent, ignorant, or otherwise unconcerned with poetic tradition and *technê* – stuck to him all his life, in spite of the obvious and mounting evidence to the contrary.

Yet being a law unto himself did not mean he was lawless: 'determinate and bounding form' was what, in his view, distinguished the great artists of all ages (*E* 550), who are likewise to be thought of as prophets, not for some speculative gift in fortune telling ('Prophets in the modern sense of the word have never existed' (*E* 617)), but as oppositional voices in the Old Testament tradition; that is, as visionaries of divine truth. His appeal to 'form', then, is not merely aesthetic, it is theologically charged, as it is also double-edged. Clear bounding lines are the precondition for creativity, but pre-existing forms and laws may also oppress the imagination, and facilitate 'lame imitators' (*E* 550). Blake recurs to the conviction that laws are necessary, but that law-breaking is too, when sanctioned by a higher insight, as Christ consistently showed through his life's example.

Whether Blake's communion with messengers from heaven is compatible with sanity and rigorous reasoning is a moot point, but it is at least clear that the prejudices of modernity run in the opposite direction. It may be surprising to discover that René Descartes (father of analytical geometry and modern philosophy) was inspired to 'lay the foundations of a new method of understanding and a new and marvellous science' by the 'Angel of Truth' who appeared to him in a series of dreams. But it will come as no surprise to learn that in discussing his paradigm-breaking *Discourse on Method* with fellow mathematicians and philosophers, he kept coyly quiet about that angel.[13] It needs also to be said that whatever one makes of Blake conversing with spirits (or indeed his claims to be a prophet, or a genius), the fierce obscurity of his work independently suggests, if not actual mental illness, then certainly incoherence and ill-discipline. That is true in the extent to which he confounds settled forms and genres, and it is also true thematically. His mythological style, thickened with allegory and symbol, can be so intensely personal as to be opaque. Notwithstanding the valiant work of Northrop Frye, Harold Bloom and others in delineating his mythological tropes, it can at times be difficult to construe his meaning. It can even be difficult to know if there is any coherent 'meaning' there to be construed in the first place. Some passages take on such vivid but at the same time elliptical life – with nonlinear plots, and an army of characters who morph into one another (in which people may also be places) – that they can look more like a wildly creative riff rather than a cogent vision, either metaphysical or artistic. Even where scholars have sought to tease out the (especially tangled) vision of his late prophecies, far fewer have attempted to advocate the narrative coherence of those poems.[14]

It may be that Blake's operating as a law unto himself as an artist was heightened by his experience of coming up against the wrong side of the law as a citizen. After his trial for sedition, his poems become markedly harder to follow; and it would make sense that, shaken as he was by his criminal trial, he sought to occlude somewhat the polemical edge of his writings. But his obscurities are as much deliberate as they are defensive. After a brush with the courts, part of him no doubt wished to avoid scrutiny; but he does also explicitly present heterodoxy as a defining feature of authenticity and originality. It is the 'crooked roads' that are, he insists, the 'roads of Genius' (pl. 9.66; *E* 38); and so his crookedness – and, consequently, his comparative neglect – gave him some comfort. In contrast to the poet-priest Gerard Manley Hopkins, who regretted the 'strangeness' of his verse style for preventing his 'creating thought' from serving in 'the campaign to win England back to the faith, or increase the fame of her literature',[15] Blake aligns himself with the figure of the 'just man' who 'rages in the wilds' (pl. 2.19; *E* 33). Idiosyncrasy is his sanction. He claims not merely artistic dignity but divine warrant for his wildness, which recalls the just but unheeded biblical prophets, as 'The Voice of one crying in the Wilderness' (*E* 1). No wonder, for Blake was surely aware that his audience was severely limited on several fronts: by the radical nature of his religious critique, by the idiosyncrasy of its expression in verse, and by the high price of some of his later, extravagantly produced poems.[16] Given all this, Robert Ryan suggests that integrity is really the only consolation he must have known, and quotes the words Blake attributes to Isaiah as relevant to his own plight as a poet: 'I was then persuaded, and remain confirm'd, that the voice of honest indignation is the voice of God, I cared not for consequences, but wrote.'[17]

So: Blake's reputation – mystic, mad or inspired – seems only to reinforce what his work already independently suggests. While he cared greatly for his vision, he apparently cared rather less about how successfully he communicated it. But to short-circuit to such a conclusion is a fatal mistake. The dissenting note he strikes could look like a protest against political engagement itself, as a Romantic escape into the unpolluted unreality of the aesthetic, except that Blake believed in the efficacy of art to shape the collective conscience and theology of Britain; his faith in poetry in particular is fired by the example of Milton's *Paradise Lost*.[18] It is important to dwell on the fact that Blake did after all choose to address his faith in (verbal and visual) art rather than a theological treatise. He was not against science, but scientism; he was not anti-enlightenment, he was opposed to the idea that reason could explain everything. By extension, art was not an excuse for him to be obscure or careless in the expression of his ideas as a blank protest against logical explication that no one else but he could riddle: it was a means of obviating the limitations of logic as exercised within propositional, proof-based thinking. Art offered Blake the opportunity to say but also to do things he could not otherwise. His choler against the oppression of capitalist materialism, and his conviction that a new Jerusalem could be built in England's green and pleasant land, 'did not lead merely to a retreat into a utopian fantasy' – Christopher Rowlands makes the point well – 'but to a desire to transform through struggle what actually exists'.[19] Whereas a treatise necessarily trades in abstractions, and seeks to stabilize its intentions, art allowed him both to *particularize* and also to *destabilize* his meanings. The purpose of his destabilized particulars – drawn out in the respective subsections of this chapter – extends beyond the expression of his vision, it aims also to provoke that vision: to awaken a 'cleansed' perception of the 'infinite' (pl. 14; *E* 39).

***

'To Generalize is to be an Idiot; To Particularize is the Alone Distinction of Merit' (*E* 641). That was Blake's response to the claim by Joshua Reynolds, first president of the Royal Academy, that the 'disposition to abstractions, to generalising and classification, is the great glory of the human mind' (*E* 641). The dominant artistic mode of Blake's day valorized, as Reynolds did, the blurred, seemingly unfinished style exemplified by Rubens. Blake instead admired, and – in his singular way – sought to emulate a kind of precision associated with the classical style of ancient Greece and Rome.[20] Such models were a sanative riposte to the imprecision of a prevailing contemporary attitude. But he does not deferentially invoke the august ancients: he specifically criticizes the greatest of the English poets for this habit, which he considers a form of intellectual-imaginative-aesthetic servitude that was at the same time implicated in a literary tradition that celebrated military Imperialism and Empire ('Shakspeare [sic] & Milton were both curbd by the general malady & infection from the silly Greek and Latin slaves of the sword' (pl. 1; *E* 95)). Blindly adhering to rules and symmetries led, he thought, to dehumanized abstraction and ideals; in life as in art, a balance must be achieved and kept in tension. While recognizing the need for a certain kind of order and discipline, he also anticipates John Ruskin's apology for savageness and grotesquery in architecture, by contrasting the sterilized 'Mathematical Form' of the Greek world view with the 'Living Form [that is] is Eternal Existence' of the Gothic style (*E* 270).

Blake's wished-for balance takes form as an arresting syncretism between Classical, concrete particulars and the imaginative liberties epitomized by Gothic. It is not always clear how he orchestrates these opposing impulses, such that it is easy to misread him, by only reading half of him: usually, by noticing his waywardness, but not his corresponding probity. There is, for instance, a generic, emblematic quality to his images from nature (especially when compared with his Romantic contemporaries), such that he does not seem invested in particularity at all. Yet his figurative language is, in mytho-poetic terms, highly specific. Perhaps the most striking example of this doubleness in Blake's verse style – highly particularized while confounding the rules of established orthodoxy or symmetry – is to be found in his prosody. Here are the first two stanzas of 'London', with stressed syllables emboldened (*E* 26–7):

> I **wan**der **thro'** each **char**ter'd **street**,
> **Near** where the **char**ter'd **Thames** does **flow**.
> And **mark** in **ev**ery **face** I **meet**
> **Marks** of **weak**ness, **marks** of **woe**.
>
> In **ev**ery **cry** of **ev**ery **Man**,
> In **ev**ery **In**fants **cry** of **fear**,
> In **ev**ery **voice**: in **ev**ery **ban**,
> The **mind-forg'd man**acles I **hear**

While Blake keeps a fixed stress count per line, he varies the position of the stress in the line relative to those syllables that are less stressed. That might seem like unbuttoning the measure; but in spite of this freedom over syllable number and stress placement (as many as three stresses in a row, or stresses separated by up to two unstressed syllables), the metre is fetched out emphatically. As readers, we are aware of significant rhythmical variation, yet we are never at a loss to know which words or syllables to emphasize over others. Untrammelled outpouring meets purposeful plangency. Such is the general character of Blake's most lyrical and best known poems collected in his *Songs of Innocence and Experience*. Forsaking models of prosodical correctness bequeathed by his Augustan forebears, Blake forges his stresses through the less 'literary' measures of the four-beat, four-line ballad stanza, as well as the tunes of the child's nursery rhyme.[21] The pay-off is clear: he may move easily between double and triple rhythms, and between shorter and longer lines, as he may have stresses collide or run across strings of less stressed syllables, while the clarity of his rhymes and the syntactical brace of his stanzas ensure that the word-picture is nonetheless sharply drawn. His boldness is thrilling but controlled, whether working in couplets, such as the much-cited trochaic opening of 'Tyger Tyger, burning bright, / In the forests of the night' (*E* 24), or in the gentler but no less haunting two-beat lines of 'The Sick Rose' (*E* 23).

Comparison with demotic, oral forms (from ballads to nursery rhymes) is a useful entry-point for approaching the paradoxical impulses in Blake's style – where precision co-exists with asymmetry, individual instance with symbol, coherence with fragmentation – but his poems after *The Songs of Innocence and Experience* require further contexts to make sense of them; especially when it comes to assessing his later, longer and apparently slacker lines that he wrote in his prophetic poems. Here we may helpfully look to other models, notably the Bible, which (following Robert Lowth's insights on its structures of poetic parallelism) succeeds in generating order out of apparent disorder, and prophecy out of poetry, without obeisance to classical literature. 'The stolen and perverted writings of Homer and Ovid, of Plato and Cicero, which all men ought to contemn, are set up by artifice against the Sublime of the Bible', Blake insists: 'We do not want either Greek or Roman models if we are but just & true to our own Imaginations, those Worlds of Eternity in which we shall live for ever; in Jesus our Lord' (pl. 1; *E* 95).

Blake's own attempt 'to justify the ways of God to man' is thus at once aesthetically revisionary and theologically re-visioning the minute particularities of Milton's style. Milton well understood the extent to which religious justification in the form of poetry required a just and judicious deployment of verse, and indeed that a certain kind of style might itself constitute a kind of bad faith; hence his polemic against end-rhyme, as 'being no necessary adjunct or true ornament of poem or good verse ... but the invention of a barbarous age'.[22] While Blake in one sense seeks to re-write Milton, then, he is also consciously following Milton's double-minded emphasis on correcting religious as well as prosodical error. Or rather, Blake shares Milton's faith that poetry can correct religious error, but only if its style is itself correct; as he explained in his preface to another of his most important visionary works, *Jerusalem* (pl. 3; *E* 145–6):

> When this Verse was first dictated to me I consider'd a Monotonous Cadence like that used by Milton & Shakspeare [*sic*] & all writers of English Blank Verse, derived from the modern bondage of Rhyming; to be a necessary and indispensable part of Verse. But I soon found that in the mouth of a true Orator such monotony was not only awkward, but as much a bondage as rhyme itself. I therefore have produced a variety in every line, both of cadences & number of syllables. Every word and every letter is studied and put into its fit place: the terrific numbers are reserved for the terrific parts – the mild & gentle, for the mild & gentle parts, and the prosaic, for the inferior parts: all are necessary to each other. Poetry Fetter'd, Fetters the Human Race! Nations are Destroy'd or Flourish, in proportion as Their Poetry Painting and Music, are Destroy'd or Flourish!

Milton is by far the most important poetic–prophetic precursor for Blake, and scholars have detected his influence throughout Blake's oeuvre, before and after *Milton*.[23] Blake's relationship with Milton cannot be exhaustively explained as anxiety of influence, however. No doubt he sought artistic independence by overmastering Milton's example, but Blake's dissenting impulse connects with a broader imperative to keep his religious vision keen and true, by challenging it through re-formation. So it is that particularity not only features as a central tenet of his creative endeavour, shaping his artistic practice, it also features within his art, as a governing thematic preoccupation (pl. 55.51–3; 60–4; *E* 205):

> Labour well the Minute Particulars, attend to the Little Ones:
> And those who are in misery cannot remain so long
> If we do but our duty: labour well the teeming Earth.
>
> He who would do good to another, must do it in Minute Particulars
> General Good is the plea of the scoundrel hypocrite & flatterer:
> For Art & Science cannot exist but in minutely organized Particulars
> And not in generalizing Demonstrations of the Rational Power.
> The Infinite alone resides in Definite & Determinate Identity

Twice framing his commitment as a form of 'labour' impresses the sense of righteous moral duty while at the same time expressing the artist's graft, which is all in some sense continuous with the work of science, rationality and divine infinity. Blake's working practices (evidence from his drafts and corrections) amply confirm that he was highly adept and self-conscious as an artist, in the way that, say, Robert Browning was; but unlike Browning, he was consumed by his work to the extent that he could not easily leave it alone, and so restlessly revised it. The passage quoted above comes from *Jerusalem*, which poem alone contains as many as nine further references to 'minute particulars'.[24] The same phrase circulates conspicuously within other poems too, and his letters as well, as 'Particulars which will present themselves to the Contemplator' (*E* 701). Blake's preoccupation with particulars – the conviction that one must move 'from Particulars to Generals' (pl. 3.37; *E* 97) – animates his entire outlook. It is an aesthetic and theological principle he believed to operate in the Bible ('The subordination of the general to the particular, with a reliance upon internal coherence among the parts rather than upon an externally imposed order', as Leslie Tannenbaum glosses it),[25] and he takes up this same principle of particularity as a continuous creed, encompassing art and poetry together with life and religion (*E* 560):

> General Knowledge is Remote Knowledge it is in Particulars that Wisdom consists & Happiness too. Both in Art & in Life general Masses are as Much Art as a Pasteboard Man is Human Every Man

> has Eyes Nose & Mouth this Every Idiot knows but he who enters into & discriminates most minutely the Manners & Intentions the Characters in all their branches is the alone Wise or Sensible Man & on his discrimination All Art is founded. I intreat then that the Spectator will attend to the Hands & Feet to the Lineaments of the Countenances they are all descriptive of Character and not a line is drawn without intention & that most discriminate & particular as Poetry admits not a Letter that is Insignificant so Painting admits not a Grain of Sand or a Blade of Grass Insignificant much less an Insignificant Blur or Mark.

Perhaps the most striking expression of Blake's formal heterodoxy as a visual artist was his refusal to paint in oils. But this decision – which was disastrous for him both commercially and in terms of his career – was not only aesthetic, it was also ethical. Or rather, his decision demonstrates the extent to which he saw aesthetic and ethical questions as entangled. He preferred the clarity that could be achieved in line engraving, which he thought impossible in the 'blotting and blurring' medium of oils (*E* 546). And this preference arises from his sense that form, rather than colour, is the most important quality ('all depends on Form or Outline' (*E* 529–30)).[26] He also repeatedly noted the practical disadvantage that oil painting is so susceptible to decay ('Oil will not drink or absorb Colour enough to stand the test of very little time and of the Air; it grows yellow and at length brown' (*E* 527; see also *E* 530, 531)). But his aesthetic and practical preference for visual art with a 'firm and determinate outline' must not be taken as an isolated opinion. The artistic vision implicates the religious and the lived experience of both (*E* 550):

> The great and golden rule of art, as well as of life, is this: That the more distinct, sharp, and wirey the bounding line, the more perfect the work of art; and the less keen and sharp, the greater is the evidence of weak imitation, plagiarism and bungling. ... What is it that distinguishes honesty from knavery, but the hard and wirey line of rectitude and certainty in the actions and intentions. Leave out this l[i]ne and you leave out life itself; all is chaos again, and the line of the almighty must be drawn out upon it before man or beast can exist.

He could hardly be more explicit: for art as for life, hard and sharp distinctions, intentions and actions are salutary, and he is every bit as committed to the ethical imperative of form in the mode of verse. Yet it remains a question of some nicety as to whether the emphatic measure of Blake's prosody, so telling in *Songs of Innocence and Experience*, finally slurs and smudges in his later poetry, in his longer lines that approximate prose. (Some of this later poetry exploits short lines, such as the books of *Urizen* (1794), *Ahania* (1795) and *Los* (1795), but it is the longer-lined poems, which are his most ambitious writings, where the stresses typically become indeterminate.) Those characteristically clear outlines in his visual art soften in his later practice, and so does Blake's presumed moral corollary (on the 'hard and wirey line of rectitude').[27] His watercolours for Dante created at the end of his life, for instance, have an atmospheric quality as well as a more varied type of outline, probably influenced by Turner, that are quite different from the linear technique of his (*c.*1810) illustrations to Milton.[28] Might it be said therefore that Blake's commitment to clear vision clearly realized abated later in his life?

Comparison between his artistic modes is instructive in many ways. But it may be that his visual art was in some ways at odds with his verse style. Praising Blake, Saintsbury argues for an 'extraordinary prosodic quality which ... distinguishes him as a poet',[29] but he goes on to speculate that Blake's quality as a prosodist was compromised by the competing demands of the other artistic medium in which he worked. 'In the two sets of *Songs* and the wide range of "prophetic" and semi-prophetic books', Saintsbury advises us, 'we have to remember the method of production, and the fact that he was evidently always thinking of the meaning or the ornament, not the poetic form ... . This, taken literally, would exclude prosody in the ordinary sense from among the minute particulars to which no doubt he did pay attention'.[30] More recently, John Beer has argued similarly, that 'the importance of such [extra-verbal] effects seem, in fact, to have deflected Blake from the craftsmanlike concerns of the normal poet'.[31]

But Blake never was a 'normal poet', and his 'craftsmanlike concerns' confound prior assumptions and established critical categories. Even Saintsbury (viewing Blake from the Olympian perspective of his *History of English Prosody*) was caught out, and in a way that is worth noting. While championing Blake's lyrical verse, Saintsbury deferred fuller discussion of his poems from *Visions of the Daughters of Albion* onwards to his prospected book on prose rhythm. But when, a few years later, Saintsbury came to write that book on prose, he was forced to conclude that Blake's prophetic books could not be domesticated into that study, either. 'I am now disposed to look upon them', Saintsbury admits, 'as belonging to a Debatable Land which is much more poetic than prosaic'.[32]

Saintsbury's hedging witnesses how unusual Blake's writings are, even when seen across the full literary history of poetry and prose. But Saintsbury also prompts a question he does not answer, as to whether Blake ultimately loses faith in poetry – and so writes instead in prose, or at least a hybrid form of it, a kind of slackened verse. Even Wordsworth, who claimed that 'there neither is, nor can be, any *essential* difference between the language of prose and metrical composition', re-affirmed that, to be classed as poetry, language must at least be metrically composed.[33] The only book-length study of Blake's poetic form, Alicia Ostriker's *Vision and Verse in William Blake*, follows Saintsbury, but goes further. Ostriker judges that Blake's early poems were, in effect, a warm-up for the main act that is *Songs of Innocence and Experience*, and that his subsequent writings veer away from poetry. Of his epigrams, 'We have no right to expect anything poetic out of these primarily splenetic jottings'; 'in form', his later lyrics 'turn gradually from beauty of sound to power of sound, from metrical control to metrical devil-may-carelessness'; by the time we come to *Jerusalem*, the last of the Prophetic Books, he 'breaks the bones of meter for the sake of something Blake called oratory'.[34]

Unlike Saintsbury, Ostriker devotes some space to debating the Land Debatable, and she finds much to recommend in it. But she is nonetheless wedded to the same system of prosodic analysis, which she describes as 'basically Saintsbury's foot-scansion'.[35] Such a system is of limited use in evaluating Blake's early poetry, but even less helpful when trying to construe his later writings. Derek Attridge has led the way in encouraging readers to hear the 'dolnik' beat in balladic poetry, where stresses play more freely but at the same time more sure-footedly than is apparent by foot-based scansion.[36] But it remains to be shown how best to audit (both in the sense of to hear, and to inspect what we hear) Blake's later verse, where the prosodical constraints are neither fixed 'feet' nor unconstrained 'beats', but rhythmic phrases, in lines such as the following, plucked from *Milton*, *Jerusalem* and *The Four Zoas*, respectively:

> Loud sounds the Hammer of Los, loud turn the Wheels of Enitharmon
> Her Looms vibrate with soft affections, weaving the Web of Life
> Out from the ashes of the Dead; Los lifts his iron Ladles
> With molten ore:
>
> (pl. 6.27–30; *E* 100)

> Embrace him tenfold bright, rising from his tomb in immortality.
> They have divided themselves by Wrath. they must be united by
> Pity: let us therefore take example & warning O my Spectre,
>
> (pl. 7.56–8; *E* 150)

> Go forth sons of my curse Go forth daughters of my abhorrence
> Tharmas heard the deadly scream across his watry world
> And Urizens loud sounding voice lamenting on the wind
> And he came riding in his fury.
>
> (27–30; *E* 346)

That briefest sample of Blake's longer lines gives a flavour of their pungency, which – for their torsions of rhythm, syntax and lineation, heightened through parallelisms of sound – could not be mistaken for prose, and yet resist calibration by established prosodic categories. Whether to parse by beats or 'feet' or by musical notation, whether to treat as rhetoric or as free verse, or whether to take the line endings as the key to his measure or its greatest irrelevance? Scholars have adduced many different and mutually incompatible ways to explain Blake's rhythms, without establishing a settled view.[37] Rather than try to pronounce definitely on Blake's prosodical system, however, it may be more productive to attend to how his style resists systemization, and thrives instead through its elusiveness: through its expressive tensions between discipline and liberty, as well as between tradition and innovation, precedent and experimentation.

Upending the critical burden in this way, seeking to inspect his method on its own terms rather than according to its apparent fit with other recognized methods, cannot be achieved by adjudicating on stresses, junctures and caesurae. We must consider more than just Blake's words on the page and their paralinguistic patterning; we must attend also to the visual appeal of his writing, not with the impatient presumption that the visual operates at the cost of his prosodical craft, but to ask after why he composed as he did in his dual mode, for both the eye and the ear. 'Blake's refusal, not just of poetic form but of standard prose form, is', Susan Wolfson suggests, 'made to seem the expressive necessity of a primary, unmediated voice of prophecy and political emergency, the ultimate "organic" form'.[38] That is a rich insight, but it is necessary to go beyond generic Romantic notions of prosody as 'organic', to ask how Blake's principles and praxes might be different from, say, Wordsworth's, who (as noted earlier) is implacable on the question of metre as the only 'essential' feature of what makes poetry uniquely what it is. The prefatory address to *Jerusalem* quoted above sets the tone for that poem and for Blake's poetics in general. Prosody must liberate and not fetter expression. Otherwise poetry suffers, as does the society for and to which it speaks. But liberty cannot be freewheeling; where form is forsaken, art (like life) is threatened by 'chaos'. Again, a balance must be struck. But given how often the word 'chaos' is pejoratively applied to Blake's poetry, it is important to press the matter of quite what this balance looks like, and whether it fulfils what it promises; and that is not best achieved by slicing up his corpus into that which is more or less definitely poetic, but by aiming instead to trace continuities in his practice.

Readers cannot help noticing how Blake recurs obsessively to the same words and phrases, which find their place again and again in quite different, unconnected poems. An industry of criticism has also shown how his mythologies and religious sympathies play across his whole work, from Swedenborgian to Morvarian to Anabaptist. Far less attention has been paid to his versification, and less still to the ways in which his prosody shapes and animates his thinking in myth and on religion. The problems that flow from this are several and significant. To read Blake's texts in a way that emphasizes their historical contexts is more problematic in his case than perhaps for any of his contemporaries; to treat the particularities of his religion separately from the particular ways in which it finds expression in his poetry is perverse. On the one hand, Blake insists that artisanal accomplishment is empty in itself, and only finds adequate purpose in the service of a religious vision; on the other hand, he locates the very origins of religion in poetry that priests abstracted into theological systems (*The Marriage of Heaven and Hell*), as he also presents institutionalized religion as in some sense the fallen form of poetry's 'most holy forms of Thought' (*Milton*, pl. 28.5; *E* 125). The point is not merely a historical one about the relationship between poetry and religion. Blake sees the artistic endeavour as vitally connected to the activity of what religion should and can uniquely do, through imaginative investment in the particular over the abstract.

Here it is well to note that though religion is what 'inspires' Blake's artistic vision, it is only rarely religious in the sense of devotional. Personal piety is conspicuously absent. His letters have moments of personal reflection, inspection and spiritual avowal; as does some of his more conventional pictorial art.[39] But coming to his poetry after, say, Donne or Herbert, or indeed the likes of Tennyson or Hopkins later in the century, his preoccupations can seem curiously impersonal. But that is not because the religious strain in his poetry lacks personal investment; it is because his vision is more determinedly outward looking: centrifugal rather than centripetal, it proceeds from the personal but extends beyond itself, taking in the whole of society. His poetry is 'religious' insofar as it is fired by protests against oppression and injustice (which includes a protest against religious thinking and practice that serves as a cause of oppression and injustice). But his poetry is religious also for its mythological vision that is far removed from worldly reference. For its doubled purview, Blake's art affirms G. K. Chesterton's conviction that 'there is no fact of life, from the death of a donkey to the General Post Office, which has not its place to dance and sing in, in the glorious Carnival of theology'.[40] While some critics have bracketed off certain poems by Blake on the basis of their overtly religious terms and themes, it makes more sense to see all his art as a continuous commentary; or more specifically, as a rumbling religious protest that is simultaneously a protest against the institutionalization and practice of religion.

Comparison with Chesterton clarifies Blake's position for the ways in which they are aligned, but also for the ways in which they are incompatible. Both were committed to a religious faith fired by the animus of lived experience: socio-economic, political, cultural and imaginative. In that respect, they stand apart from the devotional tradition exemplified by the self-exiled or self-inspecting religious writer. Both also employ their art as a way of overcoming mental inertia: rattling conventions and startling our assumptions; cleansing the 'doors of perception', 'melting apparent surfaces away, and displaying the infinite which was hid' (*E* 39).[41] But whereas Chesterton defended the institution of the Christian Church and denounced heresy, while counselling the efficacy of 'dogma',[42] Blake set his face against both these things. He granted extraordinary freedom to the imagination, as against the edicts of ecclesiastical orthodoxy, including when it comes to the interpretation of the Bible. 'I know of no other Christianity and of no other Gospel', he writes, 'than the liberty both of body & mind to exercise the Divine Arts of Imagination' (*E* 231).

By extension, Blake's own religious faith expresses itself most forcibly defying what he took to be the deleterious influence of misconceived and misapplied religious thinking besetting all spheres of modern living, via what he called state religion, and sometimes natural religion, or Deism.[43] In that sense, all Blake's poetry must be deemed religious, insofar as all of it is kindled by a sense of social justice, right living and a correct estimation of humanity, as well as man's relation to God. Substance meets style here in Blake's poetry that constitutively refuses dogmatic pronouncements, by arousing the imagination – which he consistently and in complex ways invokes in relation to Poetic Genius, Prophecy, the Lord, God, Jesus, Society and the individual – through his strategies of destabilization.

***

Blake's art is unstable – or rather, artfully destabilized – because his religious vision is one of dynamic dissent. While he stands against chaos, he also spurns absolute law, and in that sense has been rightly called antinomian.[44] Blake's law-breaking defiance does not arise merely from a sense of his own exceptionalism, by genius, inspiration or indeed madness: it is emboldened by his theological resistance to closed systems – institutional or ideational – that he views as authoritarian, hypocritical and inhibiting. In this he takes his precedent from Christ himself, whom he characterizes as a supreme rebel and rule-breaker, as against the negative exemplar offered by the Pharisee. Blake's poetry reads much of the time therefore like an exercise in 'reverse theology', designed to be maximally unsettling.

Perhaps the most obvious way in which Blake subverts assumptions in his poetry is by setting contradictory states or suggestions against each other. This method is inevitably described as 'dialectic'. But the word may not be the most useful gloss, because Blake's oppositions do not operate in the dominant, Hegelian sense whereby contradiction refines into synthesis. Tennyson's *In Memoriam* is animated by such a movement, as the poem's separate sections cycle and recycle faith and doubt, hope and despair, towards reconciliation. The process is at points ragged, and includes regressions as well as progressions, but (as will be seen in Chapter 2) there is for all that a discernible 'drift'.[45] Blake's oppositions work differently, such that it might be more helpful to think not in terms of dialectic, but of paradox. For his oppositions are not self-cancelling contradictions, but non-dual truths of the sort Henri de Lubac elucidates as irreducible antinomies defined by their perpetual elusiveness:

> When we discover it and hold it in our hands we do not have time to bring our first look of satisfaction to rest upon it before it has already fled. The eternal story of the Pharisee starts afresh in each of us. To get hold of the elusive truth again, we should perhaps seek it in its opposite, for it has changed its sign. But often we prefer to hug its rotten corpse. And we go rotten with it.[46]

'Without Contraries is no progression' (pl. 3; *E* 34), one of Blake's most quoted lines, does not imply, then, that truth might be intimated through the reconciliation of antagonistic elements. Truth might be glimpsed instead by viewing both simultaneously, by seeing opposing states as in some way coexisting and mutually defining. Recasting Swedenborg's text *Heaven and Hell, and The Last Judgement*, Blake dramatizes human beings as themselves made up of contrary states; as indeed was Christ himself, who is said to have broken all of the Commandments while at the same time being 'all virtue' (pl. 23; *E* 43); and indeed, within the poem, the devil too has wisdom to share.

Paradoxes within the poem thus confound the desire to hold still the individual elements of apparent contradiction, in order to inspect and evaluate them; they frustrate the Pharisaic urge, not by refusing outright the possibility of understanding, but by refining understanding as a function of what de Lubac goes on to describe as a paradoxical 'rhythm' of thinking.[47] Blake's paradoxical investment in the particularities of his poems is necessarily dynamic, but in a way that, as de Lubac explains, 'however necessary' the 'forward movement', 'no real progress has been made'.[48] Blake's 'progression' through contraries is not therefore an onward, teleological development, it operates rather as a perpetual interplay, as has been most amply expounded by scholars in respect of his *Songs of Innocence and Experience*. These sets of poems come down to us as a pair, with the shared subtitle, 'Shewing the Two Contrary States of the Human Soul'; and seen together they advance the notion that neither 'state' is self-sufficient as an account of the soul. 'Innocence' is clarified by 'experience', but not in a way that straightforwardly idealizes the former over the latter. Within individual collections, poems prime and speak back to each (as indeed they do as early as his first collection, *Poetical Sketches*); and similar movements occur even within individual poems. Ignorance that exists before experience is insufficient to human flourishing, such that poems of 'Innocence' include structurally opposed states of being, as in the merry sparrow's contrast with the sobbing robin in 'The Blossom'. And the compositional and publishing history of these sets of poems complicates all these things even further.[49]

From sets of poems, to separate poems, to individual words: Blake's strategies of destabilization operate at his minutest particulars. Double meanings play potently, for instance, in those first two stanzas of 'London' that were quoted above: eight short lines, forty-nine words, reverberate in ways that disquiet the scene they describe. In the first two lines, the most salient image is 'charter'd', which, accented by its repetition, invokes associations of protected rights and enfranchisement, but here prefaces the obverse sketch of dehumanization, scarred as physical 'marks' of depredation. Yet even that keyword extends beyond its own suggestiveness, by having the observer 'mark' these marks, while those who are thus 'marked' do not mark him.[50] More is at play, in the insistent inclusiveness of the triple refrain of 'every', the corruption 'cry', as Man's lament is associated with the inarticulate wail of the infant; not to mention the compacted mixed metaphor of 'mind-forg'd manacles', at once visually vivid but at the same time hard to grasp, especially as the line spills over through the third stanza.

Blake's wordplay even extends to the morpheme. Tennyson was cited above as a poet who exploits a somewhat different kind of nonlinear movement, but he is a useful point of correspondence here for the way he likewise teases at absent presences. 'Dark house, by which once more I stand. / Here in the long unlovely street, / Doors, where my heart was used to beat': that short extract from *In Memoriam* is so affecting for the way Tennyson allows the present and past to co-exist.[51] Remembering how his heart *used* to beat exhorts how it no longer does so; just as the street described as 'unlovely' invokes the present as something worse than ugly, for being an active loveliness now deleted. Another memorable example occurs in Tennyson's great poem of frustrated hope, 'Mariana', in which the poem's eponymous character wearily waits for a visitor who never arrives: 'Unlifted was the clinking latch' allows us to imagine, and indeed to hear, the absent presence of the sound of the latch that remains *un*lifted.[52] Such effects as occur at choice moments in Tennyson may be found much more commonly but at the same time more audaciously in Blake. Taking only the prefix 'un' (more might be said about, for instance, the prefix 'in', or indeed the suffix 'less'), within a single poem: *Milton* includes, 'unhappy' (x3), 'unexampled', 'unroots', 'unmans', 'unfathomable' (twice), 'Unutterable' (x3), 'unconquerable', 'unloose' (x2; plus 'unloos'd'), 'unkind', 'unknown' (x4), 'ungirded', 'unannihilated', 'unbar', 'unwilling', 'unseen' (x2), 'unnatural', 'unpermanent', 'unchain', 'Unwaken'd', 'unconvinced', 'ungovernable', 'unform'd' (x2), 'untouch'd', 'unwearied' (x2), 'Unpassable', 'unbounded', 'Unforgiving', 'unlovely', 'unexpansive', 'unfolded', 'unendurable' and 'undervaluing'.

Some of these words are outlandishly unusual, and are (the OED suggests) likely coinages, such as 'unannihilated', 'unpermanent' and 'unmans'. But even those that seem conventional read quirkily within their contexts. 'Unhappy', for instance, first occurs in the phrase 'Unhappy tho' in heav'n', which draws 'happy' and heaven' into juxtaposition through the chiming of their 'h' sounds: the semantic work performed by the prefix 'un' therefore feels all the more disruptive of the natural expectation, averred by the sound pairing, that heaven ought to be a place to excite happiness. Similarly, 'unkind' is more telling as an absolute value within its context, for being paradoxically equated with its opposite: 'To do unkind things in kindness'. Contrasts are thereby made sharper by drawing opposing elements together through their sonic similarity. Further examples from *Milton* include: '*C*upidity un*c*onquerable!'; 'un*r*oots the *r*ocks & hills'; 'And *man*, un*mans*'. But the broader point about these un-words is how they tease at limits, either by reaffirming those limits or by revealing a breach.

More might be said on this topic of Blake's contraries, drawing out the implications of the notion that (as Blake enigmatically asserts in *Milton*) 'There is a place where Contrarieties are equally True' (pl. 30.1; *E* 129). But for the purposes of this chapter, it is helpful to see Blake's use of oppositions as part of his global strategy of destabilization within his verse style. Oppositions within his writing might be usefully understood, that is, as continuous with the oppositions he stages between the eye and the ear. For the images with which he illustrated his poems are not dispensable ornament or afterthought, or even ekphrastic annotation. Even where he was commissioned to illustrate texts by other writers, his visual art offers more than secondary 'illustration': his images inform, but also challenge, so as to transform. The visual life of Blake's poems induces disparate or actually opposed elements into conjunction, in ways that (Erdman has suggested) draw upon the Old Testament prophetic tradition of dramatizing multiple perspectives.[53] Saintsbury and Beer were quoted above as cautioning the reader of the extent to which the visual illumination of his verse meant that 'he was evidently always thinking of the meaning or the ornament, not the poetic form', and that 'deflected Blake from the craftsmanlike concerns of the normal poet'. But such a worry, though understandable, misconceives the challenge Blake sought to meet, and the challenge his poetry invites us to take up. The opposition of eye and ear is not a matter of a fixed compromise but shakes out as a kind of dynamic collusion. Wolfson refers to 'a marriage of the verbal and the visual' that requires us not only to 'see … what we hear … [but also to] hear … what we see'.[54] That sound and sense might not be competing but reciprocal and integrative brings us closer to Blake's method – though Wolfson's 'marriage' metaphor needs to be understood as enabling the fullest context of Blake's starkest contraries, including heaven and hell.

Reading Blake with our eyes as well as our ears, and for the interplay between the two, certainly makes sense also in the context of how biblical poetry often works with and out of highly visual actions and prophetic descriptions.[55] But it remains problematic to engage fully the visual appeal of Blake's verse, not least for the fact that his poems are for the most part printed without his illustrations; modern readers routinely experience a sterilized version of what Blake produced. For reasons of cost as well as convention, his poems are most often encountered today as stranded on the pristine blank space of the white page. It is a form of bowdlerizing, of the sort Blake weathered in the later nineteenth century, when his prosody was routinely smoothed out in printed editions, and generally made more conventional. While that no longer still happens today, Blake does in fact continue to suffer the procrustean imperatives of his editors. For in spite of developments in facsimile, photographic and letterpress technology, Blake's punctuation continues to be normalized and modernized. Where it is ambiguous, editors inevitably interpret it one way or another, usually in favour of modernized norms. That might seem reasonable in principle. In practice, though, Blake's etching is such that it is sometimes hard to distinguish between full stops and commas, or indeed colons and exclamation marks, and editors have therefore come to significantly different conclusions.

To dwell on such tiny details might look like undue fuss. Risking what Coleridge called 'hypercriticism', however, it is well to remember that for all his circumspection on this score (not wishing to miss the wood for the trees), Coleridge was also the first to emphasize 'how little instructive any criticism can be which does not enter into minutiae'.[56] Even so, unlike attending to Blake's wordplay, the difficulty in adjudicating on the minutiae of his punctuation marks is not merely a matter of determining what he might have intended. He was not always consistent or conventional in his marks and spacings.[57] Worse: he sometimes seems to have been careless when it came to inking in what the copper plate had left out in the printing process; and at other times, he acted capriciously, making changes from the copper plate, or across different printings.[58] All of which creates a headache for editors, and might prompt readers to wonder whether the game is after all worth the candle. Why invest such energy in determining what Blake 'really' meant, when he seemed not to have taken the trouble to make that clear himself?

Without disputing the occasions where he was inconsistent, unconventional, careless and capricious, there is good reason to believe that ambiguity was, at least some of the time, his decided intention. Uncertainty in calligraphic rendering might have been a deliberate ploy on his part, that is, to keep multiple possibilities operative. Nelson Hilton argues this case suggestively, and ties his observation to the idea that multiple, including contradictory, rhetorical and syntactical variations might simultaneously be entertained if Blake's punctuation choices remain purposefully unresolved.[59] Punctuation has implications not only for rhetoric and syntax, it also affects prosody; and indeed, 'punctuation' may include more than the conventional spacings, signs and typographical devices. Visual adornments and decorations may also serve – and might well have intended to serve – to 'punctuate' Blake's texts too. Here, as David Fuller has suggested, punctuation 'is not primarily syntactic, or rhythmic, or rhetorical', it is instead a kind of 'visual jouissance'.[60] That, in turn, opens up the question of Blake's humour that critics have tended to find in his early works in particular, though it pervades his entire oeuvre.[61] From biting satire against erroneous convictions or the practices of contemporary culture to mischievous wit directed against the reader, Blake is not offering us light relief, but keeping us on our toes, or on the back foot; he's addling our flow and pattern of thinking.

From the pithy 'Proverbs of Hell' to his protracted prophetic poems, there is throughout a restless impatience with convention, which is continually put under pressure, through irony, surprise and paradox. To take a late work that has been described as one of Blake's most impenetrable, *The Four Zoas* is an extended example of where the joke is, if we are not careful, at the expense of us earnest head-scratching scholars. As with his indeterminate punctuation, we risk missing the point if we work too worthily, when it may be that his poetics are designed to resist our attempts to tame them into paraphrase. If we sweat to riddle the intricate mythology of the poem without registering its satirical force, we are liable to overlook the governing sense in which the poem is, among other things, a critique of the power of mythological narratives. Those competing voices that erupt in the poem do more than make difficult the possibility of a steady narrative line: they also help expose, through their contradictory suggestions, the incoherence of society's mythmaking narratives that inhibit individual responses in favour of prefabricated assumptions, and ultimately authorize social repression.[62]

A suggestive analogy has been advanced between his methods and those exploited by Kierkegaard (especially dialectic and irony) to explore the tensions between scepticism and affirmation, religion and nihilism, philosophy and poetry.[63] It is a useful prompt, in that both serve up highly quotable lines, but neither seeks to communicate through individual lines so much as through their interstices. Blake asserts a great deal – reading him can sometimes feel like being beaten over the head – but far more than in his individual hectorings, his poetry takes its imaginative life through the connections and collisions staged in his own writing.[64] Little is efferent as a self-sufficient theological tenet. That is not to say his poetics abet religious relativism. Binaries are consistently foxed, and categories of understanding continually renegotiated, as a way of upsetting dogmatic certainty, but in a way that provokes greater awareness of the insufficiency of static, monological thinking – not least because the world is itself provokingly contradictory in the way in which separate parts make up the whole. But that, in turn, sharpens the emphasis on particularized belief, over generalized faith or fixed institutional belief systems. Blake's faith is an endless negotiation between warring mental impulses, the goal of which is a momentary clarity of vision, because, for Blake, discord was the guarantor of religious truth and vitality. Within his provoking paradoxes nothing is beyond contradiction; no doctrine or belief is beyond criticism; belief must forge its own path, between the pratfalls of credulity and the sterility of scepticism.

But my passing metaphor of the true path is not Blake's, and it is not to be imagined as a rational mean between the irrational excesses of being either too ready or too unwilling to believe. If we reckon, with Blake, that art 'cannot exist but in minutely organized Particulars', as against the 'generalizing Demonstrations of the Rational Power', we may be forced to reimagine an opposition to rationality that does not come in the form of irrationality, but rather as transrationality. As above the rational grasp, that is to say, rather than, as it were, below it. Or perhaps beyond it, rather than a reduction of it; over-spilling rather than underwhelming. 'The merely rational mind is invariably dualistic, and divides the field of almost every moment between what it can presently understand and what it then deems "wrong" or untrue': Richard Rohr describes how the mystical mind, by contrast, outstrips the limitations of this binary.[65] Language struggles to capture that transrational perspective, but poetry may draw upon special resources to do so: from the appeal of myth and metrics to metaphorical and metonymical thinking; including the enigmatic subtlety of being both for and against. As a mode, poetry has licence and means to outwit the limitations of rational dualities; that is its milieu. If error inheres in a stable, 'single vision', art, verbal and visual (or in Blake's poetry, verbal–visual), is the needful antidote.

Curiously, then, Blake's achievement as a craftsman of minute particulars as against chaos (where 'not a line is drawn without intention', and there is 'not a Letter that is Insignificant') is not expressed in the steadiness and sureness of his creations, but in the extent to which they resist dogmatism (religious and artistic) through their destabilization. Viewed in this way, Blake's poetry is not an apprenticeship to lyricism that culminates in the *Songs of Innocence and Experience* before curdling into the long lines of his later prophecies. From start to finish his poetry attempts to unsteady familiar patterns of thought, which is both reflected in and achieved by the evolving ways he unsteadies familiar patterns of poetic expression. Correspondingly, attempts to tidy Blake up as a way to make sense of his thought and style have impoverished both.

Scepticism over Blake's craft, and the tendency to read it as chaos, has been refined on several fronts over the years since he died; while it was once orthodox to disparage Blake as a poet of strong vision but weak execution, critics have edged increasingly towards admiring his design and facture. Still, the opinion that Saintsbury articulated over a century ago remains a critical commonplace: that in his later poems, which were his most ambitious and explicitly religious works, 'he found pure verse insufficient ... for his "prophetic" exercitations'. What's perhaps most surprising in Saintsbury's view is not his contention about Blake's prosodical practice but his concomitant claim that this evolution in Blake's writing style is itself 'not in the least surprising': 'English lyric' being 'too delicate for the commands of a mysticism' that was, after all, 'somewhat chaotic and giantesque'.[66] How can this judgement – compounding the well-worn aspersion of his vision as chaotic with the notion that it was also oversized – stand against Blake's own uncompromising counter-claim that 'Spiritual Verse' is 'order'd & measur'd' (pl. 48.8; *E* 196)? Or indeed, his rider that 'prosaic numbers', if such prosaic texture there must be, suit the 'inferior parts' of the poem, complementing by contradistinction the 'terrific' passages of his white-hot religious visionings (pl. 3; *E* 146)?

We cannot simply take Blake at his word; but then, he does not ask for that. His poems are not issued as self-evidences inviting passive assent; they are designed to pique. They challenge us as readers, however sceptical or sympathetic, to engage in the drama of their unfolding styles, which challenge may include subverting our account of what poetry is. When he avows, in *Milton*, 'To cast aside from Poetry, all that is not Inspiration', he refuses to abide even the notion of what might constitute 'pure verse' in the first place, if it should not in the end prove consubstantial with his 'inspiration', which is never merely aesthetic but always animated by divinity (pl. 41.7; *E* 142). It is clear how deeply Blake's work is informed by tradition that he fashions to his own purpose, even from the very beginning.[67] But it is essential to remember that the traditions on which he draws are not only literary. His seemingly unmetrical poetry takes its cue and its authority also from the example of the prophetic poetry of the Bible, from those he described as 'Naturally free, and of too ardent a spirit to be confined by rule', being guided instead by 'the nature of the subject only, and the impulse of divine inspiration'.[68] Nineteenth-century biblical scholarship abetted Blake's artisanal audacity here. Lowth has been mentioned already, but the work of Thomas Howes was perhaps even more important, for going further in justifying the apparent 'disorder' of the sacred prophecies, demonstrating more thoroughly the aesthetic as well as discursive coherence of their oratorical styles, which may include abrupt transitions and juxtapositions, for the purposes of 'persuasive argumentation'.[69]

Cutting Blake up into the ingénue and the iconoclast, the effulgent, untutored youth and the jaded, self-exiled prophet crying in the wilderness, traduces his accomplishments and maturation as a poet. He avows his faith in poetry across his writing, and most vigorously in the ways he disturbs its very nature as verse, without ever resigning his writing to anything that could be called prose: while insisting all the more keenly, indeed, that what he produced must be taken for poetry, by implicit precedent of no less a model than the sacred poetry of the Old Testament.

For Blake's contemporaries saturated in the verse culture and hermeneutical debates of their moment, his stylistic and theological heterodoxies carried an unmistakable disruptive charge, and in this sense his earlier lyricism is continuous with his later, long-lined poetry that remembers not only the tunes of the nursery, and the rhythms of ballads and of broadsides, but also the mythic resonances of Macpherson's *Ossian Poems*, the sacerdotal valencies of the Authorized Version of the Bible, and the antinomian, revolutionary spirit of the Levellers and Ranters.[70] But even while registering the emblematic significance (or 'semantic halo') of his rhythms, and of his prosodic repertoire more generally, it is sciolistic to trace his verse style – to attempt a definitive scansion of his poems – as if its lineage were purely literary, or 'pure verse'. Blake's 'particulars' draw on the resources of literary history, as well as on a far wider set of religious sources and influences ('inspiration' not least among them), and they express themselves through the destabilizing strategies well documented by scholars, but also in ways that scholars have yet to agree upon, from his punctuation to his prosody. Destabilization is never richer here than when it exceeds dialectics and operates instead by paradoxes, the 'rhythm' of which (in de Lubac's lexicon) refuses binary thinking, while simultaneously insisting on the productive necessity of keeping opposing possibilities in play. Blake's verse style creates the conditions for truth that lie beyond the limitations of fixed, either/or thoughts; his poems stage but also elicit occasions for the more active and engaged process of *thinking*, which is ongoing.

Especially where his metres seemingly diffuse into rhythmic prose, the provenance of his poetics really is to be located in the Land Debatable. But they must actually be debated, and on the merits of their minutiae, each time, by each of us, in the act of reading: 'those who have been told that my Works are but … a Madman's Scrawls', Blake admonished, 'I demand of them to do me justice to examine before they decide' (*E* 527–8). His impatience is apt now as it was in his lifetime, perhaps more so, and rests not merely on the question of whether or not he was sane, or his works worthy as artistic objects. Where Blake demands 'justice', it is for his works to be engaged in a way that discerns how his habits of systematic unsettling inhere in the form but extend to the themes of his poetry, in which his theology of justice and just thinking is made available, however obliquely, through his own self-debating.

2

Alfred Tennyson: Word Music

Let blow the trumpet strongly while I pray[1]

At the age of eighty-two, the year before he died, Alfred Tennyson – long since a Lord and Poet Laureate – remained playfully as well as pridefully spry, revelling in long walks and waltzes, defying his friends to get up from a low chair twenty times without using their hands, while performing this feat himself.[2] In that same year, he was asked by a visitor if he might read to a young boy, and both his choice of poem as well as his style of recitation belie something of the same 'high spirits of his youth' (*M* ii. 416). He read 'Ode on the Death of the Duke of Wellington', and his son Hallam recalled how he 'dwelt long on the final words, letting them ring so to speak'; and how at the end he said: 'It is a great roll of words, the music of words', adding, 'People do not understand the music of words' (*M* ii. 417–18).

It is a commonplace to refer to Tennyson as 'musical', in the sense that his verses are winningly mellifluent, or vividly mimetic. But the same epithet is also often cast as an aspersion, where his ringing verses are said to ring hollow. 'Nay, he will write you a poem with nothing in it except music,' observed one of his contemporaries, R. H. Horne, 'and as if its music were everything, it shall charm your soul'.[3] While these views of Tennyson's musicality are obviously at odds – innocent pleasure as against sirenic deception – they nonetheless share a common assumption that his verse is primarily sensuous rather than intellectual.

Although Tennyson lacked any aptitude for music ('he was by nature shut out from it'),[4] his verses prompted a number of musical adaptations, and more generally Tennyson himself encouraged the view of poetry's essentially affective appeal. This is true when it came to his own compositions, but also when admiring others. Rather than dwell on the details of this or that philosophical nuance inscribed in particular phrasings, his headlong appreciations characteristically took the form of phatic hurrahs. Declaiming passages by heart (he had a prodigious memory for verse), he would punctuate his renditions with basking ejaculations such as, 'That's magnificent', or 'What a line!', or 'Isn't that splendid?'[5] For public readings of his own poetry he provided prefatory and running explanatory commentaries; but still, he deferred to the act of reading itself. His recitations had about them not only, as his wife recalled, a certain 'glamour',[6] they had also a burden of realization. Listeners frequently reported that they were greatly moved by his performances but also that they only really 'understood' his verses when he read them; his recitations corrected as well as enriched how listeners responded to his writing. That did not mean he always tidied things up by eliminating ambiguities. His audible readings were not offered in the service of establishing a definitive translation of what the page-bound words already and self-evidently articulated; they were as likely to insinuate further hesitations and uncertainties (William Allingham, for instance, recorded how he introduced 'a peculiar *incomplete* cadence at the end' of his readings).[7] Whereas Robert Browning's poetry inspired societies exfoliating every layer of implication in his writing,[8] Tennyson contended that his own poems might reveal themselves most truly when instantiated as word music: 'It doesn't matter so much in poetry written for the intellect – as much of Browning's is, perhaps,' he explained, 'but in mine it's necessary to know how to sound it properly'.[9]

But what was it about sounding that mattered 'so much' for Tennyson, that made it 'necessary', over and above any direct appeal to 'the intellect'? 'When I was eight, I remember making a line I thought grander than Campbell, or Byron, or Scott. I rolled it out, it was this: "With slaughterous sons of thunder rolled the flood" – great nonsense of course, but I thought it fine' (*M* ii. 93). That judgement – fine sounding, but great nonsense – curiously prefigures the adverse verdicts on his mature verse, as the line itself – its lateral, lingual and sibilant sumptuousness – offers a phonetic and rhythmic foretaste of what velvet soundings would come to be called Tennysonian. Perhaps his poetic sensibility never much matured from his childlike thrill of its sheer sounding, and that all the octogenarian with a glint in his eye 'understood' about the music of words was that versified language might slip the discipline of semantic sense, to revel in aural unmeaning. That Tennyson never outgrew his appetite for poetry's fantastical possibilities is clear from his preoccupations with mythical times and figures that run from his early to his last verses (the very final poem he wrote is, aptly, called 'The Dreamer'). It is certainly no surprise to learn that he cherished the story-teller's phrase, 'far, far away', which 'had always', he confessed, 'a strange charm' for him (III. 197. n). In his old age as in his youth, Tennyson was drawn to poetry for its aesthetic transports, and with undiminished pleasure; verse was the ideal passepartout for his escapist's longings.

So it has been said, at least, often by his most ardent admirers. W. H. Auden thought Tennyson 'had the finest ear, perhaps, of any English poet', but that 'he was also undoubtedly the stupidest';[10] and for Auden, there was no tension between these observations. 'I became Public Cultural Enemy No 1 over the Tennyson preface,' he later told a friend, noting that the backlash against him was after all 'a little comic', given that Tennyson was one of his 'favourite poets'.[11] Auden is by no means alone in his fine-ear/thick-brain testimony, nor in his presumption that Tennyson might be so neatly sliced up in this way, so as to relish his lyricism while in the same breath abjure its vacuity.[12] Others have gone further in their suspicions, to suggest that Tennyson's verbal opulence is not merely devoid of intellectual content but that it might actually be avoiding something, or covering something up.[13] But Auden's view in particular is worth pausing over, because he elsewhere widens the lens, diagnosing the tendency of nineteenth-century poetry in general to evince an 'extraordinarily high standard' of 'prosodic skill' with 'frequent clumsiness' of verbal sentiment, and because he also speculates a cause.[14] Auden attributes 'both the virtue and the defect' to an early schooling in the classics. That poets of the period inevitably had their first experience of writing verse in Latin, a language 'syntactically and rhythmically very different from their own', honed their habits of prosody while at the same time cultivating a 'habit of approximation' when it came to diction ('for two words in two languages to match exactly, to have not only the same general connotation, but also the same overtones, is extremely rare').[15] Poets inducted into such habits were, Auden argues, too easily satisfied with the first word they could think of to fit the metre or supply a needed rhyme, and insufficiently concerned with the expressive potential of words themselves.

James I. Wimsatt likewise identifies a marked formal proficiency in nineteenth-century poetry, also attributing the cause to the classical education poets of the period typically received. Differently, though, where Auden speaks of virtues and defects as immutable aesthetic desiderata, Wimsatt proposes that nineteenth-century poets in fact proceeded by a rival set of values; namely, that studying prosody in the classical tradition predicates rhythmic pattern rather than Aristotelian mimesis as the beginning of poetic life, thereby according 'verbal sound' 'a prior and positive value'.[16] Without an equivalent education today (which has been replaced by a new preoccupation with Aristotle, literary theory and vernacular literature), Wimsatt argues, readers tend to focus on poetry's discursive content (character and theme), as if verse were no more than a series of grammatical statements shaped to an imposed metrical form that regulates and ornaments it.

Taken together, Auden and Wimsatt's literary-historical conjectures may caution us against being too quick to find defects, or to forgive them as virtues, in Tennyson's verse style.[17] But we might yet wish to ask why, if classical education determined a unique habitus of writing and hearing in the period, it did not seem to have had an equivalent influence on previous generations (on such paragons of precise diction as Dryden or Pope, for instance). In the prior and positive value of sound that can be heard so potently in Tennyson, there must surely be other influences at work to have distinguished his style from other literary periods, as well as from other coeval poets. (After all, Hopkins, considered in Chapter 4, also enjoyed a classical education, but his verse is often recommended for the exactitude of its diction but dispraised for the apparent imprecision of its metrics.) Aestheticism is an obvious candidate, and its sway on

Tennyson has been well documented. But though Tennyson was early and influentially dubbed a 'Poet of Sensation' by Arthur Hallam, and subsequently folded into the movement by later literary historians, he himself baulked at the association ('Art for Art's sake! Hail, truest Lord of Hell' (III. 12. 1)). His relationship with aestheticism is more complicated than that of exponent or adversary, not only because the movement itself admitted diverse sympathies and expressions, but also because he was anxiously torn, as Seamus Perry frames it, 'between a passionate faith in lyricism and unshifting doubts about it'.[18] Whatever readers might feel about his word music, Tennyson was himself persistently troubled by the worry that his compositions might in the end express no more than their own sumptuous artistry. Kirstie Blair's illuminating account of Tennyson's ambivalent attitudes to 'form and faith' offers needful help here, teasing out the ways in which 'poetic forms were deeply implicated in nineteenth-century debates over religious forms'.[19] But a study of Tennyson's 'faith in poetry' requires a slightly different perspective, at once broader and more focused ('form' refers to both more and less than 'poetry', as 'in' specifies more and less than 'and'). Generalizing about poets and periods may, in any event, only take us so far. To get a surer grip on Tennyson's word music, it is necessary to inspect his strategies close up.

***

Everyone knows Tennyson's signature achievements in imitative harmony, in which, as one contemporary quipped, 'You are sure of a sweet sound, though nothing be in it';[20] as here, from *The Princess*:

> So waste not thou; but come; for all the vales
> Await thee; azure pillars of the hearth
> Arise to thee; the children call, and I
> Thy shepherd pipe, and sweet is every sound,
> Sweeter thy voice, but every sound is sweet;
> Myriads of rivulets hurrying thro' the lawn,
> The moan of doves in immemorial elms,
> And murmuring of innumerable bees.

(II. 287–8. 200–7)

Sweet, sweeter, sweet: these words that cascade through the stanza collaborate with rich internal rhymes to overweeningly, cloyingly, loamish effect. Lexical luxuriating of this sort may delight or disgust readers, but even if the onomatopoeic urgings are not themselves 'stupid' by Auden's standards, they threaten to make their readers so. That lush clutter of polysyllables towards the end invites us to stop thinking, to relax into sheer sounding, like Tennyson's torpid mariner who ate the lotus leaves: 'And deep-asleep he seemed, yet all awake, / And music in his ears his beating heart did make' (I. 470. 35–6). While our ears are stimulated, our minds drift off. We are not being woken to new ideas and experiences, we are being rocked to exquisite somnolence: such verses seem (quoting 'The Lotus-Eaters' again) 'a tale of little meaning though the words are strong' (I. 476. 164).

Fewer people associate Tennyson with clanging urgency; as here, also from *The Princess*:

Entering, the sudden light
Dazed me half-blind: I stood and seemed to hear,
As in a poplar grove when a light wind wakes
A lisping of the innumerous leaf and dies,
Each hissing in his neighbour's ear; and then
A strangled titter, out of which there brake
On all sides, clamouring etiquette to death,
Unmeasured mirth; while now the two old kings
Began to wag their baldness up and down,
The fresh young captains flashed their glittering teeth,
The huge bush-bearded Barons heaved and blew,
And slain with laughter rolled the gilded Squire.

(II. 250. 10–21)

Something of the same sonorous 'murmuring' recurs through 'lisping of the innumerous leaf'. But sonority is set up here to throw the harshness that follows into greater relief, and sounds are used to evoke not only other sounds but also other things. The whole passage simmers with portent, with the stridulous promise of terror that is violent only in its laughter, where unleashed passions – wagging, flashing, heaving, blowing, slaying – are anomalously contextualized as unmeasured mirth. Assonance, alliteration and rhythm fetch out a sinister-seeming set of collocations that are to be read as the opposite: from hissed whispers to strangled titters to the wryly oxymoronic pairing of civilized clamour.

It is an intricate, ironic and cumulative drama; and we thrill to the scene not so much because of the story it tells, but for the ways we are – through breathless, tongue-twisting sounds and rhythms – implicated into its telling. Our reading generates the narrative, but also an experience that itself becomes part of the narrative: we are made intimate with the event our reading describes. The poem's verbal impasto thus offers something quite different from direct proposition, and it is notable in respect of Tennyson's word textures how studies attentive to his style consistently identify repetition as his dominant trait.[21] In prose, that typically implies redundancy, but in poetry (as observed in several of the poets in this book), it may imply repletion; or indeed, it may open the possibility of renegotiation. Suffice to notice for now that Tennyson leads with a technique of writing that frustrates attempts to 'understand' his poems by abstracting his meanings outside of the poetic mode, into paraphrase. Many of his most famous lines thus play with the possibilities of replay – from 'Break, break, break' (II. 24. 1), to 'Tears, idle tears' (II. 232. 21), to 'The woods decay, the woods decay and fall' (II. 607. 1) – and the same sort of effects may be found throughout his writing. Relatedly, his style of recitation, though richly varied depending on the poem,[22] was nonetheless consistent in seeking (as one contemporary described it) to make his verses sound 'as unlike ordinary prose as possible'.[23]

Approaching Tennyson's poetry as a riposte to the instrumental and monolithic logic of prose is a good start, though it should not be overstated. 'I hate to be tied down to say "*This* means *that*" … interpretation', he once complained; but he also carped about being 'widely misunderstood even by educated readers' (*M* i. 393, 254). Between his aversion to being pinned down and his frustration with his poems being taken willy-nilly, Tennyson urged a different category of attention: he wrote of catching his poems' 'drift', whether 'allegorical', 'parabolic' or 'general' (*M* ii. 123, 127).[24] While retreating from the stringencies of propositional thinking, then, he does not thereby lapse into passive unthinking. Where Edmund Gosse wittily admitted himself a 'young coward' happy to 'let sleeping dogmas lie',[25] Tennyson was always boldly exploratory. As an undergraduate he was 'stirred ... to wrath' by the narrowness and dryness of the ordinary course of study at Cambridge, which he felt skirted the most pressing subjects of deepest human interest (*M* i. 66). And right up until the end of his life, he pursued a number of existential and religious positions and anxieties in verse, in ways that show both his intellectual restlessness when it came to ultimate questions (on the apparent Godlessness of the world, say, or damnation, or immortality), but also his openness to thinking through contemporary developments in science, and the possibility that revelation might be found across religious traditions – whereby, in the words of his friend Benjamin Jowett, 'All religions are one.'[26] Even the tidy confidence of 'Crossing the Bar' (which poem he asked his son Hallam to put at the end of each of his collections) prospects the 'hope' of meeting his maker rather than dogmatic certainty (III. 254. 15). The same might be said of a poem like 'Faith' (III. 250), which was 'written at the end of his life' as a long-delayed pendent to 'Despair'. The defiance with which it quashes doubt, through negative phrasings put under trochaic pressures at the start of five of the poem's eight lines ('Doubt not', 'Let not', Quail not', 'Neither Morn', 'Dark no more'), is acutely at odds with, say, the serene spiritual confidences styled in the poems of Christina Rossetti (considered in Chapter 3). Tennyson huffs and puffs so heartily as to insinuate the precariousness and provisionality in his attitude.

Correspondingly, it is often said that Tennyson is a poet of doubt rather than faith, and there is some truth in that. But some nuancing is required. A number of commentaries, especially more recent ones, seem determined to figure religious faith as normatively 'constant, certain, and absolute', in antithetical contrast to the 'conditional, tentative and skeptical' faith that literature inspires or demands.[27] Polarizing religious and poetic faith in this way is cartoonishly unhelpful; within the Christian tradition, faith is an act of grace and of will that comes, if it comes at all, without any such contractual expectations of absolute constancy or certainty. That is what defines its epistemological status as 'faith' in the first place; otherwise it would simply be called 'knowledge'. Tennyson registers and ratifies that distinction, as he also refines it. Treating religious faith in exclusive opposition to doubt obscures the extent to which Tennyson's religious faith is made 'vital' (Charles Kingsley's word) by his willingness to think through his beliefs, and indeed the nature of believing, in verse.[28] More than the fact of doubting itself, Tennyson's *style* of doubting brings his faith as well as his poetry alive, in the way his word music *strives*: not merely to think and to express his faith, but also to explore and experience it, through verse. That is presumably what T. S. Eliot responded to when he affirmed that *In Memoriam* – Tennyson's greatest poem, and his greatest poem on faith[29] – ought indeed to be called 'religious', not because of the quality of its faith, but because of the quality of its doubting ('Its faith is a poor thing, but its doubt is a very intense experience.').[30] But before examining that poem in particular, it is instructive to turn back to where this chapter began, to 'Ode on the Death of the Duke of Wellington', which is routinely overlooked in Tennyson's corpus, or if cited at all, typically done so as an instance of his mawkish misfiring, both poetically and theologically.

***

Tennyson is such a looming figure that before it is possible to read him adequately we must first hear past the Tennysonian stereotype of merely pleasing melody, whether according to what Christopher Ricks admiringly described as his 'mouthability', or what William Empson, less admiringly, dismissed as his 'simple and laborious cult of onomatopoeia'.[31] His 'Ode' takes us far beyond that, but the poem is not perforce, as it is often said to be, an aberration or embarrassment of his talent. His hammy recitation of the 'Ode' is important to remember not because it was exceptional but because it was representative of how he read all his verse: with high drama, typically 'lingering with solemn sweetness on every vowel sound'.[32] What is exceptional, however, is the extent to which the poem's word music is itself, by Tennyson's standards, so curiously *un*sweet. Here is the first stanza:

BURY the Great Duke
  With an empire's lamentation,
Let us bury the Great Duke
  To the noise of the mourning of a mighty nation,

Mourning when their leaders fall,
Warriors carry the warrior's pall,
And sorrow darkens hamlet and hall.

(II. 480. 1–7)

Having greɪt dju:k ring with Tennyson's thick Lincolnshire accent would give the phonetic collocation blunt force, accentuating the contrast with the softer, liquid, polysyllabic tremolo that runs through the next line – before we are brought back, by repeating the opening phrasing: 'Let us bury the Great Duke'. Then the fourth line runs away once more, gathering up the 'n', 'm' and 't' sounds of the second line, and the double end-rhyme, 'ation'. Which in turn gives way to a new movement of sound and rhythm, tolling through the flat-sounding triplet-rhyme, 'all'. A single sentence cast over seven lines is arrested into near inarticulacy: slugging, stop, starting; and repeating, as the rest of the poem continues in the same stentorious, hortatory unfluency. Here are the next two stanzas:

II

Where shall we lay the man whom we deplore?
Here, in streaming London's central roar.
Let the sound of those he wrought for,
And the feet of those he fought for,
Echo round his bones for evermore.

III

Lead out the pageant: sad and slow,
As fits an universal woe,
Let the long long procession go,
And let the sorrowing crowd about it grow,
And let the mournful martial music blow;
The last great Englishman is low.

(II. 482. 8–18)

Repetition of word and sound here reaches parodic proportions, every line being self-contained, beginning ponderously, and culminating on its rhyme – on which, we remember, he specially dwelt. All that 'or'-ing and 'oh'-ing seems self-indulgent, an adagio liberty of sighing and moaning that's more tumid than aureate. He seems to have lapsed into 'semantic satiation', whereby the iteration of identical or near-identical sounds threatens to make the words they speak meaningless. The 'Ode' does not quite curdle into nonsense in that way; it does not quite go over the cliff, but it gets vertiginously close.

'Ode on the Death of the Duke of Wellington' was Tennyson's first separate publication as Laureate, and perhaps the most public commission he would ever take, commemorating the 'last great Englishman'; it was his chance to show off the felicity of phrasing and auditory appeal for which he was feted. He seemed as well placed as anyone to produce something monumental, to satisfy a nation. The Laureateship had after all been conferred on him in explicit recognition of another elegy, *In Memoriam*, which had so impressed Prince Albert; and not even his harshest critics could deny that he wrote beautifully. Yet his 'Ode' left most reviewers wanting, and his distinguished acquaintances let their disappointment be known too. 'Perhaps the most remarkable thing about the few lines', Thackeray observed, 'is that Moxon has given £200 for it'. T. H. Huxley was even more derisive: 'I send Tennyson's ode by way of packing – it is not worth much more'. Ricks quotes both of these remarks as a preface to his own contradistinctive account of the 'sober dignity' with which the poem begins; and if that dignity seems somewhat 'stiff', Ricks suggests, the admiration for Wellington 'rings entirely true'.[33] But even Ricks – perhaps Tennyson's greatest critical champion – cannot in the end excuse what he identifies as the poem's double flaw, where it loses faith in its own convictions, leading to failure of impression. 'Whose life was work' is, Ricks thinks, honourably to the point, but then Tennyson cannot imagine what work might be like for Wellington after death, and so protests too vaguely and too much:

> ... we doubt not that for one so true
> There must be other nobler work to do
> Than when he fought at Waterloo,
> And victor he must ever be.
>
> (II. 491. 255–8)

It is right to say that 'we doubt not' insinuates the very thing it seeks to negate,[34] and indeed Ricks's complaint might be extended, by noting the modality of 'must' in the line following. If there really were no doubting, if there really *must* be nobler work, why not state this plainly, and specify what it might be? W. David Shaw objects to the same lines: 'Whenever Tennyson tries to be more assertive, he can imagine nothing more inspiring than a heavenly Bentham and an apotheosis of machine-like simplicity and practical capacity.'[35] Rhetoric compensates for argument, except that it can't. Avowing Wellington's otherworldly work to do, and his 'Eternal honour' and 'ever-echoing avenues' of fame (II. 487. 150; 481. 79), Tennyson does not entirely buy it himself, and so neither do we. But the failure of the poem is in that sense theological rather than poetic: the greater strain of the poem does succeed, and brilliantly so, as sheer lament, and perhaps more wittingly than Ricks and Shaw allow. Here is the complete sentence from which the lines above were quoted:

> Whom we see not we revere;
> We revere, and we refrain
> From talk of battles loud and vain,
> And brawling memories all too free
> For such a wise humility
> As befits a solemn fane:
> We revere, and while we hear
> The tides of Music's golden sea
> Setting toward eternity,
> Uplifted high in heart and hope are we,
> Until we doubt not that for one so true
> There must be other nobler work to do
> Than when he fought at Waterloo,
> And victor he must ever be.
>
> (II. 490–1. 245–58)

Seen in this fuller context, the negative construction of 'doubt not' and the self-witnessing 'must' take on a new aspect. Reverence – beat out three times in a single sentence – is itself rallied negatively: for one whom 'we see not', and through 'refrain' of mere nostalgic glorifying. Lamentation is compounded by metaphors of morbidity, mortality and gloom that circulate and grow through the poem, undercutting those moments that seek most forcibly to reach for consolation. Yet this prevailing negativity is not absolute; it has more positive charge than, for instance, Arthur Hugh Clough's, 'That there are powers above us I admit', in which his meditation on the efficacy of prayer to divine powers concludes with the most grudging of concessions, squeezed from a double negative: 'I will not say they will not give us aid.'[36] Tennyson's concession, by contrast, is actively willed by the transcendent promise 'Music' provides – twice mentioned in the poem already, but here idealized into a proper noun – that uplifts hearts and hopes, 'Until' such time as the negating force of doubt can itself be negated. It is a provisional kind of hope, for sure, one that is not steady and secure but must be uplifted, and may only be so while the music gestures us towards eternity. So it might, after all, be a delusion. But its quality of doubting is not thereby a fraud; it has a piercing honesty arising from its imperfect struggle, willed through its word music.

Such music is not to be sampled, though: as 'a great roll of words', it takes all two hundred and eighty-one of the poem's lines to register it potency, which is cumulative, never mind its purpose. Taken thus as a whole, Ricks's sympathetic reading of the poem's tone as 'sober dignity' does not seem at all right; intoxicated, even incontinent, is more like it, teetering at the brink of bathos. Edward Fitzgerald recalled how Tennyson used to read 'St Simeon Stylites' 'with grotesque Grimness, especially such passages as "Coughs, Aches, Stitches, etc.," laughing aloud at times'.[37] The 'Ode' is not ironically silly in that way, but perhaps it occupies somewhere between the cute histrionics of St Simeon and the aweary-dreary refrains of 'Mariana'. There is certainly some mischief in its dogged unloveliness, affronting readers' expectations – as it did at the time and continues to do so – for the unmusicality of its word music. Words do not flow but must instead be wrested into expression, and pressed to work: 'let' occurs some fourteen times, often at the opening of lines; 'and' occurs eighty-nine times, also dominating the beginning of the lines, emphasizing the paratactical labour by which the unfolding narrative is constructed through incremental conjunction, willed at every stage, rather than by organic, hierarchic or self-propelling logic. But it is at the other end of the lines, lines typically too short to contain complete statements, that the Ode's tone is established most markedly, by its sonic replays. Auto-rhymes are everywhere, and introduced from the very start,[38] encouraging the poem's claustrophobic feel as the sum of its sonic obsessiveness, returning so frequently to the same or similar sounds. Reading the poem with Tennyson's due incantatory swing and accent, it is only possible to make sense of its ending as the exhausted termination of languorous travail:

> On God and Godlike men we build our trust.
> Hush, the Dead March wails in the people's ears:
> The dark crowd moves, and there are sobs and tears:
> The black earth yawns: the mortal disappears;
> Ashes to ashes, dust to dust;
> He is gone who seemed so great.—
> Gone; but nothing can bereave him
> Of the force he made his own
> Being here, and we believe him
> Something far advanced in State,
> And that he wears a truer crown
> Than any wreath that man can weave him.
> Speak no more of his renown,
> Lay your earthly fancies down,
> And in the vast cathedral leave him,
> God accept him, Christ receive him.
>
> (II. 491–2. 266–81)

These sixteen lines only have five separate end-rhyme sounds, and the auto-rhyme at the very last is in fact a double rhyme ('l*eave him* / rec*eive him*'), which picks up the same double rhymes from a few lines above ('ber*eave him*' / 'beli*eve him*' / 'w*eave him*'). The end-rhyme of 'him' occurs earlier in the poem, in which 'With honour, honour, honour, honour to him / Eternal honour to his name', already an example of extreme repetition, is itself exactly repeated (II. 487. 149–50; 490. 230–1), though here the pronoun is pressed to supplicatory rather than celebratory intent. Wellington's 'renown' is deliberately put aside, and he is instead presented in earnest hope that God and Christ might extend to him the spiritual rather than worldly 'honour' of salvation.

Still, the poem's faith is essentially affective; and it would be too generous to claim that Tennyson is purposefully staging the collapse of theology before a tragedy that overwhelms rationality. More plainly (for the reasons Ricks, Shaw and others have adduced), he attempts a form of redemption by theology that fails because it is incoherent. But for all that, the 'Ode' has its own integrity *as* a poem. Once, listening to the choristers in Westminster Abbey, where he himself would eventually be buried, Tennyson said: 'It is beautiful, but what empty and awful mockery if there were no God. On the fields of Flanders there was no God, and the mockery and squalor of it all was relieved by no white-robed choristers, voicing a consolatory strain.'[39] His 'Ode' does not risk the same mockery, because its verse style refuses easy felicities; it purposefully undoes what Walt Whitman once described as Tennyson's 'finest verbalism'.[40] Dicey clumsiness honours the pain of the collective grief it explores, because the corrigenda of doubt are not effected through reason's cant phrasings, but through the mordant insurgences of affective stress. That is not wishful, but wilful thinking.

***

Coming to *In Memoriam* after the Wellington Ode – which is inevitably the opposite of what usually happens – we are primed to hear how far it likewise thrives through its resistance to the formal rationalizations of theology, and to the settled traditions of verse elegy itself. Lineation, rhyme and rhythm are essential to *In Memoriam*, as they are for the Wellington Ode, but in a different way. Tennyson explained how his poem's one hundred and thirty-one sections (plus Prologue and Epilogue) were written 'at many different places, and as the phases of our intercourse came to my memory and suggested them': 'I did not write them with any view of weaving them into a whole, or for publication, until I found that I had written so many' (*M* i. 304–5). Yet after an early period of experimentation (in which manuscripts show a variable stanza length of between four and five lines, and some stanzas with an alternating rhyme scheme), he established a consistent form to run through each of his separate sections, implicitly unifying the poem's diverse episodes and tones. Sections vary in length, but each shares the same stanza, according to the same rhyme scheme and metre. Pastoral and other literary elements in the poem invite associations with the elegy tradition, but rather than employ the so-called elegiac quatrain (abab), Tennyson rhymes abba. He also composed by tetrameter rather than pentameter, further distancing his poem from the formal dignities of the elegy genre, aligning his poem instead with the oral outpourings of the ballad and song, or even the nursery rhyme.

Little changes, but hardly trivial in a poet so accomplished as a stylist and in a poem so self-aware about the workings of poetry itself. Tennyson was after all the man who boasted he knew the quantity of every word in English except 'scissors'; and he had, with virtuosity, already turned his hand to the long line, from the classical-cum-medieval form of 'Leonine Elegiacs', to the breathlessly extensive catalectic trochaic octameters of 'Locksley Hall'. Styling *In Memoriam* as he does, by tumbling tetrameters and bite-sized quatrains, was, then, a highly conscious decision; and indeed he did so because he believed that his stanza form was his own innovation. He was wrong on that front (Ben Jonson, Philip Sidney and others had got there before him), but the point stands that he did not wish to compose by default: he wished to reimagine elegy's orotundities, as well as his own.[41] His stanza's comparatively short lines (four rather than five main stresses) tend to brief and incomplete suggestions, while also offering ready opportunities for post-modifying enjambments. The Prologue immediately sets a tone of firm resolve, in such stanzas as:

> Strong Son of God, immortal Love,
>   Whom we, that have not seen thy face,
>   By faith, and faith alone, embrace,
> Believing where we cannot prove;

(II. 315. 1–4)

And:

> We have but faith: we cannot know;
>   For knowledge is of things we see;
>   And yet we trust it comes from thee,
> A beam in darkness: let it grow.

(II. 317. 21–4)

End-stopped, confident, propositional. The emphatic caesura of that last line quoted above exemplifies the Prologue's steady, summative purpose. Composed after the rest of *In Memoriam* had been completed, it frames and thereby also seeks to forgive the haverings and heterodoxies that follow ('Forgive' is indeed the request issued at the start of each of the Prologue's final three stanzas). How different that steady start is to the opening of the poem proper, in section I, which hazes its syntax, twice running over the lines, feeling its way along:

> I held it truth, with him who sings
> To one clear harp in divers tones,
> That men may rise on stepping-stones
> Of their dead selves to higher things.
>
> (II. 318. 1–4)

That stanza immediately gives way to others that acerbically turn against its sentiment, from the very first word of the very next line: 'But'. Even the Prologue is a poem of productive scepticism, however, such that John William Colenso cited part of it as the epigraph to his radically controversial *The Pentateuch and Book of Joshua Critically Examined* – 'as though', Blair convincingly argues, 'Tennyson's poem provided part of the inspiration (and indeed authorization) for his exploration of biblical history'.[42] For in spite of the Prologue's assuredly end-stopped bracing, like the rest of *In Memoriam*, its prefatory reflections reaffirm a kind of faith that must be tested on the pulse of experience, rather than something readily expressed by doctrines of science, philosophy or theology: 'Our little systems' all come and go, and are 'but broken lights' of the divine image (II. 316. 17, 19). What follows, then, are fragments and broken lights, which means a kind of 'faith' that 'has centre everywhere, / Nor cares to fix itself to form' (II. 351. 3–4). Faith is frisked through diverse channels, that is, and by restless revisions, according to the vagaries of personal testimony, rather than by the rehearsal of universal, settled wisdom. At one point 'Urania speaks with darkened brow' at the poet's presumption to trench into matters of religion:

> 'Thou pratest here where thou art least;
> This faith has many a purer priest,
> And many an abler voice than thou.
>
> (II. 354. 1–4)

Instead of seeking to 'prate' on theology, or indeed philosophy or science, the poem's soundings in these domains for knowledge and comfort leave him empty-handed; and so he returns again and again to the one unshakeable conviction of his love, which alone proves sustaining, even when it appears counter to other, mounting evidence. In one scene, where he contemplates the decaying bodies of the dead that threaten the possibility of love's endurance, he resists this objective reality in the only way he can, by cussedly asserting his subjective faith:

> Might I not say? 'Yet even here.
> But for one hour, O Love, I strive
> To keep so sweet a thing alive:'
>
> (II. 352. 5–7)

Striving – effortfully performed across the line-break here, into the thin air of the page's white space – seems fragile ('But for one hour'), if not actually futile. The rest of this section answers its own hopeful question by heaping more fears of hopelessness, in the decay of the earth itself across geological time, a theme that recurs throughout the poem (notably, CXXIII).[43] 'Ulysses', written earlier than *In Memoriam*, but also informed by his immediate grief for Hallam, ends with an obdurate commitment 'To strive, to seek, to find, and not to yield' (I. 620. 70). Tennyson explained that the poem was 'written under the sense of loss and that all had gone by, but that still life must be fought out to the end', and that it 'gives the feeling about the need of going forward and braving struggle of life' (I. 613. n). It certainly does; though it is far more convincing about the 'strong' 'will' of the speaker (that persists though he has, physically, been made 'weak by time and fate' (I. 620. 69, 70)) than the likelihood that his striving, seeking and finding will be successful. We trust the sincerity of the speaker's faith, while doubting its objective foundation. In comparable ways, faith in *In Memoriam* is not predicated on the elimination of doubt but on the scoping of faith; and while doubts threaten to enervate, they ultimately spur faith, as something not proven by objective fact but willed into being. Among the poem's most quoted lines are:

> There lives more faith in honest doubt,
> Believe me, than in half the creeds.
>
> (II. 415. 11–12)

The affront to creedal authority here is consistent with what is well known of Tennyson's religious convictions, as summarized in his grandson's essay on 'Tennyson's Religion'. Namely, that he held to a few cardinal beliefs – in God and His providential goodness, in the revelation of God's love and laws through Christ, and in the immortality of the human spirit and the immutability of free will – but that he scanted further ecclesiastical details, and was indeed sceptical about attempts by established religions to claim complete authority. Although he put some store in revelation, the Bible, miracles and the authority of the Church, he was most concerned with and convinced by faith founded on lived experience.[44] Hence the push-back that comes through his parenthetical pause in that second line, which turns from recommending honest doubt to issuing his own certain testimony, 'Believe me': a rival faith authenticated by personal feeling, even if such faith sits on a knife's edge, as Perry describes it, for being 'at once a claim of conviction ("believe me, I know what I'm talking about"), and also a plea to be believed (you must believe me'), an appeal that admits the very real possibility of a reader's frank incredulity about faith on these terms'.[45]

The honesty in Tennyson's faith is thus determined by the honesty of his doubt. It is governed by a sense of scruple that (in an analogous context) Herbert F. Tucker describes as Tennyson's 'peculiarly undogmatic certitude',[46] and it expresses itself as a kind of irreverence that is at once epistemological and poetic. When Milton mourned the death of his Cambridge College mate several centuries earlier, Dr Johnson complained that his subsequent elegy (*Lycidas*), decked with mythic figures, was too ornately contrived to be convincing: 'Where there is leisure for fiction there is *little grief*.'[47] A dubious kind of cavilling (a category 'confusion', as C. S. Lewis showed),[48] but Tennyson could not at any rate invite the same, since he resists not only the systems of prefabricated thought but also the settled poetic mode of elegy itself, striking out – as he did in his Wellington Ode – to present grief, and the faith required to reconcile it, as the very opposite of leisure. He implicates his readers instead in the hard-won immediacy of what Freud called 'the work of mourning'.[49]

Thematically, *In Memoriam* is preoccupied with the efficacy of verse as redemptive, through the struggle of articulation itself: 'That out of words a comfort win' (II. 338. 10); 'To lull with song and aching heart' (II. 354. 15); that 'in the songs I love to sing / A doubtful gleam of solace lives' (II. 355. 7–8); that 'out of painful phrases wrought / There flutters up a happy thought' (II. 380. 6–7). Writing of 'verse that brings myself relief, / And by the measure of my grief' (II. 388. 2–3), he punningly parses what his rhymes bring into focus and possibility: that he is not merely writing out his 'grief' in words, he is transforming it into 'relief' through the metrical 'measure' of poetry. 'In an age of disbelief', Wallace Stevens suggested, 'it is for the poet to provide the satisfactions of belief, in his measure and in his style',[50] and there seems something of that surrogacy at work here. Tennyson's theological investment is thin, repairing to verse as an end in itself, for its meliorating metres, rather than for its capacity to mediate higher, spiritual 'satisfactions'. Another earlier section avows the same:

But for the unquiet heart and brain,
  A use in measured language lies;
  The sad mechanic exercise,
Like dull narcotics, numbing pain.

In words, like weeds, I'll wrap me o'er,
  Like coarsest clothes against the cold;
  But that large grief which these enfold
Is given outline and no more.

(II. 322. 5–12)

Where verse is here glossed as a grimly unthinking service, elsewhere it is cast as uncertain, even profaning, such as in the opening of section V: 'I sometimes hold it half a sin / To put in words the grief I feel' (II. 322. 1–2). Such sentiments gnaw the very marrow of Tennyson's faith in poetry; they flinch at the limitations of language to articulate faithfully the fullest expanse of himself: 'For words, like Nature, half reveal / And half conceal the Soul within' (II. 322. 3–4). But even this description bemoaning language's limits implicitly affirms the way in which poetry can 'reveal' more than mere language, through its versification. As the line-break separating revelation and concealment exposes the imperfection of the poetic mode, it dramatizes what it describes, performing its ability as poetry to avail itself of a semiology that exceeds the conventions of prose. In this case, the language is enriched by enjambement, but the principle applies to the whole repertoire of verse style. It is through such disruptions in settled language and in established 'systems', where orderly proposition breaks down, that poetry, though still necessarily limited, might yet 'reveal' more than prose, and whereby the broken lights of true faith might shine through.

To take another example, the mechanic exercise of versifying might offer respite by dulling, as in the passage quoted. Other sections that explicitly dwell on 'pain' (such as XIV, XVIII, XX, XXV, XXVIII, LXIV and LXXVII) also aver the opposite, paradoxical possibility – unique to the poetic mode – that Wordsworth describes (in his 1802 addition to his 'Preface' to *Lyrical Ballads*), in which language that is metered at once enlivens the pain it describes, while at the same time making its encounter more bearable.[51] But *In Memoriam* is by no means all versified wallowing; the event of versification animates some of the poem's more exultant figures too, figures that recall Hallam's observation on Tennyson's ringing recitation of his Wellington Ode. Section CVI is made of eight stanzas, in which that same verbal phrase, 'ring out', occurs some twenty-six times in only thirty-two lines (occasionally offset by 'ring in'), of which the most pointedly meta-poetical stanza is the fifth:

Ring out the want, the care, the sin,
  The faithless coldness of the times
  Ring out, ring out my mournful rhymes,
But ring the fuller minstrel in.

(II. 428. 17–20)

Such passages are high moments of optimism, in his faith and his faith in poetry, but ambivalence over the capacity of verse to engage faith is never definitively resolved; it shifts with the mood and the narrative. Half-revealing and half-concealing is picked up again at later points, notably in section XLVIII, which worries over the incompleteness of the 'Short swallow-flights of song' that sorrow allows, and worries too at the possible 'sin and shame' in attempting to draw 'The deepest measure from the chords' (15, 11, 12). Throughout, the poem grapples with the adequacy of language and verse especially to perform the work to which he would put it. Sections XXX, XXXVII, LXXV and XCV are among the most suggestive instances, though none is more poignant than LXXVII, which opens with the pressing question, 'What hope is here for modern rhyme?' (II. 390. 1), but which cannot, through twelve lines of wondering, find a secure answer. Defiantly, though, the poet commits to writing out his sorrow even in the absence of a firm faith in poetry, by repairing again to striving and sheer will: 'But what of that? My darken'd ways / Shall ring with music all the same' (II. 391. 13–14).

There is desperation here, rawly figured as regression, where Tennyson relegates his verses to 'mortal lullabies of pain' (II. 390. 5). At its darkest, the poem is and aspires to be nothing more, where it ebbs from abstract speculations to images of unmediated, inarticulate emotions, like a bird crying for its lost fledglings (XXI). Almost halfway through the poem, at the close of section LIV, he self-questions, 'but what am I?' (II. 370. 17), and his answer comes only by way of infantilized lament:

> An infant crying in the night:
> An infant crying for the light
> And with no language but a cry.
>
> (II. 370. 18–20)

Many sections are shot through with such moments that the Prologue forecasts as the poem's characteristically 'wild and wandering cries' (II. 318. 41). Tennyson repeatedly feels unable to utter words commensurate with the pain that prompts them, never mind adequate to pain's rationalization or redemption within the providential scheme ('Where truth is closest words shall fail' (II. 353. 6)). He often surprises himself, too: 'What words are these have fallen from me?' he asks at one point (II. 334. 1), unsettled by the way his expressions of grief may at times be mutable and even contradictory: 'Can calm despair and wild unrest / Be tenants of a single breast, / Or sorrow such a changeling be?' (II. 334. 2–4). Thoughts may also have commerce with thoughts, without finding direct expression in language ('And Thought leapt out to wed with Thought / Ere Thought could wed itself with Speech' (II. 342. 15–16)).

One constant faith does run through the poem, however: faith that manages to weather and take fresh purpose from his doubt; as perhaps most directly addressed in section CXXIV. Even when framed as an implacable antinomy, 'Our dearest faith; our ghastliest doubt' (II. 443. 2); even when arguments for faith by reason must fail, whether by natural theology ('I found Him not in world or sun, / Or eagle's wing or insect's eye' (II. 444. 5–6)), or philosophy ('Nor through the questions men may try, / The petty cobwebs we have spun' (II. 444. 7–8)); even, indeed, when faith has 'fallen asleep' or been assaulted ('I heard a voice "believe no more"' (II. 444. 10)), then faith yet resurges through the will to feeling:

A warmth within the breast would melt
  The freezing reason's colder part,
  And like a man in wrath the heart
Stood up and answered, 'I have felt.'

(II. 444. 13–16)

Without the warrant of intellection, he must turn to intuition, and that, not unreasonably, leaves some readers unsatisfied, even contemptuous. The idea that 'God must exist because the human heart felt an instructive need of His existence' is, Harold Nicholson demurs, a 'pathetically inadequate formula'.[52]

***

But Tennyson does not will his faith by any 'formula' that might be so readily extracted. His poem must be read as a great roll of words, as observed with his 'Ode', precisely for the way it unsteadies summary conclusions. Differently from his 'Ode', however, the personalized investment apparent through *In Memoriam* casts the poem in an insistently reflexive epistemology, and one that is humbled by an awareness of its own inadequacy. Even while he feels God's presence, doubt renders him to the condition of a fearful child, in the lines following those quoted above:

No, like a child in doubt and fear:
  But that blind clamour made me wise;
  Then was I as a child that cries,
But, crying, knows his father near;

(II. 444. 17–20)

It is, Henry Sidgwick once observed, Tennyson's 'most characteristic merit' that he can 'see both sides of a question': 'Almost any poet might have written, "And like a man in wrath the heart / Stood up and answered, I have felt". But only Tennyson would have immediately added, "*No*, like a child in doubt and fear"'.[53] Quite so; to get at Tennyson's faith, we must appreciate its inherent tensions, which refuse the pat appraisal of his metaphysical attitude as 'pious acquiescence'.[54] At once the child of the Romantics, rehearsing the authority of the heart, but at the same time the consummate Victorian, suspicious of the presumed authority of the poet as *vates*, Tennyson courts but resists universalizations: his affective witness is characteristically restless, self-questioning, on the move.

To 'understand' his poems, then, we must not unpick them line by line, to inspect how 'pathetic' or indeed 'stupid' they might be: we must read them dynamically and dialectically. *In Memoriam* finds its faith not so much through its separate moments, that is, as through its movements, by instaurations that model the untidier tendencies of human thought and feeling when under stress, pushing forward but then slipping back, changing tack, knocked by specific memories, events or anniversaries. Verse style tracks but also enables these shifts and shimmies, tracing Tennyson's 'drift', which often progresses paradoxically, by returning to its beginnings. 'No poem so obsessively remembers itself as *In Memoriam*', Isobel Armstrong justly observes,[55] and its extreme recursiveness establishes a sense of a subject thought through and felt out from all angles, at different times, in different tempers. Its repetends are not as claustrophobic or costive as those felt in his 'Ode'; greater length and thematic range allow a more thoroughgoing drama of re-imaginings, of occasion, theme and sentiment, as well as rhyme, word or phrase.

While often consciously vernacular and spontaneous-seeming, *In Memoriam* also at times ripens into what Matthew Arnold, raising an eyebrow, called 'heightened and elaborate'.[56] The poem's multi-texture is felt on multiple levels: hard-won cogency and confidence may give way to sudden unravelling, intellectual speculation to emotional reaction, easy reverie to intense fretfulness. Even cliché and stock response, bane of the poetic enterprise, finds a place in this work, yet in so doing also helps precipitate a quickened, personalized response.[57]

This poem's seven hundred and twenty-five stanzas are, then, not only marked by what Perry nicely characterizes as Tennyson's 'scrupulous imprecision' at the level of the word and phrase,[58] its words and phrases are also perpetually in flux: narratively, tonally, figuratively, and so on. Whatever poised equivocations play on his deployments of modals and semi-modals, these are doubled by his sequiturs and semi-sequiturs that join them up. At a global level, the poem's formal subdivision into sections marks a structural inconclusiveness, and allows it to take a less predictable path than is usual in classical or even English elegy. From Sidney to Spenser to Milton to Gray to Shelley, grief is negotiated in a broadly linear movement towards consolation, but Tennyson discomposes this generic trajectory for the elegy form, threatening the very possibility of its expected *peripeteia.* Loosely (and liturgically) cycling through three years marked by Christmases (XXX, LXXVIII, C), *In Memoriam* traverses in often unexpected ways, back and forth between sections, from reconciliation to renewed grief, as it also diverts from the focus of mourning itself, notably towards related questions of religious faith. There is no wrinkle in our reading when Tennyson refers to his poetic activity as 'chanting hymns' (II. 430. 10), given not only the formal similarity to his sections to hymnody,[59] but also the spiritual saturation of these sections. Nor is it a shock to learn that other titles he considered for the poem include 'Fragments of an Elegy' and 'The Way of the Soul': the former emphasizing the extent to which the poem is consciously incomplete in its elegiac account; the latter, how far the poem exceeds a meditation on mourning to be a testimony of the spirit in the broadest sense.

Still, Tennyson worried that the poem might be overdetermined by its Epilogue, making it 'too hopeful' ('more than I am myself', he suggested to James Knowles (II. 312. n)).[60] There was certainly a danger that the ending might, together with the Prologue, have compressed the textures of the sections between them. But these bookending sections – starting with a funeral, ending with a marriage – do not serve as fixed points in a straight narrative. They were both written late in the compositional process, and they are to some extent separate from the rest of the poem, and they mark a definite 'drift'. Yet they are also of a piece with the governing narrative strategy of the main poem, which is defined above all by its unfixity, its (almost Blakean) destabilizing '*No*'. That is the animating principle of Tennyson's faith in the poem that needs to be grasped above all, and before anything else can be. Scholars have noted that Tennyson carefully revised the final sequence of the poem's sections to ensure that 'faith wins out over doubt',[61] but he also latterly added new verses (XCVI), to affirm the value of doubt in quickening faith. The poem's final outcome is by no means smoothed into a steady or inevitable progress of consolation and optimism.

Ragged narrative style can mean and can do different things, of course; but in reading Tennyson, the *ne plus ultra* of orbicular euphony, we may at least be assured that his formal deformities were conscious imperfections. Charles LaPorte brilliantly parses the fragmentariness and conflictions of *The Idylls of the King* as an intervention by Tennyson on the nature, value and dangers of contemporary hermeneutical criticism (whose biblical source material was likewise fragmented and dispersed).[62] But unlike that later poem (or indeed his 'Ode'), *In Memoriam* engages religious faith in a way that is in the end more personal than universal, tracing the straits of an individual psychology more than the general state of faith, whether inflected by 'higher criticism', or anything else. *In Memoriam* certainly does have an epic range and scope, and engages the theological pressures of its moment, but its formal instabilities are focused through its troubled speaker. Verse serves not so much as an emblematic intervention in contemporary religious debates as an individuated, line-by-line tussle with such debates, stained by the pain of personal circumstances.

Correspondingly, the poem's affective power inheres not so much in the satisfactions that come where faith wins out – as if doubt were progressively chipped away – but rather in the ways doubting persists through the poem, acting as the driver through which faith is refined and emboldened. Doubt is not progressively subtracted, in other words, it is turned to positive ends. Even the stylistic feature that most conspicuously unites *In Memoriam* as a whole, its stanza scheme, has been read as expressing that same ongoing negotiation between faith and doubt, as the end-rhyme from the first line of each stanza is momentarily stranded. Tennyson suggested that *In Memoriam* 'was meant to be a kind of *Divina Commedia*' (*M* i. 304), but though Dantean influence is strongly evident thematically, and through many of his borrowings, analogues and allusions,[63] the two poems strongly diverge when it comes to the defining feature of their poem's rhyme scheme. This divergence is not an isolated, aesthetic difference: the purposeful way *terza rima* rolls inexorably, if also uncertainly forward, gathering itself up as it goes, indicates and endows a different theological mode.[64] For the *In Memoriam* stanzas necessarily fall back on themselves. Their abba structure looks like the opening of a Petrarchan sonnet, but one that never makes it to its octave 'turn'.[65] These stanzas may only re-turn, through perpetual cycles. The fourth-line rhyme offers a delayed sonic closure that does not propel the poem forward but instead remembers its beginning. As here:

> I wrong the grave with fears untrue:
> Shall love be blamed for want of faith?
> There must be wisdom with great Death:
> The dead shall look me through and through.
>
> (II. 368. 9–12)

With the 'a' rhyme reprisal, untruth is clarified, and thereby made true, as it were, in the echoing 'through and through', which insists that the dead friend does after all know the veracity of the speaker's love, and returns it undiminished. Such elegant economy in the poem's thinking here is rarely seen in the Wellington Ode. But the strategy of unsteadying and reprisal through rhyme, and of refusing easy sweetness and the apparent stupidities of onomatopoeia, is consistent across both poems. If these poems charm, they are also verses of gritty endeavour. *In Memoriam* is 'Perplext in faith', but over the course of almost seventeen years of grief-induced doubt, 'At last he beat his music out' (II. 415. 9–10).

Tennyson walks a fine line here, perhaps a blurred one. *In Memoriam* finally allayed Emily Selwood's misgivings as to his faith, such that she agreed to marry him soon after its publication. Charles Kingsley declared the poem to be 'the noblest Christian poem which England has produced for two centuries'.[66] For other readers, though, Tennyson's honest doubting has seemed dishonestly uncommitted. 'We remain undecided as to Mr Tennyson's faith,' *The English Review* concluded in 1850, 'though we opine, that, strictly speaking, *he has none*, whether negative or affirmative, and advise him, for his soul's good, to try to get one!'[67] Such a response is at once reasonable but at the same time as misguided as it is possible to be. It is correct to say that the poem's faith is not wholly nor straightforwardly either negative or affirmative, but it is wrong to conclude that this was because Tennyson was firmly undecided either way. For he was in fact firmly committed – as the reviewer would have him be – to *trying* to work through his position, which he attempts through the measure of verse itself, engaging doubt to clarify his faith, by the mode that only verse might allow.

Philosophically, then, *In Memoriam* exemplifies what Walter Houghton describes in *The Victorian Frame of Mind* as 'the will to believe'.[68] Poetically, it epitomizes what Matthew Campbell argues in *Rhythm and Will in Victorian Poetry* as the prosodic expression of self-striving.[69] But for all that, the question remains: Is willing faith adequate to faith itself, and if so, what is to distinguish Tennyson's blank credo from, say, Swinburne's, which likewise balances an antipathy to organized religion with a largely unspecified 'will to believe'?[70] These poets bear suggestive comparison on a number of fronts, not least for the fact that they are, by customary acclaim, the period's paragons of 'musicality'. Whereas Tennyson regrets of the 'intellectual' Browning that, though 'he has plenty of music in him', 'he cannot get it out', Swinburne is 'a reed through which all things blow into music' (*M* ii. 285); and as with Tennyson, Swinburne's verse was often said by his contemporaries to lack substantial content for being a mere 'trick' of sound.[71] In Swinburne's *Tristram of Lyonesse*, his greatest poem (by length as well as richness), 'one deep chord throbs all the music through', that of love and fate; and much the same might be adduced of *In Memoriam*. Yet Tennyson's faith in poetry is highly distinct from Swinburne's (which it would take another complete chapter to delineate), and extended comparison risks simplification.

'As a single line he said he knew hardly any to exceed for charm "Of Abbana and Pharphar, lucid streams," unless it were Wordsworth's great line in "Tintern Abbey" "Whose dwelling is the light of setting suns".'[72] So Tennyson's friend Knowles reported, drawing once again on the mystical-seeming category of 'charm' (III. 197. n). But Knowles goes further in his account, in a way that clarifies what might be at stake in Tennyson's sometime swooning, beyond the flush of sensuous pleasure. '"Poetry," he would say at such times, "is a great deal truer than fact"'.[73] That's an extravagant as well as enigmatic claim: hard to prove, hard even to know what it means. In 1886, William Sharp defined the Pre-Raphaelite's attention to visual detail by explaining that, for them, representation was not a matter of providing an image that was 'literally true', but one that 'would yet in another sense *be* true'.[74] Such a qualification helpfully demarcates a kind of artistic knowledge outside of the positivist's sphere, but the particular charge of Tennyson's comment may be more fully appreciated in the context of what has been argued above for his epistemology of affect, which includes a sense of its experiential contingency.

'Dreams are true while they last' (II. 706. 4), one of Tennyson's most cited lines that might be a metonym for his entire poetics, implies that the 'truth' of poetry can only be known and verified in the experience of reading itself – while it lasts. I have elsewhere argued as much for art in general: that aesthetic objects may offer us trivial forms of knowledge, and yet profound forms of knowing, as aesthetic experiences.[75] But Tennyson comes to his own position on poetry's truth-bearing capacity from a rather different path, via poetry itself, but also as informed by his particular exposure to philosophy as an undergraduate at Cambridge, where he was much influenced by both German idealism and British empiricism.

The idea of the 'waking dream' – treating aesthetic productions as if they were real, 'while they last' – preoccupied many of the most powerful and influential thinkers in the eighteenth and nineteenth centuries, infusing the criticism of drama but also literature.[76] Thinkers associated with this idea range from Schlegal to Schiller to Herder to Lessing to Mendelssohn, with a number of less obvious figures in the mix too, from Diderot to Rousseau to Erasmus Darwin. But for Tennyson, the most immediate and formative influence was S. T. Coleridge, who not only assimilated many of the diverse strands of these philosophers but also repurposed the notion of the waking dream in terms of his most significant literary-critical intervention: 'suspension of disbelief'. Michael Tomko's study of this concept refines Coleridge's position into something much more than its common praxis as 'a begrudging toleration of the fabulous'.[77] Coleridge's ostensibly literary tenet is intimately bound to his conception of 'poetic faith', in a way that loads that concept with theological import; and that is true not only for Coleridge, but also (though Tomko does not advert to him in his study) for Tennyson, who thoroughly assimilated Coleridge's poetics as well as his philosophy during his formative years as an undergraduate, notably in his reading and discussion with his other Cambridge Apostles.

To this Coleridge connection may be added another, provided by Donald Hair, who observes how John Locke likewise helped to shape Tennyson's faith in faith itself: neither as a groundless desire to believe for its own sake, nor as a reactionary fideism that refused to consider contemporary challenges to religion. Rather, in careful and thoughtful ways, Tennyson pursued arguments that gave ultimate authority to human experience of the senses and the imagination.[78] Hair demonstrates how Locke, though coming from a different philosophical tradition to Coleridge, complemented and illuminated the distinction between faith and knowledge to which Tennyson consistently repairs, at the same time giving ballast to faith as the expression of a human need from which it gains its authority. Hair's argument may be extended to the wider empiricist tradition, headed by Hume, which argues that faith is not a fixed doctrine but a way of living, and that it consists thereby of assumptions rather than facts, the truth of which is probable but never certain. As such, personal witness is by no means a 'pathetically inadequate formula', it is the best formula available; and even Tennyson's recurrent image of the crying child does not undermine his faith by infantalizing it: the cry is itself evidence and affirmation of the truth for which his faith seeks confirmation as well as comfort.

What is missing from the philosophical account of Tennyson's faith, however, is the extent to which his striving towards it occurs through and with poetry. To plug this gap, it is helpful to introduce another thinker, not this time as an influence on Tennyson, but by comparison with the ideas as well as the stylistic exigencies of the author of the greatest book on faith written in Tennyson's lifetime. John Henry Newman began his *Grammar of Assent* in the year *In Memoriam* was published, and like Tennyson's poem it took almost two decades to complete. That it took Newman so long is relevant because the difficulty he faced – what forced him to start from scratch no less than nineteen times, and what consumed his intellectual energies so fully he thought it might kill him – was not merely the book's conceptual difficulty. In ways that converge with Tennyson (Coleridge and Locke), Newman aimed to show that faith is reasonable, and yet cannot be achieved through reason alone. 'If we insist on proofs for everything', Newman avers, 'we shall never come to action: to act you must assume, and that assumption is faith'.[79] But Newman presents action as more than a pragmatic necessity in the absence of full knowledge: action may be the ratification of faith, but it may also, through its own activity, nurture faith. Trying to articulate such a thesis, Newman faced a problem. He sought to bring his thesis alive through rhythm and image, and by particularizing abstractions through thought experiments. But more than this, he sought through his style to explore and indeed elicit suggestions that otherwise resist the discipline of propositional prose. Newman is unexpectedly and fascinatingly close to Tennyson in the explicitness with which he describes his method, which is to employ language 'not by syllogistic compulsion', but in the 'full compass' of its expressive possibilities: 'to avail … of language, as far as it will go, but to aim mainly by means of it to *stimulate* … a mode of thinking' (emphasis mine).[80]

Not so fast, it might be objected: there is surely something fundamentally incompatible in the nature of religious authority – and by extension, religious faith – that Newman, the Roman Catholic Cardinal, and Tennyson, the agnostic ecumenist, envisage.[81] When it comes to religious faith, Newman surely differs from Tennyson in many important respects, and it is well to be cautious of positing equivalence, especially given the popular but unhelpfully exaggerated ways in which Tennyson's 'honest doubt' has been compared with Kierkegaard's philosophy of 'authentic' religious faith. But whereas the proposed correspondence between Tennyson's and Kierkegaard's expression of faith (suggestive up to a point, when it comes to requiring a leap beyond sheer rationality) founders on the extent to which Tennyson invests in will,[82] it is on that very question of self-determination and personal striving – specifically through literary style – that his connection with Newman is richest.

Tennyson shares Newman's conviction that if we are not prepared to commit to faith in the absence of perfect knowledge, 'we shall never have done beginning', we shall 'ever be laying foundations'. But

Newman also brilliantly figures reason as productively unstable, as an activity that, in a sermon on 'Explicit and Implicit Reason', he called 'a living, spontaneous energy with us'; an 'exercise' that implies movement and requires effort, which he likens to a taxing scramble in which the foot and hand-holds of intuitive intellection daringly perform their task of ratiocination.[83] Most suggestively of all, however, Newman ardently believed that when it comes to expressing, exploring and eliciting faith, it is not best engaged through formal argumentation, but rather through the polysemy and instability that literariness uniquely affords.[84] Newman may thus serve as a bridge between Coleridge and Locke, in the extent to which he, like Locke, proceeds from the empiricist tradition, while also, like Coleridge, recognizing that reasoning is limited, but that language can do more than express and describe thoughts and feelings on faith that already exist: that language – specifically, language that is styled – can shape and create how faith is conceived and experienced.[85]

It is in this respect above all that Tennyson's and Newman's seminal works on faith are instructively similar, and all the more so for the very reason that the connection is at first surprising. Tennyson's motivation for writing *In Memoriam* was quite distinct from what precipitated Newman's *Grammar* – Tennyson beat out his word music as a way of beating out personal grief. But as Tennyson advised his son Hallam, it is well to remember that his masterwork is, in the final analysis, 'a poem, *not* an actual biography' (*M* i. 305). While it is sometimes hard to avoid the critical convenience of eliding the poet with the poem (as has implicitly occurred at moments in this chapter), it coarsens Tennyson's achievement to imagine the poet to be identical with the speaker of his poems. Confessional verse may involve cathexis, but it always also includes confection; while Tennyson perhaps turned to writing as a way of coping, he was highly self-conscious as well as ambivalent about the nature and adequacy of his recourse. Fitzgerald's bluff complaint, 'if Tennyson had got on a horse and ridden twenty miles, instead of moaning over his pipe, he would have been cured of his sorrows in half the time',[86] figures *In Memoriam* as no more than lugubrious rumination remedied by distraction and divulgence – and presumes Tennyson's affliction could have been salved faster and with less fuss by other means. Reading public elegy as private therapy misses the extent to which the poem does not indulge its way to an exhausted equilibrium (as some critics have suggested),[87] but instead *strives* through its stylistic heurisms to make sense of the condition it seeks to express, by testing the limits of what it means to believe, and reaching for what exceeds the grasp.

Attending to Tennyson's strivings enjoins us to revise the suspicion that his poetry is stupid or merely sweet, not by attending away from the sensuous appeal of his verse, but by suggesting how far the sensate as well as sematic charge of its word music might itself prove substantial, even if its substance expires with the act of reading. That is not escapism or aestheticism by another name, it is a way of acknowledging Tennyson's investment in the different categories of knowledge and faith, and the commerce between them that his verse style allows; it is a Coleridgean but also Newmanesque act of 'poetic faith'. While Queen Victoria admitted that after the death of Prince Albert, next to the Bible, *In Memoriam* was her 'comfort',[88] George Eliot was among those contemporaries who discerned import beyond the poem's immediate prompting, 'the deepest significance' of which she located in 'the sanctification of human love as a religion'.[89] That seems about right; except that Eliot overlooks the poem's deeply significant sanctification of verse itself, as a style of testing as well as attesting Tennyson's love, whose concomitant faith must otherwise go not merely unexpressed, but unimagined.

3

Christina G. Rossetti: Practically Perfect

My faith is faith; it is not evolved out of argumentation, nor does it seek the aid of that.[1]

As a child, Christina Rossetti was known to her father as '*vivace*', or as one of the 'two storms', the other being Dante Gabriel.[2] But something changed during her adolescence, after she fell ill. The feisty, fractious, tantrum-prone girl was tamed, such that she was in her adult life known rather for her excessive temperance and scrupulosity. Her other brother, William – who was, with Maria, one of the contradistinctive 'two calms' of the family – describes the transformation in a memoir that served influentially as the preface to *The Poetical Works of Christina Georgina Rossetti* (1904):

> In innate character she was vivacious, and open to pleasurable impressions; and, during her girlhood, one might readily have supposed that she would develop into a woman of expansive heart, fond of society and diversions, and taking a part in them of more than average brilliancy. What came to pass was of course quite the contrary.[3]

What precipitated the shift in her character from squally vivacity to something 'quite the contrary' has been cause for much speculation, mostly unverifiable. But whether the cause was physical or psychological, or whether she was indeed (as she was diagnosed at the time) suffering from 'a kind of religious mania',[4] Rossetti did not share her brother's dismay. Far from her change being uninvited and regrettable, she presented it as self-willed and salutary. 'You must not imagine, my dear girl,' she once counselled her niece, 'that your Aunt was always the calm and sedate person you now behold':

> I, too, had a very passionate temper; but I learnt to control it. On one occasion, being rebuked by my dear Mother for some fault, I seized upon a pair of scissors, and ripped up my arm to vent my wrath. I have learnt since to control my feelings – and no doubt you will![5]

A temper so 'passionate' it could exercise itself through self-laceration mellowed into a 'calm and sedate' person because – she makes the same point twice in consecutive sentences – she 'learnt to control it'. Most modern biographers are prepared to meet Rossetti halfway here: to accept that she imposed a change upon herself, without conceding that it was to the good. Restraint is called repression; self-control is glossed as 'self-abuse'.[6]

In any event, a broadly similar narrative of passion-quelling control has often been constructed around her life as a writer. When Dante Gabriel shared his sister's poems with John Ruskin, he advised that for all their 'beauty and power', no publisher would touch them, 'so full are they of quaintness and offences'. He identified Rossetti's verses with 'irregular measure', which he called 'the calamity of modern poetry', and advised that she should 'exercise herself in the severest commonplace of metre', as the only way in which 'passion' might be rendered 'precious' in verse: 'she must have the Form first'.[7] The collection was published nonetheless, as *Goblin Market and Other Poems*, and the title poem especially excited much critical attention, and was diversely interpreted; but there was at least consensus over its style, which was said to revel against discipline, through what one contemporary critic called its 'fantastic jangling of words'.[8] Few failed to be thrilled by the audacity of the enterprise, though most, like the reviewer for the *Athenaeum*, deplored her 'discords' that were said to occur 'with a frequency which aims at variety but results in harshness'.[9] In a similar vein, two years later, the reviewer for *Fraser's Magazine* contrasted Rossetti's 'racy individuality' – at once 'bold, vigorous, peculiar, daring' – with the 'peculiar perfection of form' to be found in the poetry of Jean Ingelow.[10]

But then something odd happened. When Rossetti's second mature collection of poems reached the public in 1866, reviewers dramatically changed their tune, apparently in response to Rossetti having changed hers. *The Prince's Progress and Other Poems* was well received and specifically commended for being 'melodious and sweet'; what's 'peculiar' about these new verses is not their fervent intrepidity, but their 'calm'.[11] Where she is defined against another female poet, it is not any longer to clarify her 'rhetorical ardour', her 'fiery, almost volcanic torrent of thought [that] rent and scarred the inadequate channel of the form'. These qualities are granted instead to Elizabeth Barrett Browning, whose 'irrepressible vivacity' apparently throws into maximum relief Rossetti's 'close control': 'subdued, restrained, withdrawn, rippling over with faultless music in a low key'.[12] That review was from *The Examiner*, and Harry Baxton Foreman, writing for *Tinsley's Magazine*, likewise paired the same poets to the same end, recruiting the self-witnessing authority of chiasmus to underscore his contrasts: by 'impassioned bursts', Barrett Browning 'disarranges the stately folds of a woman's raiment more than we would have them disarranged', whereas Rossetti's poise is the 'purified essence of purity'.[13]

It is an extraordinary reversal of her reputation – irregularity redeemed into perfection – in which the narratives of her life and her writing become entangled, as contemporary critics speculated on why it was that she 'allowed herself, in the early days, to speak of love with the generous abandon of an ardent spirit'; but only 'in the early days'.[14] One reviewer explained that, following her personal 'crisis', her 'passionately human' poems find 'repose' in 'the rational and temperate form of faith that ministered to the failing soul'.[15] That estimation comes from 1895, the year after her death; another eulogizing account from the same year (by an anonymous critic for the *Saturday Review*) pressed the same point even more forcibly:

> she possessed, in union with a profoundly emotional nature, a power of artistic self-restraint which no other woman who has

> written in verse has … ever shown; and it is through this mastery of her own nature, this economy of her own resources, that she takes rank among poets rather than among poetesses.[16]

Rossetti is here commended (not without the standard dollop of condescension) for demonstrating 'that a woman may be trained to a special manner of workmanship'.[17] In her self-mastery – personal and poetical, poetical through the personal – she is crowned the *ne plus ultra* of her sex and her moment, as equipoise incarnate. Her slightly rocky start is hardly remembered. 'Anyone who *begins* his acquaintance with the definitive collection of 1904', observed George Saintsbury, 'would hardly notice much "irregularity" in her'.[18] A predictable lexicon of approbation actually settles down quite a bit earlier, recycling through reviews. Words like 'sweetness' and 'simplicity'.[19] Phrases like 'beautiful in form',[20] 'balanced simplicity',[21] 'secure hand on the precise medium'[22] and, 'not a word out of place'.[23] Even Edmund Gosse, self-appointed bastion of the period's prosodical correctness, came to honour Rossetti as 'one of the most perfect poets of the age'.[24]

***

'Perfect': that might seem like a positive outcome, and Rossetti herself was generally fond of the word, using it consciously as well as habitually in all genres of her writing, as noun, verb, adjective and adverb. Everything from the 'weather' to the 'summer', from 'darkness' to a 'sundial', from a 'globe' to a 'spring blossom'; all these things and many more precipitate the term.[25] She refers with similar liberality to 'perfect strangers', having 'perfect confidence', or 'perfect freedom', or a 'perfect friend', or finding a 'perfect copy' (*L* 3.335; 3.201; 2.167; 3.307; 1.253). And in addition to such everyday usages, she reverts to questions of 'artistic perfection', of having 'perfect command' of an artistic medium, of seeking 'to perfect' poetry, and wondering if 'practice makes perfect' (*L* 2.25; 1.15; 2.199; 3.60). All of which seem commensurate with the compliment of practical impeccability that she received about her own verse. Yet the idea of Rossetti as a perfect poet, transformed from ignorantly ardent to urbanely sweet, risks occluding more than it reveals about the development of her religious faith, and how she comes to express it in verse.

One of the earliest and still one of the best refutations of the perfectibility narrative is to be found in the third volume of Saintsbury's *History of English Prosody* (1910), in which he acclaims 'Goblin Market' as 'a dedoggerelised Skeltonic, with the gathered music of the various metrical progress since Spenser, utilised in the place of the wooden rattling of the followers of Chaucer'. Far from being an eccentric outburst typical of Rossetti's early immaturity, Saintsbury reads her most famous poem as exemplifying the 'various but perfectly regular music' that we might admire across her corpus, which includes long narrative poems, sonnet sequences and nursery rhymes, as well as standalone lyrical poems and devotional verses.[26] 'Read her, and read all of her', he is quite clear: 'A more charming and certain-fingered executant in English verse it would be difficult to find'.[27]

Saintsbury does Rossetti a great service by his formal analysis, encouraging us to see the continuity in her early and later style, all of which is worthy of our attention. But he also does her harm, by seeming to bracket off her achievement as merely stylistic, and by implicitly allowing readers to imagine that her later devotional verse might have no more substance than her juvenile fribbles. Accentuating her stylistic achievements, and the sense that what's admirable in her style may be detected from the earliest stirrings, abets the notion that she is a poet of daintily arrested development to be read only for her lissome technique. 'On the whole, late-nineteenth century poetry has hardly, on the formal side, a more characteristic and more gifted exponent':[28] Saintsbury's *summa* is a lavish hurrah, yet his parenthetical qualification, 'on the formal side', consigns Rossetti to the realm of mere licitude. But what's noteworthy in Saintsbury's rider is not that it is unusual or even that it has been influential, but rather that it is representative. Gosse was quoted earlier describing Rossetti as 'one of the most perfect poets of the age', and this quotation has been routinely reproduced by critics in this way, adjuring superlative praise. But Gosse's ovation is actually embedded in a sentence that makes clear that his estimation of Rossetti's perfection is severely qualified. Here is that complete sentence:

> In the following pages I desire to pay no more than a just tribute of respect to one of the most perfect poets of the age — not one of the most powerful, of course, nor one of the most epoch-making,

> but to one of the most perfect — to a writer toward whom we may not unreasonably expect that students of English literature in the twenty-fourth century may look back as the critics of Alexandria did toward Sappho and toward Erinna.[29]

Skip over the parenthesis and the tribute is generous to the point of prodigality. But those 'not' and 'nor' clauses immediately following are essential concomitants. They hollow out Rossetti's achievement, leaving us to admire only the husk of her enterprise, her style alone, which apparently supports little but its own edifice as verse. Most devastating of all, perhaps, is the casualness of Gosse's 'of course', as if his qualifications are at once indispensable and indubitable, while at the same time so obvious as to be redundant. The perfect poet turns out to be not quite perfect after all. She falls short, she is only *practically* perfect, because she is perfect only in her prosodical practice.

There are gender politics at work here, cutting both ways. On style: contemporary reviewers propagated the notion that Rossetti's poems are perfect insofar as they are seemly. That means sweetly, by graceful discipline, as against the indecorous example set by Barrett Browning. Dante Gabriel even warned his sister against attempting to emulate such 'falsetto muscularity'.[30] On faith: reviewers seemed unwilling to imagine that an unworldly woman could have the intellect and temperament or education and experience to produce much more than personalized emoting or prettified devotion. Rossetti's contemporaries routinely believed her poems laid bare her romantic longings, and perhaps also gave a clue to the identity of her unnamed lover. Modern scholarship has come some way since; but while it is certainly less complacently sexist when it comes to adjudicating on Rossetti's style (though not always),[31] feminist readings have themselves often unwittingly distorted and diminished her achievements as a poet too.[32] Modern scholars are doubtless better informed about Rossetti's actual circumstances, and so no longer entertain the possibility that she conducted secret relationships; and yet, incited by psychoanalysis, critics have persisted in speculations about her love life, with the difference being that she is now presumed to be sexually frustrated rather than secretly fulfilled: her poetry is not taken to be a coded record of her dalliances but a sublimation of those appetites she was unable to express. Either way, her poems are still routinely read now, as they were in her lifetime, as more or less coyly or consciously confessional.

There are conspicuous exceptions to these literary-critical trends, and the twenty-first century may indeed herald a new reception for Rossetti among critics who are prepared to suspend the hermeneutics of suspicion, and to take sensitive account of the integrity and importance of her faith. A crop of recent book-length studies has paid careful attention to the ways her writing assimilated and expressed Tractarian and Anglo-Catholic ideas and practices.[33] But the challenge of reading Rossetti aright extends beyond any corrective that might occur through a 'religious turn' in literary studies, whereby expressions of faith might be taken seriously in poetry. Such a corrective is necessary and welcome, as is that against reading by gender stereotypes – but these reparative readings are not in themselves sufficient. Stereotypes around verse style need to be revised too. Work on Rossetti's faith tends to have a biographical and historicist emphasis, such that her devotional poems have received fresh attention from religious scholars mining for 'content' – whereas literary critics have not mustered a comparable revisionary interest in their 'form'.[34] The problem here is not merely aspectual, as if we need to read Rossetti both for what she says and for how she says it: more radically, we need to read these twin aspects of her verse as interpenetrating. There can be no adequate division of labour between critics interested in the substance and others in the style of her faith, as if metaphysics and aesthetics could be cleanly cut: when it comes to the particularities of poetry, each defines the other. Rigorous attention to Rossetti's religious life and contexts must, in other words, be matched by a corresponding sensitivity to the mode wherein and whereby her faith finds its singular expression as verse. That means thinking hard about individual verse instances, but it also means thinking more broadly about how poems work, and what they can uniquely do as poems. Readings driven solely by Rossetti's gender or her religion necessarily simplify, or worse.

That there might be something more at stake than gender or religious bias alone in the ambivalent evaluation of Rossetti's seeming 'perfection' is suggested by the fact that her brother needed to be defended against the same charge, and that his defence came from an avowed atheist. 'It is said sometimes that a man may have a strong and perfect style who has nothing to convey worth conveyance under cover of it': so begins Swinburne's review of Dante Gabriel's poetry, in which he attempts to champion his friend by countering that such is 'a favourite saying of men who have no words in which to convey the thoughts which they have not'.[35] Swinburne's waspish contempt is no doubt apt. But more needs to be done than insisting that the burden of proof lies with the detractors 'to prove as well as assert that beauty and power of expression' are indeed incommensurate with 'depth and wealth of thought'.[36] Another contemporary poet, Matthew Arnold, perhaps offers more than Swinburne on this topic, because he concedes more. 'People do not understand what a temptation there is,' he confessed, 'if you cannot bear anything not very good, to transfer your operations to a region where form is everything':

> Perfection of a certain kind may there be attained, or at least approached, without knocking yourself to pieces, but to attain or approach perfection in the region of thought and feeling, and to unite this with a perfection of form, demands not merely an effort and a labour, but an actual tearing of oneself to pieces, which one does not readily consent to (although one is sometimes forced to it) unless one can devote one's whole life to poetry.[37]

Arnold's generalized comments here gain exemplifying force when elsewhere, in a private letter, he disavows one of his poems in particular. 'The Scholar-Gipsy' had been favourably reviewed for the very reason that Arnold had in that poem abandoned his high-minded theorizing and instead offered himself directly, speaking (as one reviewer put it) 'straight out of things which he has felt and tested on his own pulses'.[38] But Arnold could not stomach this compliment, and turned on his literary friend and confidant, Arthur Hugh Clough, who presumed to praise it on the same score. 'I am glad you like the Gipsy Scholar—but what does it *do* for you?', he demanded to know: 'Homer *animates* – Shakespeare *animates* ... the Gipsy Scholar at best awakens a pleasing melancholy. But this is not what we want.' What men do want, Arnold countered, 'is something to *animate* and *ennoble* them – not merely to add zest to their melancholy or grace to their dreams'.[39]

Instead of zest and grace, Arnold prescribes harsher stimulants; he wants to wake his readers up, not cosy their dozing. Such earnestness is registered in Henry James's observation that Arnold's poems appealed to readers who 'like sometimes to perceive just a little the effort of the poet, like to hear him take breath'.[40] Readers will find no such satisfactions in Rossetti. Even where her lines are thickened with symbols, allegories and intertextual allusions, as they very often are (sources include Plato, the Bible, Barrett Browning, L.E.L., Hemans, Crabbe, Saint Augustine, Dante, Scott, Blake, Pope, Petrarch, Herbert, Crashaw, Maturin, Coleridge, Keats, Tennyson and troubadour traditions), the prosodic snap, slide and chime of her post-'Goblin Market' poems seem as blithely untroubled and effortless as her nonsense and children's verse. It is as if she had learnt too well Ruskin's lesson that 'she must have the Form first', such that prosody takes absolute priority:[41] both in that patterns of sound and rhythm have an uncompromisingly insistent role in her poems, but also in the sense that these prosodic patterns seem to be driving the compositional process in the first place. Here is a sonnet Dante Gabriel considered to be 'as good as anything' his sister had written:[42]

Methinks the ills of life I fain would shun;
   But then I must shun life, which is a blank.
   Even in my childhood oft my spirit sank
Thinking of all that had still to be done.
Among my many friends there is not one
   Like her with whom I sat upon the bank
   Willow-o'er-shadowed, from whose lips I drank
A love more pure than streams that sing and run.
But many times that joy has cost a sigh;
   And many times I in my heart have sought
For the old comfort and not found it yet:
Surely in that calm day when I shall die
   The painful thought will be a blessed thought,
And I shall sorrow that I must forget.[43]

There is much to extol: from the arresting austerity of the opening conundrum (that to shun life's ills would be to shun life itself); to the emphatic *volta*, which (recalling the uncompromising 'But' of the opening dilemma) upturns what's gone before, spinning the octave twice through 'many times'; to the castling conclusion, where 'painful thought' switches places with 'blessed thought', and sorrow lies not in remembering, but in forgetting. As a whole, at the level of thought and feeling, word and phrase, rhythm and rhyme, the poem's foxy reversals and reprises afford the pleasure Wordsworth once described as 'the great spring of the activity of our minds, and their chief feeder'; that is, 'the pleasure which the mind derives from the perception of similitude in dissimilitude', and indeed 'dissimilitude in similitude'.[44] What in the end turns out to be most remarkable about this poem, however, is not so much this or that localized effect, but the fact that Rossetti completed the whole thing in seven minutes.

Seven minutes! It was a product of *bout-rimés*, a game in which she would race against one of her brothers to compose according to the rhyme-endings provided by the other. Dante Gabriel thought this particular production so good that it was 'well worthy of revision', and the manuscript notes suggest he took some part in this himself. No more than tweaking, though; what's quoted above is substantially the same as Rossetti's first dash.[45] Nor is this poem exceptional of its kind. Her twenty surviving *bout-rimés*, all written in under ten minutes, some as fast as six, bear the same qualities – working through keen complements and contrasts without ever losing their rhythmical groove – even when the rhyme-words demanded considerable ingenuity (such as 'meander', 'heaving', 'lances' or 'slime').[46]

We might marvel at these *bout-rimés* specimens as curiosities. Except that William Michael suggests that whether or not his sister was writing *bout-rimés*, her habits of composition were 'entirely of the casual and spontaneous kind, from her earliest to her latest years':

> If something came into her head which she found suggestive of verse, she put it into verse. It came to her (I take it) very easily, without her meditating a possible subject, and without her making any great difference in the first from the latest form of the verses which embodied it;[47]

Such comments appear to explain how she wrote – spontaneously, quickly, easily – and by extension, how she could have written so much. It is certainly hard to see how she could have produced more than a thousand poems if she had adopted Arnold's strenuous and potentially self-annihilating method. Which forces the conclusion niggling away at even her most fulsome admirers, such as Saintsbury and Gosse; namely, that she was a consummate stylist, but little more. But that cannot be right. Other evidence shows that Rossetti cared deeply about her compositions, especially in the period up until 1870 (which were the most poetically productive years of her life), and that she had earnest ambitions to be recognized as a poet.[48] Digging deeper into William Michael's memoir of his sister, there is a less-quoted passage recording that she was 'very resolute in setting a line of demarcation between a person who is a poet and another person who is a versifier', and that 'she never could see any good reason why one who is not a poet should write verse in metre'.[49] It is a hard line, the severity of which William Michael emphasizes ('Pleadings of *in misericordiam* were of no use with her'), and she here converges with Arnold's sentiment in 'The Study of Poetry' (1880) that, 'a nation may have versifiers with smooth numbers, and yet may have no poetry at all'.[50] Poetry amounts to more than versified prose; it is its own mode, for which accomplished prosody is the minimum condition, but which cannot itself suffice. There needs to be substance too.

For all these reasons, it is important not to make too much of her *bout-rimés*, which after all she rarely played again after 1848, and which she did not choose to publish, even though she did print poems from this period in her life, and some from even earlier. Reports of Rossetti's casualness (her brother is not the only person to comment on it) need also to be explained as part of her self-fashioning: it was a pose she cultivated, especially as she turned increasingly to religious themes in her writing. Her attitude was something more than modesty, or indeed the false modesty of *sprezzatura* phrase-making. The best contemporary critics recognized that Rossetti's 'art consists in a seeming disregard of art'; that she is only 'seeming artless', where the verses achieve 'aesthetic and finished perfections'.[51] But there is something else going on as well. Downplaying her compositional effort was an expression of her religious faith; specifically, her Tractarianism. As John Henry Newman never tired of insisting that 'the art of composition is merely accessory',[52] Rossetti likewise sought to de-emphasize the pains of literary composition, and literary achievement, to emphasize instead her commitment to poetry as a piously selfless endeavour. For what's 'literary' in Tractarian poetics is never the desired end but only the required means. Tractarianism helps also to explain Rossetti's commitment to poetry as such, insofar as it was the form of language that proponents of that movement regarded as most suited to the expression of religious devotion and yearning, having a unique capacity to guide the mind to worship and prayer.[53] She shared John Keble's faith in poetry as having the power to 'express thoughts and feelings beyond the power of prose to describe'.[54]

It is hardly surprising, then, that we can find in Rossetti's poems examples of where she seeks expression for something beyond aesthetic perfection as an end in itself, and beyond what could be expressed even in the purplest prose. 'Up-hill' (1858), which William Michael identified as 'the first poem by Christina which excited marked attention',[55] provides a ready test case. A long, wearying journey serves as an allegory for the salvic path to heaven; but, crucially, this allegory is not merely described, it is dramatized. Rossetti is revealing about her instrumental ambitions for her prosody when the poem comes to be set to music, noting that 'day long interferes with the rhyme', thereby affording 'a clue to the correct reading'; and the same might be said of what she describes as the 'ruggedness' of her metre.[56] Where an abstract notion of formal perfection is disrupted as it is in this poem, it is done so in the service of a higher perfection, whereby the poem might show as well as tell its tale. Here we see emerging Rossetti's specifically religious sense of perfection, which she sometimes refers to as the spiritual 'road to perfection',[57] or the 'progress towards perfection' (*L* 4.228), that she knew to be hard but worthy. And worthy for the very reason it was hard, because that honourable struggle would yield 'the bliss and perfection of eternity' (*L* 4.380).

Reversing the terms, 'Amor Mundi' (1865) entrammels the reader in the easy journey that leads to imperfection. The poem opens and ends with the same line, but where that line first presents as liberation ('We shall escape the uphill by never turning back' (I. 213. 4)), when it reappears at the end of the journey, it designates entrapment:

> 'Turn again, O my sweetest, – turn again, false and fleetest:
>
> This beaten way thou beatest I fear is hell's own track.'

> 'Nay, too steep for hill-mounting; nay, too late for cost-counting:
> This down hill path is easy, but there's no turning back'
>
> (I. 214. 18–20)

Having careered by triple rhythm to the destination from which there is no return, having ridden the poem's extravagant inter- and intra-lineal alliterations, assonances, consonances, full rhymes and double rhymes, the hard landing at that implacable final conjunctive, 'but', feels like devastation. No wonder Rossetti chose to pair the poem with 'Up-Hill' in her collection of 1875. The mimetic virtuosity at work in each clarifies the differing theological thrusts of both. But Rossetti could also use her verse style for more personalized spiritual testimony, to create atmospheres as well as delineate arguments. 'Yet a Little While' was written after she had already weathered many personal disappointments and difficulties, and the impatience of her religious appetency rings through:

> Heaven is not far, tho' far the sky
> Overarching earth and main.
> It takes not long to live and die,
> Die, revive, and rise again.
> Not long: how long? Oh, long re-echoing song!
> O Lord, how long?
>
> (II. 266)

Parallelisms and polarities, verbal, phrasal, rhythmic and sonic: like her much-anthologized 'Echo' poem, 'Yet a Little While' is an intense reverberating chamber that recognizes itself as such; a short piece that never seems to end. Closing with a question, the poem is at once centripetal – turning back on itself (recalling but also reimaging its preoccupations, from 'not far' to 'far'; from 'live' to 'die', to 'revive' and 'rise again'; even the final question has been previously posed) – but at the same time centrifugal, flinging itself outwards, as 'not long' primes the anxious, already unanswered, 'how long?' Narratively, the poem does not go anywhere, but that is the point. It explores a mood of longing that is painful precisely because it is continuous, where echoes multiply into re-echoing, and repetition is a condition of re-petitioning. Is there anywhere in English a poem that is simultaneously so dense yet so light, so concise yet so circumlocutory? In the haunting beauty of its own economy, we encounter (to borrow a line from Coventry Patmore) 'The song that is the thing it says'.[58]

***

Such an apology for Rossetti's perfect practice could be considerably elaborated, but it can only take us so far, and where it stops short anyway tends in the wrong direction. The imitative force of her style is often remarkable, but a great number of her poems, perhaps the majority, do not only, or principally, employ style in a way that straightforwardly sharpens a theological thesis or heightens spiritual testimony. Her verse style seems often indeed to inhibit such possibilities, by a combination of open-endedness and self-referencing that threatens to parody what makes 'Yet a Little While' so potent. Inscrutability, even when posed as an urgent concern, may be a kind of facetiousness, of the sort with which Rossetti ends one of her letters written in purple rather than her usual black ink: 'Now why have I written this letter in such a hand? Echo answers nothing but "why," and I merely re-echo Echo's "why"–' (*L* 3.60).

Re-echoing may after all be to no end. Just as riddles may have no solutions, ghost poems may be insubstantial, and nonsense verses may be no more than that. Even her many poems about dreams – from 'Dream-Love' to 'Dream-Land' to 'A Nightmare' – might have no purpose but whimsy, such that to take them as anything more must be a joke at the reader's expense. Critics have had a Freudian field day with 'My Dream', and the poem was a favourite with Rossetti and her family (leading to long-running jokes about her penchant for crocodiles), but we may wish to pause at the note she later appended to the poem's manuscript: 'Not a real dream'.[59] Perhaps the idea that the poem is no unconscious sublimation but a more self-aware channel of expression for Rossetti only encourages those determined to read all her poetry as sexual ache and death wish. 'Goblin Market' has invited even more speculation in this line, as well as an ingeniously wide variety of other interpretations: engaging everything from proto-feminist and homosexual politics, to a polemical (perhaps anti-Semitic) commentary on economic exchange, desire, consumerism, commercialism, localism, marriage markets, advertising, drug addiction, the Christian communion service, anorexia and vampirism. No consensus has emerged, which might just be the most compelling clue to the poem: that it is not meant to be read as interpretable allegory at all.

Another popular poem, 'Winter: My Secret', holds its advertised 'secret' so tightly that we cannot construe it. 'What?' is a title-teasing example in the same vein, a puzzle inside a 'bitter dream' from which the speaker wakes in the final stanza, in a head-scratching twist without a resolution. 'Hollow-Sounding and Mysterious' likewise announces in its very title the unfathomable elusiveness that is its subject, at the same time perhaps hinting at its method: just mysterious enough to draw us in, to divert us, but evacuated of content. As a child, Tennyson could declare, 'I hear a voice that's speaking in the wind', and he would spread his arms and cry back to it.[60] But Rossetti's poem, published in her comparatively late collection, *A Pageant and Other Poems* (1881), does not arise from or even remember her childhood imagining, and it is prototypical of what comes to be associated with her perfect style: rising and falling in a way that invites us to listen, but without a purpose that can be obviously, easily or definitively extracted. 'Hollow-Sounding and Mysterious' even ends by owning its activity: 'Ever beginning, / Ending, repeating', 'Ever for ever / Teaching and preaching' allows of us 'no replying' (II. 97. 8–9; 98. 20–1).

If it is possible to resist the psychoanalytical approach, the elusive and mysterious quality in these poems about dreams, fantastical events and undisclosed secrets ('From House to Home' is another choice example) may alternatively be read as an extension of Rossetti's delight in language itself, encouraged by both her parents. She clearly relished punning and riddling from an early age, and it makes sense that this might inform her enigma verses and charades.[61] More fundamentally, as it applies to all her poems (not only those staging mysterious themes or events), we might read her playful verse style as the natural outcome for a child so in love with language on its own terms, for its intransitive rather than instrumental intensities. 'Perhaps the nearest approach to a method I can lay claim to was a distinct aim at conciseness,' Rossetti once explained, before appending the concession that 'after a while I received a hint from my sister that my love of conciseness tended to make my writing obscure'.[62] What's hard to construe in her poems is not typically or mainly a question of their subject matter. It is her style that makes them so much more dense and indeterminate than if the same ideas or feelings were to be expressed in prose. Or rather, her same ideas or feeling could not be expressed in prose, since the restlessly mobile symmetries of her writing achieve a charge and complexity that is unique to the poetic mode.

Although Rossetti's self-awareness about her habits of concision chastened her 'to avoid obscurity as well as diffuseness',[63] in practice, the former vice is felt far more keenly than the latter. Explanatory contexts are absent from many poems, and her manuscripts show that she often deleted the beginnings and endings of her poems in ways that enhance their dramatic life but prejudice their propositional clarity. That kind of trade-off might seem to bring Rossetti towards aestheticism, and Walter Pater (author of that movement's 'golden book'[64]) certainly recognizes in principle a paradox that Rossetti's poetry consistently realizes in practice; namely, that her habits of concision might collude with those of re-echoing, to create poems that feel at once highly wrought but at the same time over-brimming. 'Self-restraint, a skillful economy of means, ascesis, that too has a beauty of its own', Pater suggests: 'There will be an aesthetic satisfaction in that frugal closeness of style which makes the most of a word, in the exaction from every sentence of a precise relief, in the just spacing out of word to thought, in the logically filled space connected always with the delightful sense of difficulty overcome.'[65] Pater did not have Rossetti in mind when he wrote that, but it is hard to imagine a better gloss on her verse; and he goes further, in a way that is even more illuminating:

> Different classes of persons, at different times, make, of course, very various demands upon literature. Still, scholars, I suppose, and not only scholars, but all disinterested lovers of books, will always look to it, as to all other fine art, for a refuge, a sort of cloistral refuge, from a certain vulgarity in the actual world. A perfect poem ... has for them something of the uses of a religious 'retreat'.[66]

What's the difference between a refuge and a *cloistral* refuge, a retreat and a *religious* retreat? Nothing, according to the leading literary critics of the early twentieth century. William Empson and

F. R. Leavis offer retrospective accounts of late nineteenth-century poetry that diagnose an irresistible need to 'escape' or go 'on holiday' from the 'business' of life,[67] to take 'a holiday from serious aims and exacting business'.[68] Yet Pater strains – in his recalibration from 'refuge' to 'cloistral refuge', and his careful ushering in of 'retreat' with speech marks – to dignify poetic perfection as something more than mere escapism. He is an interesting advocate, given that he became increasingly in thrall to religious rite and ritual through his life, but could not ultimately assent to its theology – such that, for him, 'It doesn't matter in the least what is said, as long as it is said beautifully.'[69] How much more invested might Rossetti be in the aesthetics of perfection and its possible religious 'uses', given that, for her, saying something 'beautifully' within a religious context carried incarnational and sacramental significance?

Answering that question is tricky, not least because, at this juncture, several of the protagonists in the chapter become embroiled. Leavis's totalizing dismissal of Victorian poetry as sheer escapism is, for him, exemplified by a single poem, and that poem just so happens to be Arnold's Scholar-Gipsy. He was seemingly unaware that Arnold had already repudiated it in the same terms. But the poem (and Arnold's wider poetry and poetics) is pertinent to recall here for that very reason, to clarify the religiously minded perspective that Leavis obscures. 'Much of what passes with us as religion and philosophy will', Arnold believed, 'be replaced by poetry'.[70] Poetry serves by this schema as substitute for rather than a spur to faith. But where Arnold approaches poetry through fretful agnosticism, Rossetti takes up her pen steadied by her high Anglicanism. She responds to the 'melancholy, long, withdrawing roar' of the sea of faith, not, as Arnold does, by personal withdrawal ('Ah, love, let us be true / To one another');[71] her retreat is instead universalized as a 'retreat'. No need, then, for the raggedly unruly prosody of 'Dover Beach'; Rossetti's religious faith allows her to meet the encroaching vagaries and vulgarities of the world with winsome equanimity.

That might look like disengagement from the world: repairing to the emotional reassurances of poetic symmetry and sensuousness – where it doesn't matter in the least what is said, 'so long as it is said beautifully'. Even those in Rossetti's lifetime who were most committed to their religious faith wrangled over the question of how poetry might serve that faith, or might need to. Less than a year after Newman left his Anglican community for Rome, he spiked his review of Keble's *Lyra Innocentium* with the Tractarian-deflating assertion that, 'poetry is the refuge of those who have not the Catholic Church'.[72] But leaving aside such ecclesiastical tussling, Rossetti herself certainly believed that her verse might be useful if not actually needful to her religion. Not merely as 'a method of relieving the over-burdened mind', 'a channel through which emotion finds expression, and that a safe, regulated expression',[73] which was Newman's account of Keble's rationale for religious verse. More pointedly, as Emma Mason describes it: the 'mysterious ritual atmosphere' characteristic of Rossetti's poetry encourages readers to enter 'a reflective state' in which they might 'think deeply' about their beliefs.[74] And more pointedly still, Rossetti delineates and directs particular beliefs, not by the subtending method of mimesis, noted above – where form seemingly echoes content – but by a more indirect strategy Newman did fully endorse (both as Anglican and Catholic) in his conception of 'style' as a mode of 'thinking out into language'.[75] Here are the final two (of four) stanzas from a poem Rossetti composed when she was just eighteen, called 'Dream-Land':

Rest, rest, a perfect rest
Shed over brow and breast;
Her face is toward the west,
  The purple land.
She cannot see the grain
Ripening on hill and plain;
She cannot feel the rain
  Upon her hand.

Rest, rest, for evermore
Upon a mossy shore;
Rest, rest at the heart's core
  Till time shall cease:
Sleep that no pain shall wake;
Night that no morn shall break
Till joy shall overtake
  Her perfect peace.

(I. 27. 17–32)

Perfect rest closes to perfect peace, as ratified by immaculate prosody. We cannot miss what Saintsbury calls the 'exquisite regularity' of the poem's form here,[76] and its title appears to grant the reader indulgence to reverie. Yet the poem's title actually adverts to the doctrine of 'soul sleep' (the state of the soul between death and Judgement when the soul dreams of paradise), to which Rossetti was committed.[77] A wealth of extra-textual information (from the coloured designs with which Rossetti illustrated the lyric, to biblical sources, to Rossetti's own letters) supports a reading of the poem as an exploration of this doctrine.[78] But if the creed that animates this poem is so important to Rossetti, why does she engage it in a way that risks being overlooked? Just as Tractarianism – a movement that predicated an intellectual grasp of doctrine as a bedrock for faith – endorsed her investment in poetry as a means of explicating theology, it also helps explain her countervailing wiliness. For her obliquity is itself a conscious theological praxis, performing the Tractarian theology of Reserve, whereby divine laws are to be purposefully hidden from all but the already initiated and faithful, who alone might be able to read the poetic metaphors, figures and analogies for their true significance.[79]

Some scholars have gone further, to argue that Rossetti does not merely reflect but refashions these Tractarian ideas, to accommodate (among other things) her personal subjectivity, her female subjectivity and female communality, and Pre-Raphaelite influences.[80] It has even been suggested that Rossetti dwells on the enigmatic and unknowable as a way of subverting the riddle tradition to religious ends: deploying poetic clues that have no definitive answers as a way of directing readers to 'the vanity of human knowing and to point her readers instead to faith in the beyond'.[81] Each of these arguments demonstrates how Rossetti's religious faith positively informs the style as well as the themes of her verse; they exculpate her from the double imputation of being uninterestingly trivial and distastefully repressed. Yet there is still some work to do, to show how her religious faith might be reconciled with her commitment to perfect form, which commitment seems more obviously aligned to the secular self-sufficiency of aestheticism. Every literary movement exhibits more various and subtle sympathies than might be captured by its tag line (whatever Pater wished to advocate, it was hardly identical to Wilde, say, or Swinburne); yet there remains something curiously conflicted about the transcendent nature of Rossetti's religious faith, and the faith she puts in the immanence of poetic experience.

***

Back, then, to the most extreme case of form for form's sake, where Rossetti explicitly reverse-engineers her writing. To take Rossetti seriously, it was earlier suggested, to recover her as a poet who cared for more than sweet-sounding verse, and who composed more intelligently than by numbers alone, we must play down her dabbles in *bout-rimés*. But such a defensive move, diminishing the agency of form in composition, continues to accept at face value Arnold's model for versifying, whereby the poet's job is to recognize that there is a difference between the logical content of pre-verbal thought and feeling and the alogical form of prosody, and to 'unite' the two – by having the latter mimic the former. Rhythms, rhymes and the whole paralinguistic pyrotechnics of prosody may be brought out, so long as they subserve the poem's content. Too much of a stylistic side-show can distract from the poem's verbally directed thoughts and feelings, and the wrong sort can introduce unwitting ironies. For 'the only secret of style', according to Arnold, is: 'Have something to say, and say it as clearly as you can.'[82] Verse obliges what writers have to 'say' by replaying their words, acuminating them through rhythm and sound.

By this rationale, Rossetti's practice of *bout-rimés* is obviously derelict. Leading with prescribed rhymes (the metre and sonnet form is also predetermined), and indeed making the whole enterprise a competitive race, travesties even the more liberal notions of how substantial poetry comes into being. Arnold, to be fair, was too good a poet and critic not to have sensed (with Hegel) that versification may be no 'mere hindrance to the free outpouring of inspiration', and that, for the best writers, the discipline associated with poetic form, 'neither hinders nor oppresses, but on the contrary … uplifts and carries'.[83] Yet he could not tolerate the more extravagant leaps of faith Rossetti routinely took in her writing, composing so much, so quickly and so opportunistically – and neither can most readers. Scholars do increasingly acknowledge the extent to which Rossetti's faith is erudite, thoughtful and articulated in earnest.[84] But even her devotees shy from imagining that the very predeterminations of form with which Rossetti plays, and indeed the act of playing with language itself, might offer a rival form of Arnoldian 'high seriousness'.

Rowan Williams, however, imagines exactly that, in his description of the enterprise of writing as 'a remarkable act of *faith in language*, an act of faith which assumes that words can be persuaded to say more than they initially seem to mean'.[85] Persuasion is effected through 'pressure', Williams argues; that is, by administering 'carefully calculated shocks' to language. His formulation here – 'pressure', 'shocks' – is more obviously applicable to the habits of other poets considered in this book; notably Hopkins, and to a lesser extent, Eliot and Blake. But Williams goes on to note that, in addition to writers persuading language to behave in surprising ways, language may have persuasive surprises in store for us too. By playing with language, we may not only find out unexpected ways of saying what we wish to 'say', we may find out thoughts and feelings we never knew we wished to think or feel in the first place: '[B]ecause language is connected in opaque and sometimes untraceable ways with what it talks about, it will generate new perspectives when we are not looking, so to speak – when we are not preoccupied with reinforcing habitual and normal idioms and practices.'[86]

Re-enter Rossetti and her *bout-rimés*, this time accompanied by the archly ingenious lyricist-rhymer, W. S. Gilbert. Williams gives them a line each in passing, pairing them in consecutive sentences, as the purest example of how writers may complicate what seems normal – 'to uncover what "normal" perception screens out', through the simple search for rhyme.[87] It is a deft insight, though it leaves Rossetti ambivalently stranded in the knockabout company of comic opera. But if the substantial import of Williams's thesis may be recovered – that faith in language can operate not only by carefully calculated interventions, but also by consciously uncalculated play – then Rossetti's facility and endeavours in *bout-rimés* might have implications for the rest of her verses too. Form for its own sake, the springe of aestheticism, might be re-cast as play for its own sake, which provokes unexpected purposes, potentially of the weightiest kind.

Rossetti understood that conventions of rhyming are merely conventional. Dante Gabriel 'would not allow *dawn* to rhyme with such words as *born*', she advised a friend, at the same time noting that various other critics would agree. Yet she does not herself think such principles are inviolable, and so invites her correspondent to make up her own mind: '*you* judge' (*L* 4.157). On occasion, she implies that word choice might find its justification in fulfilling the rhyme scheme alone: '"taught" is scarcely the word wanted', she objects, before appending the concession, 'except viewed as a rhyme to "thought"' (*L* 4.218). But Rossetti also knew that what's 'wanted' in a rhyme-word might be more than warranted in the poem's established sense; or rather, the rhyme might itself be the warrant for a new kind of sense.

It was her (allegedly) less-perfect prosodical partner, Barrett Browning, who claimed that 'we want new forms, as well as thoughts', and who elsewhere mischievously explained that 'reverie serene' was the best phrasing because 'the rhyme *lets* me say – "sweetest eyes were ever seen"'.[88] Although Rossetti was herself no prosodical iconoclast – the music of her verse being shadowed by the epithet 'perfect', where Barrett Browning's is, at best, euphemistically called 'strange'[89] – her play of sound is in its own way committed to strategies of estrangement. Dreams, secrets, echoes: these are the recurring themes and moods of her poems, and they are actuated through her style that embraces where Barrett Browning sabotages incantational consummation. In a letter to William Bell Scott on 12 September 1887 (*L* 4.52), Rossetti offers a roundel that she has written, the last three lines of which request the reader to:

> Condone the barbarous rhymes that will not sound well
> In building up, all Poets to amaze,
> A roundel.
>
> (III. 339. 9–11)

Sounding well, rather than barbarous, is not a matter of sound alone (as was noted in the chapter on Blake, who responded to Milton's aspersion of all end-rhyme as 'the Invention of a barbarous Age'). Rhymes sate or grate also, Rossetti knew, for the ways in which they link words together. Rhyming may therefore be perfect on its own terms: 'Do you recollect the ready wit with which Gabriel suggested "viperous" as rhyme to "Cyprus" when the matter was mooted?', Rossetti reminisced with William Michael (*L* 4.144). But rhymes may also achieve what has been identified above as a higher perfection, where they 'sound well' because they sound out a new connection: 'I think your "cabbage and cabbage rose" both "witty," and pretty: reason rules the rhyme,' she advised Caroline Maria Gemmer (*L* 4.64). That might look like Rossetti is backsliding to Arnoldian poetics. But even if reason apparently 'rules' the rhyme once it is in place, the rhyme has not here 'united' with but has actually generated the reason, by the synergy W. K. Wimsatt influentially outlined in his essay, 'One Relation of Rhyme to Reason'.[90] Rossetti implicitly understands that what's witty in the connection constitutes a new kind of reasoning that cannot be separated from its prettiness.

In the manuscript for one of Rossetti's sonnets there is a note added in pencil in William Michael's hand: 'must be Bouts rimés'.[91] That seems like a confident bit of identification, but the modal construction cannot help insinuating some doubt; if there were none, 'must be' would be unnecessary. Reading the poem in question ('Have you forgotten?'), it is not clear why William Michael pegs it as an example of *bout-rimés*. Perhaps he had other circumstantial reasons to suspect so, because the sonnet (which is not included in the principal collection of her *bout-rimés* known as the 'Troxell Collection')[92] is not obviously overdetermined by its form. The end-rhymes are not inert placeholders; they earn their place, creatively interacting with the rest of the poem, especially where lines run on ('both light / And darkness; not embarrassed yet not quite / At ease?' (III. 173. 4–6). However much rhyme might have 'ruled' reason in the act of composition, the finished poem presents a relationship that is mutually shaping.

Rossetti wrote to William Michael on 24 September 1849, coaxing him to play again at *bout-rimés*, suggesting that she will select rhymes from one of her own sonnets: 'In the certainty that you cannot possibly equal that work of art' (*L* 1.27). The tone is affectionate jockeying, of the sort that runs through much of her correspondence with her brothers.[93] But the competitive edge is revealing of the fact that her faith in poetry is not one of blind serendipity: linguistic chance must be converted by writerly skill. Hence her confidence that, although adhering to an identical metrical and rhyme scheme, her brother could not equal her own poem. It is not surprising that she was confident, since the rhymes she supplied come from 'Remember', which soon became the most celebrated sonnet she ever wrote. Indeed, her choice of rhymes might seem like a cheat, given that 'Remember' was not only one of her best poems, it was not itself a product of *bout-rimés*. That Rossetti does not herself register this, however, is further revealing of the essential continuity she imagines between the generative possibilities of form in all contexts of her writing. Faith in the game, its fun but also its creative productivity, is less salient than her overarching faith in verse style itself: not merely to reflect, by cunning mimesis, the prior claims of verbal content, but itself to excite us to new ways of thinking and feeling. Sonic play is not a superadded mechanism of sense-making, a dispensable supplement to semantics; more radically, it is a *donnée* that occurs as a possibility – opportunistic and serendipitous – for the very fact that it cuts across the syntactical logic by which language ordinarily operates.[94] Rhyme's sonic sequiturs disrupt rather than mime or augment what the words already express. But the burden of the argument here is not that Rossetti's breathless compositions by fixed rhymes are in fact neither better nor worse than her more patient, self-propelling poems. What is being argued here is something more fundamental about how she could write so much, and why her finished poems are not stifled but catalysed by the arbitrary conventionalities of formal discipline. Her experiments in *bouts-rimés* rarely rival her finest writing, but they may tell us most about what makes her finest writing so fine.

Having renounced Arnold's 'secret of style', and his anguished conception of prosody as poetry's merely 'mechanical part',[95] it is tempting to return to Swinburne's implicit faith in the perfection of Dante Gabriel's poetry. Pre-Raphaelite poetics, which Dante Gabriel epitomizes, have been a useful lens through which some critics have viewed his sister's poems too; and Swinburne himself – perhaps the closest there is to French Symbolism in English – offers another instructively different model for thinking about verse style's possible relations to substance. Yet such allegiances are necessarily limited. Although Swinburne admired Rossetti's verse craft (dedicating his *Century of Roundels* to her), their personal and poetical outlooks were multiply incompatible. The breach is more fundamental than might be inferred from her priggish flinching over certain of his poems (pasting strips of paper over passages she deemed indecent), and separates her from her brother too. For unlike either of these men, Rossetti's faith in poetic perfection seeks to reflect, explore and glorify what she calls 'the Perfection of God's Goodness' (*L* 4.111). Perfect form in poetry is not, for Rossetti, an idolatry of aesthetic self-reference (form for its own sake). On the contrary, as Rossetti idealizes perfection into a proper noun along with 'Goodness', she reads this quality as an essential attribute of God Himself, to which we are enjoined to aspire. Correspondingly, her impeccable verse style is not merely the prolegomena to her faith, but its reverent practice.

There is no hubris here, only humility. She observes in *Seek and Find* (1879) that 'while all the good creatures of God teach us some lesson concerning the unapproached perfections of their creator, that which they display is a glimpse, that which they cannot display is infinite'.[96] By extension, how much fainter, she knew, must be the glimpses that her own creations in verse might provide. But all this talk of straining towards a perfect creator through the unapproachable endeavour for perfect creation may be hard for us to hear now. Not only because we live in a largely secular age, such that the religious admonitions of a poem such as 'Up-Hill' are now popularly read as 'a thing to shudder at',[97] and the personalized spiritual yearnings of her writing are predictably labelled libidinous. It is hard to hear also because we live in a postmodern age, which assumes that beauty and truth and goodness are entirely contingent and probably oppressive constructions, without any objectivity or essential relationship. The poetry-as-escapism thesis repines the extent to which poets exploit 'a sort of tap-root into the world of their childhood';[98] and when it comes to verse style, special distaste is reserved for the 'childish titillation of riming'.[99] But if we reimagine the equation of childhood with childishness, and instead see the value – theological as well as aesthetic – in the recovery of what's childlike, a quite different perspective emerges. Wordplay may be redeemed into profundity.

To take just one tiny illustrative instance, there is something more potent than mimesis in the replay of 'long' that we hear in Rossetti's re-echoing 'song': something different from the retroactive uniting of rhyme with reason that Arnold imagines, something that exceeds even Wimsatt's more subtle, but still semantics-driven account of the mutuality of rhyme and reason. Connecting 'long' and 'song' is not a single, isolated link in the poem's verbal or prosodic chain; it is a metonym for the entire poem's impatient waiting, already inscribed in its title, which recalls both the Old Testament prophecy of Jeremiah and also Paul's address to Hebrews, that salvation will come in 'yet a little while'. And as the rhyme plays its entire poem in miniature, it might also be said to perform what's characteristic in Rossetti's entire corpus, which is – as William Michael observed of Rossetti's own character – 'replete with the spirit of self-postponement'.[100] Widening the lens yet further: as the long-song percussion reverberates with what's particular in Rossetti's poetics and person, it simultaneously re-echoes what she took to be universal in the postlapsarian yearning for a reunion with God that feels perpetually and painfully out of reach.

Prosodic symmetries may prompt us to notice lexical correspondences, then, and to thrill to local mimetic triumphs. But they may also implicate us into sounding out correspondences and realities that reach further than can afterwards be rationalized into propositional paraphrase. Seen – or rather, heard – in this way, simplicity in Rossetti's verse style, and its pervasive playfulness, is no embarrassment to be got past before we can admire her. The winning stringency of her style is essential to her perfection in the fullest sense – not because it precisely represents reality, but precisely for the reason that it often doesn't even try. It is only by forsaking the delusory ambition of representing lived experience in language that she manages to re-present it with such vitality, by appealing to what (also remembering Gilbert's comic-operas) G. K. Chesterton called the 'romance of rhyme'.[101] 'In the innermost part of all poetry is the nursery rhyme,' Chesterton advises, and 'the true enjoyment of poetry is in having the simple pleasure as well as the subtle pleasure'; 'or yet more truly, the first pleasure inside the second':

> What is the matter with the modern world is that it is trying to get simplicity in everything except the soul. Where the soul really has simplicity it can be grateful for anything – even complexity.[102]

Here, finally, we may come full circle to agree with Saintsbury's judgement that the best of Rossetti is to be found in her earliest as well as her last verses, in her silliest sing-songs as well as the most earnest expressions of her religion.[103] For it is only through recognizing this continuity in her repertoire that we may fully appreciate why a poem such as 'Sleep at Sea' 'ranks among the half-dozen greatest devotional poems in English'.[104] Not because its aesthetic greatness lies in its sophistication 'on the formal side', but rather that its devotional greatness is realized *through* its seeming simplicity of form, out of which more subtle pleasures and complex implications emerge. Nursery rhyming adduces something of the pleasure of religious ritual; or perhaps, recalling Pater, the pleasure that attends stylistic patterning, ludic as well as instrumental, assumes something of the uses of a religious 'retreat'. Tolling repeats not only beat out a narrative, they do so from *inside* that narrative, educing an atmosphere conducive to spiritual reflection and transport. The poem is certainly as much meditation as argument; it ruminates its lament that those addressed cannot after all be roused from their slumber of sin. Whether or not the poem animates and ennobles, and notwithstanding its obliquities of Tractarian Reserve, its closing lines – compounding the hypnagogic pungencies of the ten previous stanzas – confirm that we are reading a poet whose practice of perfection wagers nothing less than everything:

No voice to call the sleepers,
  No hand to raise:
They sleep to death in dreaming
  Of length of days.
Vanity of vanities,
  The Preacher says:
Vanity is the end
  Of all their ways.

(I. 81–2. 81–8)

4

Gerard M. Hopkins: Counter Stress

... to recognise the form you are employing and to mean it is everything.[1]

'Surely one vocation cannot destroy another', Canon Dixon counselled his friend (*C* I.496). But Hopkins was not so sure. Six months before he was to begin his novitiate in the Society of Jesus, he explained to his old school mate Alexander Baillie that he wanted 'to write still and as a priest', and that he 'very likely can do that too', though 'not so freely' as he should wish: 'e.g. nothing or little in the verse way, but no doubt what wd. best serve the cause of my religion' (*C* I.175). It is an elaborate bit of hedging – 'very likely', 'not so freely', 'nothing or little', 'no doubt' – but his resolve soon hardens. Cessation becomes complete and unequivocal within a few months, and takes the form of purgation, as he burnt his early poems. He does not pretend to be sanguine about it. There is something histrionic, and knowingly so, in his description of his poetry-pyre as the 'slaughter of the innocents', and in his confession that he should yet like to sing his 'dying-swan song'.[2] But he honours his self-imposed quiescence for some seven years (during which he did not write more than 'two or three little presentation pieces which occasion called for' (*C* I.317)), until, unexpectedly, his position shifts once more; almost by accident. Happening to read an account of a shipwreck in *The Times* newspaper on 11 December 1875, he happened to mention to his Rector how much it had affected him, and the Rector happened to say that 'he wished someone would write a poem on the subject'. 'On this hint I set to work,' Hopkins recalls (*C* I.317). It was an unleashing.

Except that it wasn't. Because it turns out that he never really gave up on poetry at all. And even after he took tacit permission from his Superior to devote himself to verse, he continued to feel painfully troubled by the effort to reconcile his priestly practice with his practice of poetry.

That Hopkins kept faith with poetry even after he disavowed it is evident from several sources. Burning his poems was a symbolic concession to the discipline of his vocation rather than a thoroughgoing attempt to erase all poetry from his life. He was aware that Robert Bridges had kept many of his poems in manuscript, and he actually sent Bridges corrected versions of some of them three months after the 'slaughter'. Hopkins's letters from this period are, it is true, less rich in discussions of literature, but that was largely because in the early stages of his training his correspondence was limited to one missive per week, which he generally reserved for his family. In spite of the great demands that the novitiate term made upon his time and energy, he evidently still read as well as studied poetry in earnest, as seen in his attempts at learning Welsh – which was, he conceded, not undertaken 'with very pure intentions perhaps' (*C* III.602). There was no 'perhaps' about it; even after coming clean to the Rector that his language work was not 'purely for the sake of labouring among the Welsh', he persisted in translating and emulating Welsh poetic forms.[3] No surprise, then, that when he eventually produced 'The Wreck of the Deutschland', the poem with which he shattered his avowed silence, it contained 'certain chimes suggested by the Welsh poetry' (*C* I.317).[4]

But there must have been more than the tintinnabulation of Celtic vowels at play in Hopkins's imagination to have precipitated his new poetics, the flinty originality of which is marked above all by its rhythmical torsions and sonic collisions. While his earlier poems had a sub-Keatsian sweetness about them, 'The Wreck' trades sweetness for 'stress', in a measure that has no direct precedent in Welsh or indeed in English poetry.[5] Nor is it possible to trace its prosodical origins in Hopkins's own versifying,[6] or even in his verse theorizing.[7] But his innovation was not after all *ex nihilo*. He had indeed stopped writing poetry after taking his vows, but he had also, it seems – in a highly Jesuitical compromise – continued to compose in his head. Not that he was constructing complete poems; rather, he was tracking and trialling patterns of rhythmic sound, such that when it came for him to write again, he was by no means starting from scratch: 'I had long had haunting my ear the echo of a new rhythm which now I realised on paper', he explained to Dixon (*C* I.317). Hopkins's metaphorical language here is suggestive, not only regarding the provenance of his verse style (haunting, echoing), but also about its readerly appeal. A couple of years later Dixon falls in with Hopkins's formulation by explaining that he's 'haunted' by certain lines (*C* I.383). Even Bridges, who hated 'The Wreck' (having read it once, he said he would not for any money do so again (*C* I.282)), was unable to resist possession, to the extent that he brought 'echoes' of it into his own writing. The poem 'could not help haunting your memory', Hopkins advised him, with vindicatory satisfaction (*C* I.406).

Still, many critics 'can hardly help regretting' those lost seven years in Hopkins's career as a poet.[8] But that period is better understood as one of creative gain, in which he was able to nurture his prosodical innovation without having to justify its idiosyncrasies on paper. Sprung rhythm might otherwise never have come into being as poetry. By extension, it was a happy misfortune that Hopkins could not readily find a sympathetic editor, insofar as that allowed him to write without having to accommodate prevailing tastes. 'I need not alter what I cannot publish,' he told Bridges (*C* I.138).[9] As far as the quality of his poetry is concerned, it was perhaps most fortunate, too, that Hopkins felt a positive need to write against the verse style of his moment; specifically, against what he took to be the poetics of Protestantism. Walter Ong first staked this claim in the mid-twentieth century, and since then a number of scholars have elaborated the argument that the characteristic abruptness of Hopkins's verse (his very definition of sprung rhythm is that it 'means something like abrupt' (*C* I.346)) was an attempt to recuperate the pre-Reformation, strong-stress ruggedness of Old English poetry.[10] That Hopkins's disruptive rhythmical style served simultaneously as a kind of religious antagonism is a suggestive idea, but it is one that has proved vulnerable to overstatement, as if (to read some critics) Hopkins conceived of his poems and constructed them as one might select and assemble flat-pack furniture. Composition is never so determinate, not for decent poets anyway, and it is clear that Hopkins did not simply find his verse style as a ready-made Catholic resource already existing in the canon. Rather, he founded it, from the poetic practice of diverse exemplars, foremost of which included the notoriously Catholic-baiting Milton. For all that, Hopkins's self-consciousness about his particular religious identity is keenly relevant to his poetics, if viewed in more subtle and less schematic terms, according to what Eric Griffiths nicely frames as the 'reciprocal adjustments of social locution and liturgical forms' that were a central part of learning to live as an English Catholic rather than an Anglo-Catholic.[11]

While there can be no suggestion, then, that Hopkins shipped in a prefabricated Catholic poetics in his mature verse (whatever that might look like), his theology does surely make itself felt in the style as well as the subjects of those poems he wrote as a Jesuit priest. On the heels of 'The Wreck', he produced a number of rapturous sonnets, including 'God's Grandeur', 'As kingfishers catch fire', 'The Windhover', 'Pied Beauty', and 'Hurrahing in Harvest'. This is a period when he sensed divine presence and purpose everywhere in creation. 'I do not think I have ever seen anything more beautiful than the bluebell I have been looking at,' he records in his journal, before appending the meditative corollary: 'I know the beauty of our Lord by it.'[12] Hopkins amply ratifies that incarnational knowledge in his poetry too, and not by merely rehearsing his Catholic creed. Instead, his verse assays that creed as converging with his particular, lived experience. More radically: his poems labour to instantiate his faith, to make us feel what he feels, in the fact and the joy of God's presence. Clouds or cows, weeds or trees, stars or dragonflies: wherever he turns his eye, from the earth to the sky, he inevitably approaches existence – 'All things counter, original, spare' – through his conviction that the world is 'charged with the grandeur of God', for which poetry becomes a mode of wonder, testimony and, by extension, praise.[13]

But it doesn't last long. Within a couple of years, he suffers once more a crisis between his vocations. Although he complains that his life leaves little opportunity to compose, he knows the problem is 'far more than direct want of time' (*C* II.914). He explained his conundrum in a letter to Dixon of 5–10 October 1878: 'After writing ['The Wreck'], I held myself free to compose, but cannot find it in my conscience to spend time upon it; so I have done little and shall do less' (*C* I.317). This comment connects with his concerns that versifying was not 'belonging' to his 'profession' and that 'poetry is unprofessional' (*C* I.317; *C* II.681). We seem to be back to his worry that poetry might be justified only insofar as it served his priestly office.

Recent work in 'historical poetics' has emphasized the extent to which Hopkins among other nineteenth-century writers imagined poetry emblematically and instrumentally – for what it represented and for what it might do in the world – and Hopkins is among those who provide quotable pronouncements of this sort.[14] On stray occasions, he implies that the only point of writing would be to publish ('even the impulse to write is wanting, for I have no thought of publishing' (*C* I.318)), and the only point of publishing to make a difference to society: 'To produce then is of little use unless what we produce is known, if known widely known, the wider known the better, for it is by being known it works, it influences, it does its duty, it does good' (*C* II.813). The good he has in mind here is: 'To educate, to be standards' (*C* II.813). In a couple of other comments, this 'good' extends to furthering England and the Empire: 'A great work by an Englishman is like a great battle won by England,' he hurrahed to Bridges (*C* II.813; 785–6). But that triumphalist military metaphor is not representative of Hopkins's thinking on this question. His conception of what poems can and should do was for the most part far less chauvinistic and *partis pris*, and is better captured by the inclusive figure of modelling divine goodness that he focuses through an allusion to Matthew's Gospel (5:16): 'Let your light shine before men that they may see your good works (say, of art) and glorify yr. Father in heaven' (*C* II.813).[15]

However Hopkins imagines poetry's efficacy, and the need to subordinate compositional efforts to worldly ends, he seems curiously ambivalent about publishing anything himself. Perhaps after a few early knock-backs he talked himself out of the possibility of ever finding his way into print.[16] But between his decision to leave the fate of his poems to his Superiors (*C* I.333), and his later opinion that they would actually best be left in God's hands (*C* I.502), there seems more to his uneasiness than the confidence-shaking resignation at being previously rebuffed. On 15 February of the following year, he wrote to Bridges offering a fuller rationale for how he could feel 'free' to write, and yet not (*C* I.333–4):

> I cannot in conscience spend time on poetry, neither have I the inducements and inspirations that make others compose. Feeling, love in particular, is the great moving power and spring of verse and the only person that I am in love with seldom, especially now, stirs my heart sensibly and when he does I cannot always 'make capital' of it, it would be a sacrilege to do so.

Hopkins writes to express his love in response to feeling loved. His faith in poetry falters, then, with his religious faith. Or rather, poetry falters where he finds it hard to integrate his religious faith – his avowed belief in the tenets of the Catholic Church – with his everyday experience of that faith, in which he is seldom stirred by the benison of a personal God. When God feels absent, he is creatively sterile, and it seems to him opportunistic, even sacrilegious, to divert into verse what inklings he does have of divine presence.

He continued to write poems, on and off, after 1877, but with costive effort, and generally without the intensity of the earlier work. Yet there is one further twist in the tale. In 1885, poems suddenly come again, 'like inspirations unbidden and against my will' (*C* II.743). Not because he finds his spirits revivified, nor because his sense of God's love feels more present. For the opposite reason: because God feels entirely absent. Or worse, where he suffers, as he imagines, from God's own hand (at 'dark heaven's baffling ban' (*P* 101.12)). In this new phase of creativity he revives the oral priority for composition, being creatively 'haunted' once more ('such verse as I do compose is oral, made away from paper, and I put it down with repugnance' (*C* II.883)), and with the nervy puissance of his earlier style. Another stream of sonnets follows: 'To seem the stranger', 'I wake and feel', 'No worst, there is none', '(Carrion Comfort)', 'My own heart let me more have pity on' and 'Patience'.

It is a return to his finest form, but with a decisive variation. Whereas the earlier poems that came thick and fast were animated by joy, these later verses are welters of despair; 'written in blood', as he said of one of them (*C* II.736). But the most significant difference is not in the end thematic. Poetry has, for Hopkins, changed its function. As he edges into his second phase of self-described 'inspiration', poetry ceases to serve as religious testimony: it becomes instead a site for testing his faith against the recrudescence of angst. The shift is marked; expression gives way to exploration. Poetry becomes a mode for rationalizing, even reparating, his religious faith – through his faith in poetry. As will be seen in what follows, however, unpacking Hopkins's poetics in the end reveals something deeper, and less easily defined, about the relationship between his earlier and later verses, as correlative channels for inspiration and as forms of prayer.

***

'Do you know, a horrible thing has happened to me,' Hopkins – still a fresh-faced undergraduate – wrote to Baillie: 'I have begun to *doubt* Tennyson' (*C* I.67). But it's not all bad news. Felling the Laureate has, it turns out, a salutary side-effect. Learning to doubt Tennyson serves in a roundabout way to reaffirm Hopkins's faith in poetry in general. Perhaps there are hints of Oedipal eagerness to cut down the literary patricians of his day, to make room for his own incipient ambitions.[17] But he has a more disinterested and general point to make as well. Only 'inspiration', he goes on to explain, produces 'poetry proper' (*C* I.67). Great poets who compose without it lapse into the autopilot of self-plagiarism, where the ticks and tricks of cultivated repertoires produce verse that may be passable but ultimately 'palls'. He labels this kind of poetry 'Parnassian', and gives Tennyson's predecessor in the Laureateship an even harder time for falling into this custom ('no author palls so much as Wordsworth'). There is also, according to Hopkins, a lower rank of poetry still, below the Parnassian, occupied by poets who have neither talent nor inspiration, and so produce writing that is 'merely the language of verse as distinct from that of prose' (*C* I.71).

Hopkins's science of the beautiful, dividing poetry by some totalizing schema into three kinds – and then subdividing these kinds yet further, as he does, 'into a higher sort of Parnassian which I call Castalian, or it may be thought the lowest kind of inspiration' – risks tipping into travesty.[18] As does his bluff reassurance that 'The word inspiration need cause no difficulty' (*C* I.67–8):

> I mean by it a mood of great, abnormal in fact, mental acuteness, either energetic or receptive, according as the thoughts which arise in it seem generated by a stress and action of the brain, or to strike into it unasked. This mood arises from various causes, physical generally, as good health or state of the air or, prosaic as it is, length of time after a meal.

Poetry is prosaic indeed when index-linked to our gastrointestinal conditions, and so, sensibly, he cuts short that hypothesis too ('I need not go into this' (*C* I.68)). But if he scants the explanatory details, his conclusions are nonetheless emphatic and suggestive: 'poetry of inspiration' may only be written in this 'mood of mind', where inspiration, by definition, defeats our expectations. 'In a fine piece of inspiration every beauty takes you as it were by surprise'; 'not of course that you did not think the writer could be so great', but rather that 'every fresh beauty could not in any way be predicted or accounted for by what one has already read'. Whereas with Parnassian poetry one could conceive oneself writing it if one were the poet, works of inspiration refuse that conceit. Do not say, then, that *if* you were Shakespeare you could imagine yourself writing *Hamlet*, because, Hopkins insists, 'that is just what I think what you can *not* conceive' (*C* I.69).

It is easy – perhaps too easy – to dismiss Hopkins's thoughts on inspiration in this letter, written while he was only a few months out of his teens, and long before he composed the poetry for which he is known. For its naiveties, however, it is a seminal document in the development of Hopkins's poetics, setting out his thoughts on 'poetry proper' that he would worry away at for the rest of his life. Here is the very last poem he ever wrote, dated 22 April 1889, just seven weeks before his death:

> To R. B.
>
> The fine delight that fathers thought; the strong
> Spur, live and lancing like the blowpipe flame,
> Breathes once and, quenchèd faster than it came,
> Leaves yet the mind a mother of immortal song.

Nine months she then, nay years, nine years she long
Within her wears, bears, cares and combs the same:
The widow of an insight lost she lives, with aim
Now known and hand at work now never wrong.

Sweet fire the sire of muse, my soul needs this;
I want the one rapture of an inspiration.
O then if in my lagging lines you miss

The roll, the rise, the carol, the creation,
My winter world, that scarcely breathes that bliss
Now, yields you, with some sighs, our explanation.

(*P* 108)

Hopkins's plaint that he lacks creative vitality is confounded by the energy with which he expresses it. The octave's cascading fecundity – fathering, strong spur, live and lancing, flame-like, mothering – sets up the contradistinctive desolation of which the sestet despairs. But the 'turn' at the *volta* is not an about-turn. The figurative treatment of desiccation is itself positively fecund in its yearning for what's lost: sweet fire, sire of muse, rapture of an inspiration, roll, rise, carol, creation. The sestet is not therefore, as might be expected, the enervated opposite of the octave; it is its counterpart. Absence reads as absent presence: the second part of the poem speaks back to the first. This happens implicitly but also explicitly, notably when 'Breathes' from the third line (linked to 'immortal song') finds its dark pendent in the symbolically 'winter world' in which he 'scarcely breathes that bliss'.

References to breath are also etymologically connected to 'inspiration', which occurs in the most important line of the poem that erupts with first-person vulnerability: 'I want the one rapture of an inspiration'. Caught between the double meanings of 'want' – as deficiency but also desire – Hopkins confesses (once again, with both meanings intended) 'my soul *needs* this'. Yet if one enquires after 'the particulars of rapture' here (to borrow Wallace Stevens's phrase),[19] it is clear that what Hopkins wants and needs is to be found in the 'immortal song' of the poem itself. More precisely, it is founded in the act of poetic creation to which the poem attests.

But the poem is not only about inspiration. 'Nine months she then, nay years, nine years' moves from the metaphor of pregnancy's natural term to the Horation notion that a poem should – to allow second thoughts and revisions – be kept for nine years before publication.[20] The 'live and lancing ... blowpipe flame' is checked by the cooler processes of lucubration. 'Now this is the artist's most essential quality,' he advised Dixon, 'masterly execution' (*C* II.792). That means choosing words with sufficient 'point and propriety', making images 'brilliant', and the prosody 'highly wrought' (*C* I.265; 482; *C* II.544, 748, 749, 919). Though the poem poses as a meditation on lustreless lacking, the image of the 'hand at work now never wrong' counters with the reassurance of the faultless artisan. Which, in Hopkins's lexicon, implies a faith in law as against licence. As he wryly intimates to Bridges: 'Only remark, as you say that there is no conceivable licence I shd. not be able to justify, that with all my licences, or rather laws, I am stricter than you and I might say than anybody I know' (*C* I.280). Hopkins's metanoia throws waspish emphasis on the corrected statement. What might look to be licences in his poetry are actually higher laws that bind him with unprecedented stringency. That imperative has its origins in his undergraduate studies; notably, in his essay 'On the Origin of Beauty: A Platonic Dialogue', where the professor leads his pupil in the discussion of a chestnut fan. Its structure and order determine its beauty, which depends upon the relation of each part to the whole, balancing complexity and variety. The former quality encourages 'the concentration, the intensity' of the artistic experience;[21] the latter, as he would subsequently explain it (in his 'Author's Preface'), to prevent the form becoming too 'same and tame' (*P* 46).[22]

While some licences are established as law through convention,[23] others can be compensated for within the individual form itself, which is why he asserts that 'apparent licences are counterbalanced, and more' by his 'strictness'.[24] But Hopkins goes further: 'In fact all English verse, except Milton's, almost, offends me as "licentious". Remember this' (*C* I.281). It is a provoking boast – and not only for its teacherly caution not to forget, and so not to repeat the libel. Whereas previously Hopkins demands that his poetics be reappraised by way of inversion – aesthetic licences must in fact be read as aesthetic laws – here he switches the ground from aesthetics to moral theology, as licence becomes associated with 'licentiousness'. There are theological overtones, too, in the way he advocates the strictness of form for the paradoxical reason that it might enable greater freedoms ('why, if it is forcible in prose to say "lashed: rod", am I obliged to weaken this in verse, which ought to be stronger, not weaker, into "láshed birch-ród" or something?' (*C* I.282)).

Critics disagree on the extent to which Hopkins's poems are indeed governed by law over licence, but there can be little doubt about his investment in prosodical discipline as such.[25] His impatience with the formal habits of some of his contemporaries (Whitman and Swinburne especially) has often been interpreted as a merely defensive gesture, because he knew he was exercising similar liberties himself. But that is to ignore the substantive differences in his verse theory and practice,[26] as well as the fact that he reserved the same disapprobation for his own writing, on such occasions where he judged his poems to have lapsed into being 'licentious in form', and 'unpardonably' so (*C* I.475).

Although we may rightly be sceptical of Hopkins's *ex post facto* attempts to justify his innovative prosody by classical ('logaoedic') precedent, that is not to say he was seeking to delude anyone by his explanations, nor that he was deluding himself. The most thoroughgoing attempt to categorize his prosodic repertoire confirms his own assertion that his metre was indeed, as he claimed, stricter not looser than common metre.[27] It would take another chapter to appraise the assumptions of generative grammar on which this proof is founded. But at the very least, it may be said that Hopkins invested deeply in the process of composing according to the intuitive principles of strictness he had established, even if he struggled adequately to explain them. Bridges, who knew him best as a writer, affirmed that 'no one ever wrote words with more critical deliberation than Gerard Hopkins', and subsequent critics have argued the same.[28]

Yet he does not fetishize form for its own sake. He is dismissive of the fiddly contemporary taste for the villanelle, sestina and triolet,[29] and more broadly, he is wary of cramping, stilting or exhausting inspiration by making it work too hard, or work against its originary impulse. Picking up on Hopkins's cue about leaving his poem for nine years rather than nine months, Norman H. Mackenzie closes his insightful gloss of 'To R. B.' by regretting that the circumstances of Hopkins's death 'prevented a poem which has many beautiful phrases in it from being subjected to the maturing agencies of time and critical discussion' (it was sent to Bridges 'a bare week after it was written').[30] But Mackenzie underestimates how delicate the balance was for Hopkins between writing and overwriting. Maturation by mediation easily becomes meddling, and damages the 'freshness' that is, for Hopkins, inspiration's primary recommendation. Poetry's beauties are, Hopkins thinks, all the more valuable for being delicate; liable to perish. While execution is required to refine inspiration into poetry, too much of it would, he knew, spoil 'the freshness' he 'wanted and which indeed the subject demands' (*C* II.552).

For a poet as obsessive and precise as Hopkins – his drafts are a thicket of carets and corrections – over-engineering is an ever-present risk. Of 'The Sea and the Skylark', he confessed to Bridges: 'There is, you see, plenty meant; but the saying of it smells, I fear, of the lamp' (*C* II552). Ripeness needs to be cultivated, but can easily become over-ripe; virtue quickly curdles into vice. He called 'Tom's Garland' 'a very pregnant sonnet and in point of execution very highly wrought. Too much so, I am afraid' (*C* II.919). Hopkins is keenly alive, as well he might be, to 'the danger and difficulty of making more than verbal alterations in works composed long ago and of a bygone mood not being to be recovered' ([*sic*] *C* II.610-11).

Freshness has a theological as well as thematic place in Hopkins's several poems on innocence and vitality, from the Edenic afterglow he finds in 'Spring' to the 'fresh thoughts' of the uncorrupted child in 'Spring and Fall', to 'the dearest freshness deep down things' in 'God's Grandeur'. For the atheist William Morris, 'talk of inspiration is sheer nonsense, there is no such thing. It is a mere matter of craftsmanship'.[31] For the Jesuit priest, by contrast, figuring inspiration as progenitive refuses the notion of poetry as mere 'making' (*poiesis*). Hopkins did not quite believe that his poems were 'begotten, not made', as if grafted straight from the Nicene Creed. But from his earliest investigations into the genesis of 'poetry proper', he reveres inspiration as a necessary matter alongside craftsmanship. And following his conversion, he comes to reimagine inspiration's aetiology as having less to do with physical or even mental state than with divine gift.

There is of course a well-worn classical tradition of invoking the muses, and it might look at times as if Hopkins is falling back on this habit, such as when he complains of trying to compose without Minerva's blessing. But the fact that he makes this aside in Latin ('*graviter invita Minerva*') suggests he is (like many Christian poets before him) alluding to the classical tradition rather than advocating it. He is sensitive to the etymological connection of inspiration with *spiritus*, and should there be any doubt that the divinity he has in mind is centred in his Christian faith, he immediately recalibrates his thoughts on Minerva. The sentence continues, via a semi-colon, 'rather I am afraid it may be Almighty God who is unwilling: for if I could conscientiously spend even a little time every day on it I could make great progress'.[32] 'Conscientiously' here means not only scrupulously, but also in good conscience, the force of which word for Hopkins has already been touched upon above.

Hopkins presses his faith in poetry as divine gift in his poems too, notably in 'The Blessed Virgin compared to the Air we Breathe', and his sermons prospect the same as well: that 'even the sigh or aspiration itself is in answer to an inspiration of God's spirit and is followed by the continuance and expiration of that same breath which lifts it ... to do or be what God wishes his creature to do or be'.[33] Man is said to receive inspiration, in the fullest sense, as a form of grace, which is God's own 'finger touching the very vein of personality'. Hopkins goes on to suggest that man can do so little to 'respond' to this gift ('by no play whatever, by bare acknowledgement only'), and that he can summon no more than 'the counter stress which God alone can feel': 'the spiration in answer to his inspiration'.[34]

Flicking back from 'To R.B.', the last of Hopkins's poems, to 'The Wreck of the Deutschland', his first in sprung rhythm, it is clear that his theology of inspiration – as grace, mediated by breath and stress – operates powerfully even from that earliest time. 'The Wreck' opens with the very same figure of God's intimate finger-touch ('Over again I feel thy finger and find thee' (*P* 51.8)), and the poem as it gets going includes several charged references to breath (stanzas 2, 5, 6, twice) and stress (stanzas 1, 23, 25, three times, and 33). Taking these two terms together, he explained that to do his sprung poetry 'any kind of justice you must not slovenly read it with the eyes but with your ears, as if the paper were declaiming it at you'. Why? Because: 'Stress is the life of it' (*C* I.296).

In another, more expansive definition, he suggests that sprung rhythm 'applies by rights only where one stress follows another running, without syllable between' (*C* I.346). Not, then, a metre of individuated stress so much as of perpetual 'counter stress'; that is, stress upon stress, rather than alternating stress with slack: 'if you counterpoint throughout ... what is written is one rhythm only and probably Sprung Rhythm' (*P* 47). This apparent connection between his theology of 'counter stress' and his prosodical principle of counterpointing is more suggestive than conclusive. But it is suggestive beyond the coincidence of word choice on Hopkins's part. It helps to make sense of his poetry as a response to God's grace, 'bare acknowledgement' though it may be;[35] what, with Hopkins in mind, Hans Urs von Balthasar calls 'man's inchoate sigh of assent'.[36]

That 'Man was created to praise' has been identified as Hopkins's cardinal text from the *Spiritual Exercises*,[37] and – in ways that link him suggestively with Dante – his poetry is indeed at times explicitly cast as a species of prayer: 'This air, which, by life's law, / My lung must draw and draw / Now but to breathe its praise' (*P* 94).[38] Some compelling work has already been done in linking Hopkins's investment in 'stress' to his understanding of affective grace,[39] and more might yet be said about his theological phenomenology of stress ('take breath and read it with your ears, as I always wish to be read, and my verse becomes all right' (*C* I.355)). Any further consideration of Hopkins's breath-stress poetics needs, however, also to register the competing demands that his poems make upon our eyes as well as our ears, and on our reflective thinking as well as our immediate feeling. 'Neither of course do I mean my verse to be recited only,' he reminds us: 'True poetry must be studied' (*C* II.748).

***

Studying Hopkins's poetry, mindful of the dialectic between execution and inspiration, it is instructive to consider how and why his poems differ from his writings in other genres. Here is an extract from his retreat notes written just a few months before 'To R. B.':

> I began to enter on that course of loathing and hopelessness which I have so often felt before, which made me fear madness ... . What is my wretched life? ... I am ashamed of the little I have done, of my waste of time, although my helplessness and weakness is such that I could scarcely do otherwise ... what is this life without aim, without spur, without help?[40]

Sheer wretchedness: all the more for the fact that these sentences written in 1889 are done so on 1 January, the day of the year ordinarily associated with renewal. Yet how differently these sentiments read in the subsequent poem ('To R. B.'), even where he uses identical words. 'Spur', for instance: what in prose reads as unqualified withdrawal (along with the sense of 'aim' and 'help' of which he is also 'without') is in the poem linked to 'strong'. Not merely because it is adjectivally described as such, also because the grammatical relationship that affirms it is broken across the line ending, with 'Spur' then held immediately by a comma. Enjambment is not an adequate gloss here; sense does not simply 'run on'. The effect is of *rejet*: the percussive potency of 'Spur' is not flatly described as 'strong', its strength is impelled through its stress ('Stress is', in Hopkins's definition, 'the making a thing more, or making markedly, what it already is; it is the bringing out its nature' (*C* II.629)), and it brokers the way to a sharply different movement. As the poem winds up, we may notice how the *rejet* of the final line performs quite contrary work, countering rather than reinforcing the thrust of the seemingly complete phrase ('scarcely breathes that bliss'): 'Now' brings us up short as we turn the corner of the line, post-modifying the sense by the revision it announces.

In these pivotal moments, Hopkins puts his faith in poetry's defining character. Whereas prose extends to the margin, verse (from 'versus') *turns* across each of its lines, inscribing expressive – in this case, opposing – relationships and tensions. Few poets have exploited this possibility as boldly; he even outdoes Milton in the extent to which he uses the line-end to 'turn' the direction of thought and feeling. While the poem opens, then, with a description of 'fine delight' well matched by its filigree sounding (crisp dentals and fricatives, and delicate /ai/ assonances), the new 'strong / Spur' clause that follows – which initially promises some kind of symmetry with the first – is wrenched by the lineation, and the alliterative clatter and counter-stressing collision announces a new kind of urgency. The poem takes flight, as the richness of the sonic recall is amplified by the abruptness of sprung rhythm.

What has happened between Hopkins's prose and his poetry? His prose writings describe what he thinks or feels: his poems propel, inspect and refine the act of thinking and feeling. That is not to say that his prose style is not suggestive; it is extraordinarily so.[41] The passage quoted above continues with the devastating sentence, 'All my undertakings miscarry: I am like a straining eunuch.'[42] That compacted mixed metaphor stops us in our tracks, as the image of aborted life – the male poet as barren mother – degrades into another figure of absolute impotency, compounded by the frustrated, embarrassing delusion of potency, in which the castrated male *strains*. But while this prose identifies Hopkins's condition of creative sterility with wincing vividness, the poem actively evinces the attendant pain. More than a dark act of anamnesis, or indeed mimesis, his poetry is an event actualized on its own terms, in the present continuous, into which we are implicated in the act of reading. Teeming with its own images or frustrated fathering, mothering, gestating, birthing and siring, the poem *spurs* itself and us through its verse style, in the way it *strains* to engage the fervour of 'want' and 'need': bewailing the negation of absence into impassioned presence, as desire.

Revealingly, Hopkins also fashions himself as a eunuch in two separate letters, both addressed to Bridges. The first makes it clear that the source of pain is not so much that he has failed to produce poems as the knowledge that he *cannot* do so (*C* II.774):

> For it is widely true, the fine pleasure is not to do a thing but to feel that you could and the mortification that goes to the heart is to feel it is the power that fails you … . So with me, if I could but get on, if I could but produce work I should not mind its being buried, silenced, and going no further; but it kills me to be time's eunuch and never to beget.

The second letter likewise casts Hopkins as gracelessly miming the act he cannot perform. But it is troubled by another and yet more painful kind of 'strain' as well, by the possibility that Hopkins's uninspired state might after all be divinely sanctioned (*C* II.914):

> Unhappily I cannot produce anything at all … . All impulse fails me: I can give myself no sufficient reason for going on. Nothing comes: – I am a eunuch – but it is for the kingdom of heaven's sake.

Hopkins's poems obviously speak back to these letters. The reference to 'fine pleasure' in the first gestures to the 'fine delight' that will be explored in the poem later dedicated to Bridges; and the image of 'time's eunuch' also anticipates the moment in another poem, '*Justus quidem tu es, Domine*', which closes with Hopkins's pained witness to the fertility in which he cannot participate:

> . . . . See, banks and brakes
> Now leavèd how thick! lacèd they are again
> With fretty chervil, look, and fresh wind shakes
>
> Them; birds build—but not I build; no, but strain,
> Time's eunuch, and not breed one work that wakes.
> Mine, O thou lord of life, send my roots rain.
>
> (*P* 107. 9–14)

In addition to the moments of continuity between his poetry and his prose, what's intriguing in these examples is the generic particularity of their expression: that the same thoughts and feelings are treated differently in their respective modes. In the second letter, there is a peremptory return from complaint to faith: 'but it is for the kingdom of heaven's sake'. By contrast, the poem, '*Justus quidem tu es, Domine*', works the other way around. Opening (in the Latin title and English first line) with the assertion that God is 'just', it then urges a contradiction: 'but, sir, so what I plead is just'. Reworking the just man's lament from Jeremiah, the preliminary act of faith (God as just) does not soften but instead harshens the sense of grievance that follows, by coaxing the question of how, given Hopkins's personal experience, God can indeed be called equitable. So while the letter closes down its protestation by reasserting his faith in divine providence, the poem culminates by demanding that justice be served: 'send my roots rain'.

In the retreat notes quoted at the head of this section, he goes on to explain how the 'hopelessness' that made him 'fear madness' stymies all action: 'I could therefore do no more than repeat *Justus es, Domine, et rectum judicium tuum* and the like.' Yet two months later, when he comes to write a poem with the title drawn from that same refrain, he does find a way of addressing his fearful stupor: engaging his confounded faith directly and fully, without retreating into the mechanical, restitutive assertion of providential goodness.

While there is, then, an instructive biographical, psychological and thematic connection between Hopkins's prose writings and his poems, they are, at their deepest level, incommensurate, non-fungible modes. In verse, he is bolder; doubt is allowed fuller play in the dialectic with faith. In prose, he can 'do no more' than revert to a fixed formulation of faith ('Justus es, Domine et rectum judicium tuum and the like'; 'but it is for the kingdom of heaven's sake'), as if returning to that formulation might itself prove efficacious. But through poetry his statement of faith may serve as a beginning rather than an end. Through verse he exfoliates his suffering in glutted detail within open, unresolved, dramatic space; and he can challenge the justness and the judgement of the God who oversees it ('but, sir, so what I plead is just'; 'send my roots rain'). Yet more audaciously – and it turns out, more often – Hopkins puts faith in poetry, as he cannot in prose, not merely to explore, contest or assuage but even to resolve the anguishes that attend his religious faith. This is seen most poignantly in his poems that have variously been described as his 'dark', 'terrible' or 'desolation' sonnets.

Hopkins wrote quite a number of sonnets (thirty-six in total), partly for practical reasons, because when he was under most pressure of time and least motivated to write he could find 'no inspiration of longer jet than makes a sonnet' (*C* II.914). He also thrilled to the symmetries that the form demanded, which affirmed his principled fidelity to law and strictness ('I have put the objections to licentious forms and I believe they hold' (*C* I.505)), while at the same time quickening his creativity, both in meeting and tweaking received models. Several of his experiments are risky – he claims 'the longest sonnet ever made' (*C* II.840), as well as three of the shortest ('curtal'), and three more still with codas – but none is reckless. He insists on the orthodoxy of each of his sonnets, especially those that diverge from the received paradigm, to the extent of supplying mathematical equations, scansion cribs and recherché prosodical precedents.[43]

A number of scholars have shown how the devotional sonnet dramatized the paradox of freedom advocated by the Christian tradition in general and, when it comes to forms and rituals, to Catholicism in particular, indicating 'a willed acceptance of constraints set by a higher law'.[44] This is well noted in respect of Hopkins. But his allegiance to the sonnet connects with his religious faith more parlously too, in ways that have not been granted critical attention. If the form served for Hopkins as an aesthetic symbol of a theological tenet (freedom realized through constraint), it also tendered a theology of redemption. He responds powerfully to the sonnet's promise, established through convention, to resolve the problem that is its occasion for being. 'To seem the stranger', which lays out most explicitly and rationally the causes of his estrangement, ends as it opens, with Hopkins cast in a state of baffled alienation, 'a lonely began'.[45] Which seems to support the claim that only the early, exultant sonnets may 'turn' their meditations into 'action' – and that when, conversely, he dwells on his suffering and helplessness, he cannot perform this pattern of Ignatian meditation, and so ends 'not in action, but paralysis'.[46] But though he does not always achieve resolution, the writings that tell of his bleakest hours certainly do realize a 'turn' and 'action' too, in which 'paralysis' is overmastered through the willed vitality of 'passion' limned as poetry.[47] It is indeed precisely when at the limit of what he can take, when he is not merely lonely but terrified, that he puts his greatest faith in poetry – to wrest him from vertiginous distress:

> No worst, there is none. Pitched past pitch of grief,
> More pangs will, schooled at forepangs, wilder wring.
> Comforter, where, where is your comforting?
> Mary, mother of us, where is your relief?
> My cries heave, herds-long; huddle in a main, a chief-
> woe, world-sorrow; on an age-old anvil wince and sing –
> Then lull, then leave off. Fury had shrieked 'No ling-
> ering! Let me be fell: force I must be brief.'
> O the mind, mind has mountains; cliffs of fall
> Frightful, sheer, no-man-fathomed. Hold them cheap
> May who ne'er hung there. Nor does long our small
> Durance deal with that steep or deep. Here! creep,
> Wretch, under a comfort serves in a whirlwind: all
> Life death does end and each day dies with sleep.
>
> (*P* 100)

Much might be said in praise of this poem, and has been. Specifically in terms of its status as a sonnet, however, one might note its Petrarchan purity, the formal exigency of which serves to exacerbate rather than (as John Keble imagined sonnets might) 'soothe and compose' emotional and psychological distress.[48] This effect is perhaps seen most arrantly in the way the metrical and rhyme scheme is fulfilled by rupturing the word 'ling- / ering', which secures its rhymed reasoning by performing its own undoing. Yet the movement into the sestet, as acknowledged by the end-stop (so different from, for instance, Barrett Browning's octave-sestet run-ons, after Wordsworth and Milton), does not usher in a new movement: it is a variation on the same wretchedness. Charles Taylor notices that some of Hopkins's sonnets operate by 'two modes of access', according to a formal division of labour, whereby the octave articulates experience which the sestet attempts to reconcile with doctrine, but that this fusion is not always 'fully successful'.[49] Partial success may nonetheless be a 'relief' in the context of overwhelming unhappiness, and also the more honest expression of faith, religious and poetic. The sonnet cannot be expected to solve everything by generic reflex, but it might yet effect some kind of shift, through its residual force as a poetic form. The sonnet above, while its narrative runs straight into the sestet, thus strains to achieve a *volta* – even though it is not effected till the closing moments, where the syntax of the penultimate line this time connects by *contre-rejet*, to establish the merest analogical 'comfort': that life ends with death as days end with night. So while suffering cannot itself be relieved, ontological and diurnal processes insist that some relief must come with death, and with the death of each day.

Even where this cold comfort is undone by another of his poems, improbably, Hopkins's impassioned faith in poetry persists:

> I wake and feel the fell of dark, not day.
> What hours, O what black hours we have spent
> This night! what sights you, heart, saw; ways you went!
> And more must, in yet longer light's delay.
>
> With witness I speak this. But where I say
> Hours I mean years, mean life. And my lament
> Is cries countless, cries like dead letters sent
> To dearest him that lives alas! away.

I am gall, I am heartburn. God's most deep decree
Bitter would have me taste: my taste was me;
Bones built in me, flesh filled, blood brimmed the curse.

Selfyeast of spirit a dull dough sours. I see
The lost are like this, and their scourge to be
As I am mine, their sweating selves; but worse.

(*P* 101)

This sonnet's 'turn' is delayed as it was in the previous poem, but even more perilously. The penultimate line is still caught up in the sense of personal misery, and indeed contains the poem's most harrowing analogy for that misery, in which he has come to 'see' – but to see what? The line-break from the antepenultimate line ensures maximum tension and theatre in this revelation: to see that his condition is like those in hell. It is some claim, and we have to wait till the last two syllables of the poem before 'comfort' comes. Even then, it is comparative and expressed negatively. His condition is not called *better* than those in hell; theirs is *worse*. Closing the poem on such a word almost presents as a further extension rather than a mitigation of the poem's agonizing witness, at the same time remembering the opening of the previous poem: 'No worse'; 'but worse'.

It is worth asking whether we, as readers, are satisfied by these staged redemptions. Does the sonnet's form over-determine the shape of the sentiment, by inevitably tending towards melioration in a way that undercuts its credibility? Can we extend the same faith as Hopkins in the sonnet's capacity to wring last-gasp redemption, however feeble, from his impassioned tenebrosity? 'The very disproportion of the two Parts of the Shakespearean sonnet', writes Paul Fussell, 'the gross imbalance between the twelve-line problem and the two-line solution, has about it something vaguely risible and even straight-faced farcical: it invites images of balloons and pins'.[50] Fussell has a point, in principle; but in practice, Hopkins's poems do not read risibly, whether they offer 'abrupt changes of perspective between octave and sestet',[51] or whether the *volta* comes in the last two lines; or even in the last two words. There is no cheap fix. No dash of intellection or epigrammatic twist to outwit emotion in the Elizabethan fashion. The breathlessness of his verse style, its ragged ardour, authenticates both the depth of his unhappiness and also the consuming effort to square his faith in God with that experience. It exceeds mere representation; his verse is a mode of working through his faith, the success of which rests on the efficacy of his poetry *as* poetry.

The nearest sonnet to farcical might be 'Carrion Comfort', the last line of which has a playfulness about its revelation that Hopkins had, like Jacob (Gen. 32.22-32), unwittingly been 'wrestling with (my God!) my God'. But this move in the end feels more ludic than ludicrous; the joke, such as it is, is at Hopkins's expense, and has been wrought hard and long: from the limit of suffering through desperate tenacity ('*I can no more*. I can'), even if all that 'can' be achieved is to 'not choose not to be' (*P* 99). That his tormentor is God, and his suffering divinely ordained for his own good, also actually emerges much earlier, at the traditional Petrarchan pivot-point, as the poem shades into the sestet, such that the reflexive parenthesis of the final line ('my God!') constitutes a climax of self-awareness rather than a clownish coda.

***

Local examples of the specifically poetic 'turn' offer vivid illustration of Hopkins's faith in poetry to generate special ways of thinking and feeling through verse. Examples have been given of these movements at the line-end, and at the sonnet's *volta*, and there are many other such moments in his poems. The ninth line of 'Spring and Fall', for instance ('And yet you *will* weep and know why'), positioned where a *volta* might be expected in a Petrarchan sonnet (the poem would be fourteen lines long if not for this interpolation), first poses as an afterthought, with its conjunctive opening, and unexpectedly swelling the run of rhyming couplets into a triplet (*P* 88–9). As one reader observed: 'An extra line seems to have dropped into the middle of the poem as it were by mistake.'[52] But the drafts independently confirm that the line's inclusion is a highly conscious move,[53] calculated to refuse and reimagine what has gone before, and the line is all the more powerful for exerting its reversal ('yet you *will*'), by exceeding what Hopkins suggestively called the sonnet's 'beaten bounds' (*C* II.903). Another example, and perhaps the most startling *volte-face* in all Hopkins's verse, occurs in 'The Leaden Echo and the Golden Echo', which he called his most 'musical' poem (*C* II.822). I have analysed this poem at length elsewhere,[54] but here it may suffice to note the extent to which it is 'musical' in its thinking, in the way its sounds tumble phrase by phrase, culminating in a reversal from the 'Leaden' to the 'Golden' voice, as 'despair, / Despair, despair, despair, despair' is won not by sheer ratiocination, but through a homophonic spin: 'Spare!' (*P* 91–2).

It is convenient to look for transition points of these sorts as a way of tracking Hopkins's counter-stressing in action: focusing not on individual words or sounds or rhythms, but on the interstices they broach or breach, through effects of abruptness, and sharp 'turns'.[55] Hopkins's late poems exhibit stark examples of such transitions when he feels more 'inspired' by despair than joy, and puts faith in poetry to conciliate as well as to console. Such has been argued in this chapter, though these ideas are, it is well to emphasize, at odds with the settled view of Hopkins's later poetry as effectively interchangeable with the spiritual throes documented in his prose. One of the most influential studies on Hopkins's religious faith reads passages from the late poems as 'an exact description' of his 'almost constant condition during his later years' that he reveals in his letters, journals and notebooks from the same period, during which he describes himself as lying in a 'coffin of weakness and dejection … without even the hope of change'.[56] 'Not only poetry fails' during this period, J. Hillis Miller claims, but almost every project to which Hopkins turned his fraught and depleted energies.[57] But this is deeply misleading. It is truer to say that only poetry does *not* fail. Because only poetry offers the 'hope of change', and for the very reason that his verses do not attempt an 'exact description' of his condition. Because they seek instead to work through that condition; and, if possible, to redeem it.

Yet the exaggeration should not, either, be repeated in the other direction. It is heuristic to separate out his early and later poems, as a short-hand. But a closer look across his corpus suggests that distinctions between his poetic modes are of emphasis rather than kind. Among his later poems, for instance, 'Spelt from Sibyl's Leaves' and 'That Nature is a Heraclitean Fire' are steadier on their feet than the terrible sonnets. Among his earlier writings, even his poems of richest testimony also conspicuously test themselves against the limits of 'poetical language'. The poem he thought his best, 'The Windhover', which offers such an excited vision of 'ecstasy', is nonetheless to some extent dependent (as his agonistic sonnets are) on working itself out *as* poetry. From its very first line, in which the bravura line-break forces the essential paradox of Christ as 'minion' and 'king-', to the aposiopesis of the octave's end (drafts show that 'the achieve of' was a late and deliberate addition),[58] to the – ultimately – rationalized, analogical explication announced by the final triplet ('No wonder of it'), the poem does not merely state or even show its thoughts and feelings (*P* 69). It probes, scouts, trials; opening with an experience of inspiriting intensity, it is driven by a will to self-understanding, and in peculiarly poetical ways, as each consecutive word takes its cue and colour and significance from the way it concatenates (semantically but also sonically) with each other, across each line, construing itself – as we must construe the poem in the act of reading – on the move.

Refining, then, the broad-brush claim offered at the end of this chapter's first section, while Hopkins's faith in poetry comes into special relief when his religious faith comes under most pressure, it is apparent in his most joyful verses too. Expression is always, for Hopkins, also a form of exploration. Even after granting this continuity as well as the contrast between his early and later poems, however, the fuller picture of his faith in poetry remains incomplete, and beyond the scope of this book. For while his localized transitions or 'turns' in his poetic thinking are suggestive in themselves, they still need to be accommodated within his diverse aesthetico-religious claims about breath and stress, and his many other meta-poetical observations too – which exceeds what can be attempted here.[59] The greater challenge is not that Hopkins's writings on poetry are scattered and piece-meal, but that he appears to say mutually incompatible things. Notably, he seems at times to adopt a strictly neo-Aristotelian line, making an absolute distinction between form and content; whereas on other occasions, he apparently espouses the reverse view of poetry, as a 'figure of spoken sound'.[60]

Readers (this reader speaks for himself) may find relief and guilty pleasure in Hopkins's observation that 'sometimes one enjoys and admires the very lines one cannot understand' (*C* I.295). But it is not immediately clear how to accommodate that critical hands-up with Hopkins's wider poetics that asseverate 'seriousness' as 'a kind of touchstone of the highest and most living art' ('not gravity but the being in earnest with your subject – reality').[61] Having allowed himself to doubt Tennyson, Hopkins may grant with one hand that 'his gift of utterance is truly golden', while taking away with the other: 'but go further and you come to thoughts commonplace and wanting in nobility' (*C* I.374). Similarly, he may admire Swinburne's prosodical prowess, but complain that 'words only are only words' where there is 'a perpetual functioning of genius without truth, feeling, or an adequate matter to be at function on' (*C* II.990). Or again: he worries that, beautiful though it is, Dixon's 'Mano' lacks 'a leading thought to thread the beauties on' (*C* I.621), or that Richard Crawley's 'Venus and Psyche' is 'not serious', because 'the story [is] treated as a theme for trying style on' (*C* II.782).[62]

Such comments demonstrate Hopkins's keenness to distinguish between a poem's achieved form – the transporting hum and bruit of its sounding – and its impoverished content, which brings us down to earth with a bump. That distinction is key for Hopkins, and avails even where he sails closest to aestheticism; such as when he defines poetry as 'speech framed for contemplation of the mind by the way of hearing or speech framed to be heard for its own sake and interest even over and above its interest in meaning'. 'Some matter and meaning is essential to it,' he concedes, 'but only as an element necessary to support and employ the shape which is contemplated for its own sake'.[63] Repeating 'for its own sake' is an emphatic signal: that 'matter and meaning' subserve the poem's shape. Yet Hopkins clearly believes that the 'shape contemplated for its own sake' has 'matter and meaning' too. It cannot have meaning solely in terms of its 'shape'; some 'matter and meaning' is 'essential' to support that shape. But the 'matter and meaning' can no more exist without shape than the shape can without it. Poetry succeeds through this mutually supportive combination, as Hopkins intuited as early as his undergraduate essay on 'Poetic Diction': 'It is plain,' he writes – and in a style whose plainness angles towards impatience – 'that metre, rhythm, rhyme, and *all* the structure which is called verse *both* necessitate *and* engender a difference in diction *and* thought': 'The effect of verse is one on expression *and* on thought' (*C* IV.120; emphasis mine).

That is why he insists that poetry requires 'an emphasis of structure' and 'an emphasis of expression' stronger than in prose, which in turn necessitates and engenders an emphasis of thought stronger than that of common thought ('viz. Concentration and all which is implied by this' (*C* IV.121, 120)). He takes this view not as an abstract elevation of poetry as a genre but rather as a matter of phenomenological fact: that 'an effect is nothing but the way in which the mind ties together, not the sequences, but all the condition it sees'; that 'a condition of a thing considered as contrasted with the whole thing, an effect a whole as contrasted with its conditions, elements, or parts'.[64]

In this respect, Hopkins is only too aware of how hard his poems can be to construe as a 'whole' – structure and semantics – for the 'queer' singularity of his style, how it 'errs on the side of oddness' (*C* I.334). But his opalescence is not wilful. He did not, with T. S. Eliot (writing a few decades later), believe that 'poets in our civilization, as it exists at present, must be *difficult*'.[65] Nor does he have any patience for difficulty arising accidentally, from flabby thought or execution (Dixon's 'obscurity is a great fault', where he descends 'from remarkably clear speaking' into 'gibberish' (*C* I.341)). 'Obscurity I do and will try to avoid', he reassured Bridges, but then asserts his essential caveat, which is also his sanction. He would avoid obscurity, but only 'in so far as is consistent with excellences higher than clearness at first reading' (*C* I.298). Partly it is a question of genre: 'Epic and drama and ballad and many, most, things should be at once intelligible; but everything need not and cannot be' (*C* II.904–5). The needfulness of obscurity may, however, extend beyond this (*C* II.905):

> Plainly if it is possible to express a subtle and recondite thought on a subtle and recondite subject in a subtle and recondite way and with great felicity and perfection in the end, something must be sacrificed, with so trying a task, in the process, and this may be the thing at once, nay perhaps even the being without explanation at all, intelligible.

Excellences higher than clearness at first reading are the subtle and recondite expression of subtle and recondite thoughts, for which clarity may be 'sacrificed'. Yet the matter is not so 'plain' or 'plainly' stated as Hopkins implies. The figure of immolation obscures what it aims to illuminate. Sophistication is not brokered over intelligibility. Lexical-grammatical clarity may be arrested, but it must come.

Must be overcome, rather, in the way that Wordsworth and Pater variously thrilled to 'the sense of difficulty overcome'.[66] The 'more difficult' something is 'to effect', Hopkins argued ('other things being alike'), 'the more valuable when effected' (*C* II.591). He is writing on this occasion about unity of action and plot in drama, but the principle holds more widely, as seen in his affection for complex-but-strict poetic forms ('an effect of the whole as contrasted with its conditions, elements, or parts'),[67] from the sonnet to *cynghanedd* to the paeonic foot ('recommended by the complexity of its ratio').[68] 'Distinctiveness' is, by Hopkins's reckoning, the 'virtue' of inscape; and since complexity of 'design' or 'pattern' creates distinctiveness, his poetic inscapes are inevitably going to be complex, and by extension, caliginous (*C* I.334).

Complexity, distinctiveness, even obscurity: none of these is salient so much as the readerly value to be had from getting past them. 'One of two kinds of clearness one shd. have,' he explained to Bridges, 'either the meaning to be felt without effort as fast as one reads or else, if dark at first reading, when once made out to explode' (*C* I.367). In the same letter Hopkins criticized one of Bridges's poems for failing to explode in this way (*C* I.367; see also *C* I.376). Obscurity is an oblation to, not the negation of, sense. It is a propitiatory to 'poetical language': conceived as an aesthetics of delay, and offered in the expectation of a greater reward. He does not always get it right, even by his own account. Sometimes 'the sense ... gets the worst of it' (*C* II.551). When style resolutely impedes comprehension, however, an explanation should be forthcoming, such that, though he knew it would expose him to 'carping', he resolved 'to prefix short prose *arguments*' to his poems (*C* II.904). Or else to write differently.[69]

Temporarily obscuring the semantic 'meaning' of his poetry allows that meaning to be transformed through the filter of its rhythmic and sonic pulse and texture: 'where the structure forces us to appreciate each syllable it is natural and in the order of things for us to dwell on all modifications affecting the general result or type which the ear preserves' (*C* IV.121). That is the process by which his verse might 'haunt' us, which is why he recommended that 'lines and stanzas should be left in the memory and superficial impressions deepened'; and that time and effort would allow readers to become 'more weathered to the style and its features' (*C* I.295).

Obscurity, by that reasoning, is not a regrettable sacrifice but a purposeful function of the demands of the poem's 'design' or 'pattern', or what he was in the habit of calling 'inscape' (*C* I.334). But these constructivist terms should not encourage us towards Aristotelian or Arnoldian architectonics. They refer to Hopkins's concept of 'instress', which, far from envisaging verse form as a static structure or inert mimetic emblem, effects the poetical 'turns' of counter-stressful animation: heightening, haunting, exploding. Like his theology, though his style demands to be 'studied', it must also be experienced as incarnational and processive, given body and life in the act of reading. Hence his experiments with as many as twenty-one different diacritical recitation marks derived from musical notation and direction. These marks, he admits, 'are always offensive' (he admits also that he uses them inconsistently); and yet, 'there must be some': because 'if the lines are not rightly scanned, they are ruined' (*C* I.252).[70] Taking this comment seriously, together with others gathered in this chapter, perhaps Hopkins's faith in poetry might after all be better understood as faith in versifying and reading. Whether expressing or exploring ecstasy or desolation, his poems offer a mode of believing that is vividly immanent, informed by lived experience and rendered dynamically through time, and dialectically – between inspiration and execution, text and performance – in poetry's straining towards realization; or else ruin.

5

T. S. Eliot: Failing Better

There is only one higher stage possible for civilised man: and that is to unite the profoundest scepticism with the deepest faith.[1]

There is something mischievous, perhaps wilfully so, about T. S. Eliot's dedication to *The Waste Land.*[2] While honouring Ezra Pound's artisanal savvy as informal editor, '*il miglior fabbro*' at the same time affirms the poem itself as a crafted object; as it also (by threading the compliment through an allusion to Dante) asserts the value of craft in poetry as such. But then we come to the poem itself, the poem Pound called 'the justification of the "movement," of our modern experiment, since 1900',[3] and it seemingly undermines all that its dedication implies. Thematically as well as formally – from its apocalyptic title and variegated verse style to its unstable shifts in voices and perspective – *The Waste Land* revels in the fraught decay of poetical conventions rather than conventional virtuosity. Overwhelmingly, it is preoccupied with 'broken images' and 'fragments' (*CP* 55.22; 71.430); and Eliot himself would indeed, in later years, disclaim its four hundred and thirty-three lines as 'structureless'.[4]

Reading *The Waste Land* through the lens of its dedicatory sentiment provokes a paradox at the heart of Eliot's poetry, a paradox that animates the entire movement and modern experiment to which

Pound refers; namely, that poetic craft might be expressed through the apparent rejection of poetical craftsmanship as previously conceived. That's hardly the edgily unfamiliar proposition it was, a century ago; what had once been shockingly counter-cultural and counter-intuitive is now canonical. But for this very reason it is salutary to ask the innocent question of whether Eliot's poetics are not, when it comes down to it, founded on a perverse hoax, whereby the self-appointed champion of poetry actually damaged its distinctiveness and power, by blurring it with prose.

Eliot's rationale for serving as Pound's chief henchman in the 'heave' to 'break the pentameter' was highly self-conscious: that he only wished poetic forms to be 'broken' so they might be 'remade', as he was convinced they needed to be.[5] Not because of the exceptionalism of the early twentieth century – he is impatient with the millenarian talk sometimes associated with modernism – but rather because poets have throughout literary history recognized the futility of 'pouring their liquid sentiment into a ready-made mould'.[6] His literary-historical moment demanded, he thought, a new verse style – but he presents this need for innovation as something that is itself traditional. As Wordsworth and Dryden, or Shakespeare and Horace, had each revolutionized poetry by purging its stale poeticisms, so (Eliot rationalized) the revolt in verse form he abetted likewise sought to preserve and enhance poetry, rather than dilute or destroy it.[7] While the name '*vers libre*' might present as 'a battle-cry of freedom' (and in the English rendering of 'free verse', even more so), 'there is no freedom in art'; and, by extension, poetry worthy of the name that is exercised under this banner is 'anything but "free"'.[8] Far from an attempt to flatten poetry into prose, Eliot's experimentations were, he believed, a needful means of vivifying a poetic mode that had worn itself out. Without a fixed metric, rhythm may thus find fresh purpose; just as, Eliot claimed, the 'liberation from rhyme might be as well a liberation of rhyme. Freed from its exacting task of supporting lame verse, it could be applied with greater effect where it is most needed'.[9]

Later in his life, Eliot regretted that 'a great deal of bad prose' had been written 'under the name of free verse'.[10] Tellingly, though, even where he concedes this, he does not dignify the results as 'bad poetry'. Branding it instead as 'bad prose' reaffirms his conviction – first publicly expressed some twenty-five years earlier (in 'Reflections on *Vers Libre*') – that 'no verse is free for the man who wants to do a good job'.[11] Likewise, where Eliot suggests that 'no poet can write a poem of amplitude unless he is a master of the prosaic' (*CP* 882), he presses the paradoxical rationale that a retreat from what's recognized as poetry is in the interest of the poetic. Verse must vary in 'intensity', according to its own 'rhythm of fluctuating emotion', but that actually enables the poetic mode, he claims, where passages are 'deliberately intended to give an effect of flatness for purposes of contrast' (*CP* 882).

If Eliot's poetics have an iconoclastic dash to them, then, that is not because he wished to smash the poetic tradition; it is because he wished to vitalize it, by smashing false idols. *The Waste Land* is probably the most influential poem in the early twentieth century, but Eliot's 'Tradition and the Individual Talent' has also fairly been described as the most influential essay in poetics from the same period, and in it he argues what, despite first impressions, his modernist-defining poem also ultimately ratifies: that true originality must enter into dialogue with tradition. He comes back to the same point repeatedly. There can be 'no escape' from versification, 'only mastery'; 'freedom is only truly freedom when it appears against the background of an artificial limitation'; poetry is a distinctive and strenuous craft, and 'the poet who wishes to continue to write poetry must keep in training'.[12]

The reactionary accent of Eliot's poetics thus rests not so much on his will to free himself from form as in his repudiation of the freedoms associated with organic emoting. He denied that poetry was either a Wordsworthian spontaneous overflow of powerful feelings, or a channel for expressing 'personality' at all. He speaks instead of establishing an 'objective correlative' for emotion, placing the emphasis on what the poetry might evoke in the reader rather than what it might express of the author.[13] It is with this sense of 'objectivity' in mind that he humbles the poetic endeavour into an executive rather than an inspired activity: 'a task in the same sense as the making of an efficient engine or the turning of a jug or a table-leg'.[14] In an article for the *Times Literary Supplement* revealingly entitled 'Professionalism in Art', he reported that the poet is 'impatient of all the talk about inspiration', because 'he knows that, though nothing can be done without it, it comes only with command of the medium. And this command, like all craftsmanship, is traditional, handed down from one generation to another'.[15]

Eliot makes a thoroughgoing case, and returning to *The Waste Land*, there cannot be any doubt (not since the drafts were published as facsimiles in 1971, anyway) that his compositional process was skilled and thoughtful. But here's the rub. As well as attesting to Eliot's gimlet-eyed attention as a writer, the drafts also confirm why the finished poem in the end feels more chaotic than crafted: because so many of the editorial decisions, both radical cuts and fiddly tweaks, were attempts to distress if not sever the poem's prosodical and narrative lines. Rhythms that had settled into received forms – those Pound disparaged as 'too penty' or '[t]oo tum-pum'[16] – were deliberately unbalanced; scenes were distilled, and transitions between them made less clear and more abrupt. All of which re-prompts the question that remains unanswered in spite of Eliot's urbane vindications. The question of why, after all, he should expend such care in crafting something that reads as incoherent. Or to put the matter more bluntly: Why does Eliot make poems designed to fail?

For if Eliot's poems evince any one thing, it is failure. Possibilities are forever being glimpsed but not converted; yearnings recur for what is painfully out of reach; desires are overtaken by gaucherie and diffidence, enervation and paralysis, or else lapse into irony. Old, dried-up, hollowed-out men dominate the landscape, and so, correspondingly, do expressions of impotence, indecision and the dying fall; entelechy proves entropic. But it is in the language of the poem itself where failure is felt most keenly: where communication and comprehension stutters, remains incomplete or is undercut by the 'false note' (*CP* 11.35). 'I myself can hardly understand,' admits the speaker from 'Portrait of a Lady' (*CP* 13.21); 'It is impossible to say just what I mean!' exclaims Prufrock (*CP* 8.104). Incognizance and aphasia are everywhere, and they are not only registered in the characters who populate the poems. In the puckerings and pleatings of his verse style – juxtapositions without connections, and unattributed allusions; multi-lingual quotations and ragged lineation; rhythms that refuse metricality, but are yet haunted (as he put it so memorably) by 'the ghost of some simple metre'[17] – Eliot's poems wittingly fail to achieve coherence; and it remains for us to work out why.

***

One possible response is that his poems dramatize failure as an act of mimesis, staging the irredeemably alienated condition of modernity that confounds perfect understanding or communication. But Eliot's achievement is paltry if so, aesthetically as well as philosophically. By this account, he falls foul of what, with the modernists in mind, Yvor Winters decried as 'the fallacy of imitative form', whereby *The Waste Land* performs nothing more than the sheer wastedness to which it refers.[18]

But Eliot's own example as a critic invites another approach. For he asks more than what a poem is 'made of and the causes that brought it about': 'It is also necessary,' he advises, 'and in most instances still more necessary, that we should endeavour to grasp what the poetry was aiming to be'.[19] That means more than determining whether a poem is or is not structured; it means asking *why* a poem takes the shape that it does. *The Waste Land*, by this account, might be said to do more than merely imitate. Its reticulated unboundedness may aim to explore and make sense of the broken and barren moment with which it engages: feeling its way towards an epic vision, by comparison (as has been well argued by Pericles Lewis) with the 'mythical method' Eliot admired in Joyce's *Ulysses*. Far from passively recording the disintegration of the present as against the past, such a method is, in Eliot's words, 'a way of controlling, of ordering, of giving a shape and a significance to the immense panorama of futility and anarchy which is contemporary history'.[20]

There is also a larger question to address that relates to what, in more general terms, Eliot sought to achieve by writing in poetry rather than prose. But here we must confront the extent to which his impulses as a poet appear mutually incompatible. On the one hand, his poems demand that we work hard to come to terms with them; on the other hand, they work hard to resist us from doing so. This peevish tension in Eliot's poetics goes a long way to explain why, on choice occasions, even the best critics have been caught out. At the publication of the drafts of *The Waste Land*, William Empson admitted that he was 'one of the mugs who hoped that the story of the poem would be unveiled when the lost bits were restored'.[21] His self-diagnosed naivety is arresting, given that he was typically so shrewd as a critic, and that he was indeed the great cognoscente of poetic 'ambiguity'. Donald Davie well knew that Eliot 'leaves spaces, and he wants them left',[22] and yet he also found himself on the wrong side of the exegetical fence. 'The Dry Salvages' was, he felt, out of joint with the rest of *Four Quartets*, parts of it descending into 'faded and shop-soiled locution', 'stumbling trundling rhythms', 'inarticulate ejaculations of reach-me-down phrases' and 'the debased currency of the study circle'.[23] Itching to straighten out this 'incantatory gibberish', Davie rationalized that the poem must be bad because Eliot intended it to be so; and as such, it must actually be good – as parody: 'It is thus' – Davie announced with a flourish of relief – 'that the incompetence turns out to be dazzling virtuosity'.[24] It took Davie some time to sober up to his own audacity here. Thirty-five years further acquaintance with the poem in the end convinced him that he had been dazzled by the virtuosity of his own critical ingenuity rather than the poem on which he put it to use. Repenting that he had been 'too sophisticated', he disavowed wholesale his 'devious and schematic argument to show that what was wrong was after all quite right'.[25]

Eliot always seems to have us on the back foot in this respect, worrying if his inspissations and opalescences have been read with sufficient sophistication, or too much, and whether we are 'mugs' either way. Only one thing seems certain: that we cannot opt out. His use of allusion, perhaps above all, refuses that possibility. Not that his poems necessarily contain more allusions than those by other poets; Milton or Spenser may use as many, or more.[26] But Eliot makes the burden of recovering his allusions both unusually taxing (because they are often obscure and elliptical) and also pressingly necessary, if we are to catch the poem's tone or direction (especially in his earlier work). Robert Graves and Laura Riding suggest of 'Burbank with a Baedeker: Bleistein with a Cigar' that the epigraph might be written 'by some obscure diarist or by Mr Eliot himself', before adding, with cute irreverence, 'we cannot be bothered to discover whom'.[27] One sympathizes, but mannered indifference hardly stands up as literary criticism. As a reader of Eliot, a refusal to risk 'failing' is nothing less than a refusal to read him.

Nor are we free from these risks today, after a century of accumulated critical wisdom on Eliot. Since the publication of Ricks and McCue's authoritative and annotated edition of Eliot's complete poems (2015), readers need no longer wonder what they might be missing in 'Burbank with a Baedeker'. That poem alone yields no fewer than eleven pages of small-type-annotation, including a full page glossing the poem's epigraph (which is apparently made up of six different literary sources). Yet it is sometimes hard not to be more confused than enlightened when one turns for critical assistance. Looking up the identity of 'Pipit' in 'A Cooking Egg', for instance, reveals that Eliot once followed a scholarly dispute on this subject, and groaned that 'the nadir of critical futility had been touched' (*CP* 508). Perhaps fretting over the identity of a minor character in one of his minor poems might not be worth the effort, and that's the mistake. But even the poem with which he first made his reputation earns the same weary headshake. The very first line of 'The Love Song of J. Alfred Prufrock' is glossed in the commentary by a letter from Eliot regretting that there had been 'some quite astonishing over-interpretation of this poem' (*CP* 376).

The conundrum for the contemporary reader is not therefore so much whether it is possible to fill in the spaces and the story, nor whether the reader can be bothered to do so. The contemporary reader is faced rather with the quandary of whether glossing Eliot's poems might do more harm than good, through the well-meant betise of 'over-interpretation'. The impulse to reconstruct the 'story' is certainly not a historical pratfall from which we can now feel ourselves safely exempt.[28] If anything, the goad towards critical 'sophistication' is stronger today than ever, for the very reason that so much scholarship on Eliot has already been laid down, such that critics must work that much harder to offer anything original.

But if Ricks and McCue's edition, which provides encyclopaedic assistance at the turn of a page, provokes with fresh urgency the question of how much scholarly help readers need, their edition also goes some way to answering it. Because in addition to the extensive commentary (and textual history), the edition prefaces the poems with quotations from Eliot on how he wished to be read, and on this matter Eliot is, for once, unambiguous. 'I am averse to the publication of any of my poems with explanatory notes'; 'I will not allow any academic critic ... to provide notes of explanation with my poems'; 'I want my readers to get their impressions from the words alone and from nothing else' (*CP* xv, xvi–vii, xvii). The irony is glaring, but it cannot recoil upon the editors, who after all present Eliot's distaste for commentaries front and centre of their own. Ricks has also elsewhere issued severe warnings against getting too cosy with Eliot, observing that when his poems first came out, they 'ruffled people', that this was his intention, and that there remains today 'something missing from any criticism which comes across as entirely unruffled, as if rufflement were for other people'.[29]

What is most taxing, even vexing, about coming to terms with Eliot's poems is not so much that they ask a lot from us, as they certainly do. What's more riling is the sense we get in reading Eliot that he does not, in the end, want us to succeed. His notes to *The Waste Land* exemplify the situation, for even in offering a crib, he continues to tease us with incomplete leads and mis-directions. Later in his life, he called these notes a 'remarkable exposition of bogus scholarship' included for the sole reason of making the 'inconveniently short' poem publishable on its own.[30] Yet even such a disclosure must be taken under advisement, as must his other retrospective claims about the poem itself.

Eliot offers more comprehensive comments on poetry and poetics than the four other writers surveyed in this book, but he is also in some ways the hardest to pin down. He alerts us to the extent to which his criticism shadows his own aspiring poetical practice, and even goes so far as to say of his criticism that 'its merits and its limitations can be fully appreciated only when it is considered in relation to the poetry I have written myself'.[31] His views and practices – both as a poet and a literary critic – changed over time, however, and in ways that mean it can be dicey to apply isolated critical axioms to his poetry in general.[32] The older Eliot winced at some of his earlier poems; and he did the same with his criticism too, repenting for the braggadocio of his juvenile pose (which he also called pontifical, arrogant, cocksure and dogmatic), and changing his position on certain matters of substance, even over things said in his most influential and celebrated essays (such as 'Tradition and the Individual Talent' and 'Hamlet and His Problems').[33] But in allowing for Eliot's changes of heart over time, it is also important to observe his changing tones at any one time, from donnish impatience to barbed waggery, such that some of his most inciting remarks – such as when he called *The Waste Land* an 'insignificant grouse' and mere 'rhythmical grumbling'[34] – may, if taken without context or qualification, also prove to be the least helpful.

Returning, as a reference point, to Eliot's notes to *The Waste Land*: if used as an interpretative crutch, they will surely collapse, leaving us flat on our faces. But while they are not intended to bear a full explicatory burden, they are not devoid of relevance. Eliot explained that he highlighted his references to Dante in the notes, for instance, 'to make the reader who recognised the allusion, know that I meant him to recognise it, and know that he would have missed the point if he did not recognise it'.[35] While it misses the point, then, to imagine that Eliot's poems might submit to exhaustive explication, like his notorious notes, his poems do after all have a point to them – and it is quite possible to miss that too.

***

To advance further on Eliot's conflicting aims as a poet – both demanding and repelling readerly 'sophistication' – it is expedient to return to his investment in poetic craft, but from a different angle. His references to the 'task' of poetic production by comparison with engines, jugs and table-legs only tells one side of the story. That composition requires knowledge and skill is a fundamental article of his faith in poetry. But he does not really believe that verses can be knocked-up on demand,[36] or according to a fixed mould or blueprint.[37] He knew that there was, at root, something mysterious about poetry, its origin and its potency. The 'analytical study of metric' may not be 'an utter waste of time', he concedes, wryly affirming that it largely is – for the reason that it treats only 'the abstract forms which sound so extraordinarily different when handled by different poets'.[38] When he admits that he has 'never been able to retain the names of feet and metres', what might be taken for a confession of deficiency is more like a matter of pride and principle, especially when coupled with the rider that he has 'never been able to pay the proper respect to the accepted rules of scansion'.[39] We are not to read incapacity here so much as impiety; 'proper respect' and 'accepted rules' are set up like coercive conventions at a dusty remove from individual verse instances and the vital act of reading itself.

Eliot's investment in the crafted forms of poetry thus moves beyond a notion of the aesthetic object (he is no late Parnassian, fetishizing verse repertoires as ends in themselves), to consider how individual poetic forms enable a distinctive kind of experience. More than this (in a way that also distinguishes him from the Victorian aesthetes who exulted experience as an end in itself), Eliot implies that poetry might include or enable a distinctive kind of thinking. Whereas prose requires us to construe language by the requisites of the school teacher (a correct grasp of vocabulary, grammar and syntax), Eliot insists that poetry invites comprehension of a different order. He stakes this claim on the personal witness of reading verse in a foreign language, where it conveyed to him 'something immediate and vivid': 'something which I could not put into words and yet felt that I understood'. Eliot does not allow us – as we might reasonably wish – to bracket off his testimony here as vapid speculation. He can be sure that his 'impression' was not after all an 'illusion', because on later learning the language, he confirmed that it was not something he 'imagined to be in the poetry, but something that was really there'.[40]

'So in poetry', Eliot goes on to universalize, 'you can, now and then, penetrate into another country, so to speak, before your passport has been issued or your ticket taken'.[41] Secret, forbidden and accelerated access to 'another country' of consciousness, of understanding, is a highly suggestive idea, even thrilling, and he argues the same in a number of places; notably, in an essay he published a year earlier, 'The Music of Poetry' (1942), and in *The Use of Poetry and the Use of Criticism* (1933), in which he invokes the same figure of piercing or passing through the border-control of our consciousness: to 'the deeper, unnamed feelings which form the substratum of our being, to which we rarely penetrate'.[42] He elsewhere goes so far as to call it a positive 'test' of 'genuine poetry' that it can 'communicate before it is understood'.[43]

While we might wish to know more about how he is distinguishing 'communication' from 'understanding' here,[44] it is clear that he prioritizes – in both sense of that word – the open-eared reading experience. We should be readers before attempting to be scholars. 'Indeed, if we worry too much about it first as philosophy we are likely to prevent ourselves from receiving the poetic beauty.'[45] Returning to Eliot's suspicion of academic annotations for poetry, the fuller context for his comments suggests that he was by no means opposed to applying interpretative rigour to his verses as such. What he opposed was the idea that scholarship might come *before* the sensuous, so as to sterilize the reading experience into an exercise in parsing. 'Good commentaries can be very helpful,' he allows, 'but even the best commentary on a work of literary art is likely to be a waste of time unless we have first read and been excited by the text commented upon even without understanding it'.[46] Excitement and understanding are not exclusive possibilities, but the latter risks impairing the former.

Uncogency by the standards of prose might yet make sense as 'poetic beauty'. More radically, Eliot intuits a possible commerce between the apprehensive categories of beauty, the pleasure it inspires, and philosophy. 'For that thrill of excitement from our first reading of a work of creative literature which we do not understand is itself the beginning of understanding.'[47] Notoriously, Eliot pronounced that 'poets in our civilization, as it exists at present, must be *difficult*'.[48] But this comment needs to be balanced against his proposition that he would like 'an audience which could neither read nor write'.[49] These sentiments appear to be at odds, but he pairs them in his prescription for the poet as 'more primitive as well as more civilized than his contemporaries'.[50] Poetry's appeal is linguistically difficult but also primitively paralinguistic, and these two aspects encourage each other, through a feedback loop. The poem's words are hard to render semantically, which directs us to attend more fully to its non-lexical qualities. But part of what makes the poem's words hard to construe in the first place is that they are thick with sounds and quickened by rhythms; and yet how the words must ultimately be understood – how they 'mean' – is bound up with their styling as patterns of sound moving in time. Linguistic and paralinguistic modes may be separable for the purposes of analysis, but they mutually inform each other in the act of reading. Versification does not therefore ornament, it 'invigorates': 'It works through meanings, certainly, or not without meanings in the ordinary sense.'[51]

Eliot explained that the kind of poetry he needed to find his own voice 'did not exist in English at all; it was only to be found in French'.[52] He seems from the outset to have thrown his poetical lot in with the Symbolists, who were, as Paul Valéry put it, 'nourished in music', where poetry might express itself as pure, self-determining form, 'extracting from language the same effects, almost, as were produced on our nervous systems by sound alone'.[53] As a way of explaining his own work, Eliot certainly favoured comparisons with 'musical form' over all others (*CP* 893). But it would be wrong to conclude from this that he was therefore an English Symbolist. He compares poetry to music partly to assert that poetry, like music, may offer us more than 'an appreciation of virtuosity': 'something that we call its meaning, though we cannot confine it in words' (*CP* 895). But Eliot also warned that 'it is dangerous to press the resemblance between poetry and music too far' (*CP* 893). When writing of poetry's 'music', he often referred not only to qualities of versification but also to 'recurrent themes' – 'a music of imagery as well as sound', the 'contrapuntal arrangement of subject-matter'[54] – that is, he says, 'as natural to poetry as to music' (*CP* 894).

What's at stake here for Eliot is the belief that poetry's 'music' must excite our minds as well as our ears; or, more specifically, our minds through our ears, in a kind of sensate intelligence: 'if we are not moved, then it is, as poetry, meaningless', and yet you cannot have great verse music that makes 'no sense'.[55] For: 'while poetry attempts to convey something beyond what can be conveyed in prose rhythms, it remains, all the same, one person talking to another; and this is just as true if you sing it, for singing is another way of talking'.[56] Put another way, 'ambiguities' of interpretation 'may be due to the fact that the poem means more, not less, than ordinary speech can communicate'.[57]

Viktor Shklovsky wrote influentially of how 'difficulty' in art may extend the 'length of perception', and his observation illuminates why Eliot's verse claims our fullest attention. But it was another contemporary, W. B. Yeats, who offered the more salient cue when he wrote of 'difficulty' as the poet's 'plough' that might drive us 'under the surface'.[58] Eliot uses similar imagery when he writes of how poetry activates the 'auditory imagination'; that is, 'the feeling for syllable and rhythm, penetrating' – that word again – 'far below the conscious levels of thought and feeling, invigorating every word; sinking to the most primitive and forgotten, returning to the origin and bringing something back, seeking the beginning and the end'.[59]

When talking of productive resistance in Eliot's poetry, it is important to be clear that difficulty should not mean impossibility. Taking him for a sharp-elbowed elitist, John Carey among others has impugned Eliot's poetics as an attempt – through '[i]rrationality and obscurity' – to alienate those 'masses' of readers not elevated into the same educational coterie.[60] This view of Old Possum as intellectual braggart remains tenacious (as does that fabled figure of the 'general' reader), and purports to explain Eliot's allergy to explanatory notes for his poem – because such notes might tear the veil of his cultivated superiority. But while Eliot wrote primarily for 'the most intelligent and sensitive reader', 'for the hundred or so best readers', he calls it 'a common error', and 'an irrelevance based on political premises', to distinguish between 'poetry for "the few" and poetry for "the many"' (*CP* 890–1):

> Poetry should be written, not for the 'few' in the sense of a small group of highly refined, or socially superior, triflers who are trained to enjoy the obscure and the eccentric and the perverse: but for the 'few' in the sense that there are never more than a very small number of people who are competent to judge poetry at all.

The 'few' whom Eliot deemed competent to judge poetry may well still turn out to be highly refined and socially superior. Politics is hardly irrelevant. But Eliot's distinction is not thereby voided. 'To aim directly at "the people" is', he clarified, 'to aim to write the ephemeral because that is what the people wants' (*CP* 891); whereas Eliot aimed to write with less mind to his audience than to his poetry, which demanded a style commensurate with the complexity of lived experience. Facing the same charge of elitist obscurantism later in the century, Geoffrey Hill stressed the everydayness of 'difficulty' ('We are difficult. Human beings are difficult. We're difficult to ourselves, we're difficult to each other'), such that it would be 'demeaning' to expect these things to be simplified in art.[61] Abiding this principle that only 'genuinely difficult art is truly democratic', Eliot's poetry is not constructed that we might truckle to the poet's erudition but that the poem might tussle authentically with its subject – and that we might too, in the act of reading. Difficulty is not an optional verse-extra for Eliot (in the sense in which end-rhyme or metre might or might not be employed), nor is the incompleteness of our comprehension as readers. 'If only a part of the meaning can be conveyed by paraphrase,' Eliot cautions the impatient exegete, 'that is because the poet is occupied with frontiers of consciousness beyond which words *fail*, though meanings still exist'.[62]

But what exactly are these non-linguistic 'meanings' that might only find profitable purpose by and through failure? Eliot notes that versification is 'a definite concession to the desire for "play"',[63] but he also believed that poetry must offer something 'besides pleasure': 'for if it were only pleasure, the pleasure itself could not be of the highest kind'.[64] Swinburne's style left him breathless, but offered little beyond the affective transport in the moment of reading, because in his verse 'the meaning and the sound are one thing'.[65] Eliot emphasizes that meaning and sound should bear directly on each other, which is part of the reason 'poetry must not stray too far from ordinary everyday language which we use and hear': to ensure that 'the music of poetry is not something which exists apart from the meaning'.[66] What Eliot experiences in Swinburne is not the interpenetration of 'music' and 'meaning', however, but its conflation, such that he produces only 'the hallucination of meaning', where 'language, uprooted, has adapted itself to an independent life of atmospheric nourishment'.[67]

Straining to give credit where it is due, Eliot lauds Swinburne's diffuseness as 'one of his glories' – he is astonished by his capacity to use 'an amazing number of words' while employing 'so little material' – and twice in a short essay categorizes his style as the function of 'genius'.[68] Yet Swinburne flunks Eliot's 'more important' test, because his verse music is not 'struggling to digest and express' something beyond itself; it is a 'singular life of its own'.[69] Even Tennyson, whom Eliot calls 'the master of Swinburne', falls short on the same score. While asserting the Laureate's 'technical accomplishment', which is 'everywhere masterful and satisfying'[70] – even going so far as to claim he has 'the finest ear of any poet since Milton', and the power to make him 'shudder'[71] – Eliot's praise is tartly circumscribed. He avows fulsome credit for the prodigality of Tennyson's rhythms, which is itself enough to make him a 'great poet'; yet Tennyson cannot be counted among the 'very greatest', because his style does not sufficiently refine itself to communicate beyond its own 'mood'.[72]

Eliot never let his readers forget that whether something counts as literature in the first place can only be determined by 'literary standards', but he also repeatedly reverted to the codicil that the 'greatness' of literature cannot be determined 'solely by literary standards', either. 'Literary criticism should be completed by criticism from a definite ethical and theological standpoint'.[73] Yet in his essay on Dante from 1929 (where he stresses how important it is to discern the theology that animates Dante's verse), he takes elaborate pains to assert the difference between what he calls 'philosophical belief' and 'poetic assent'. He proposes something like Coleridge's 'suspension of disbelief', though he is in fact calling for something starker. To read 'poetry as poetry', he opines, 'you suspend both belief *and* disbelief'.[74] It turns out that Eliot could not quite practice his own high principle, and it says much for his intellectual honesty (which is frequently impugned, notably by those who have him pegged as a self-promoting snob) that he owns the disjunction between what he attempts and what he achieves. In a long, involuted coda note to the Dante essay, he admits that he cannot always 'wholly separate' his 'poetic appreciation' from his 'personal beliefs'. But that confession makes all the more acute his allegiance to the principle to which he (and we) ought to aspire.

Whatever the imperfect reality of his practice as a reader, it is at least his intention to take poetry on its own terms, with the caveat that the 'very greatest' poetry must rouse itself beyond its own sonic, rhythmic and verbal atmosphere or mood. Hence his impatience with I. A. Richards's estimation that *The Waste Land* effected 'a complete severance of his poetry and *all* beliefs'.[75] Eliot's counter-position, 'I cannot see that poetry can ever be separated from something which I should call belief,'[76] invites us to judge all of his poetry on the basis of its animating faith, including his early, bleaker, verses that might easily be taken as the willed negation of systematic thought. The poems that bookend his first collection, *Prufrock and Other Observations* (1917), provide convenient touchstones here. The first announces itself as a 'song' in its title; and though the poem itself reveals that it is a love song only in a darkly ironic sense, the lines as they unfold are nonetheless amply lyrical, from its famous opening:

Let us go then, you and I,
When the evening is spread out against the sky,
Like a patient etherised upon a table;
Let us go through certain half-deserted streets,
The muttering retreats
Of restless nights in one-night cheap hotels:

And sawdust restaurants with oyster-shells:
Streets that follow like a tedious argument
Of insidious intent.

(*CP* 5.1–9)

It is an odd kind of lyricism, for sure, tripping itself up, surprising itself into melody. Conversational and syntactically halting, the first line is unexpectedly swept up into verse by the second, which effloresces rhythmically, and clinches them together as a rhyming couplet. But then the third line (still pursuing the same sentence) unbalances things again, as its simile debases the romantic atmosphere previously primed by talk of the evening sky. Then the fourth line revives the opening invitation ('Let us go'), and tracks the rest of that ongoing sentence to its conclusion in similarly giddy ways across the next five lines: rhyming separate lines into couplets, and playing sibilants against dentals, and rhythms against each other, language is heightened into something ear-catchingly 'poetic'. Such alluring 'music' operates uneasily with the sinister images it enlivens ('half-deserted streets'; 'muttering retreats'; 'restless nights'; 'cheap hotels'; 'sawdust restaurants'; 'tedious argument'; 'insidious intent'). There is something seductive in these soundscapes, but we are never allowed to relax into them as self-governing atmospheres or moods. They demand we think about the unsettlement we feel. As 'Prufrock' is led to an 'overwhelming question', so we as readers want to know more than is divulged by the poem's prosody or by its words.

'La Figlia Che Piange', the closing poem from the same collection, is an instructively different case, for stimulating what Eliot sniffed at as, 'a certain low popularity' (*CP* 451). While the lyricism of 'Prufrock' engages the reader through its troubling unevenness, 'La Figlia Che Piange' attracted attention for the opposite reason. It was taken up by anthologies for 'schools and general readers', Eliot noticed, because it was judged to be the 'mildest' of his productions, and because, relatedly, 'it seemed to many people to be more like poetry' than his other work (*CP* 451). Easy elasticity and interlacing of rhythms and rhymes evidently dulled rather than refined the 'popular' response. The poem insinuates a 'troubled' experience of memory, loss and regret, but many evidently found its 'music' narcotic. Or else, and perhaps worse, its music encouraged lazy suppositions about the occasion for the poem's composition. Mostly people wanted to know whether the girl was someone Eliot had loved and lost, to which the answer was no (or NO!), the poem was prompted by an artwork described to him as 'the weeping girl', but which he had never seen. But even if readers had hit on the correct origins of the poem, they would still have misfired, because the poem itself would still have been lost in the process.

***

Eliot's poems thus invite us in, but also to keep us at bay; they demand 'sophistication', but also the 'primitive' response. We must tune into his verse, but not treat it as mere tunefulness. Which brings us back to difficulty and failure. Eliot wrote in his doctoral thesis that 'the life of a soul does not consist in the contemplation of one consistent world but in the painful task of unifying (to a greater or lesser extent) jarring and incompatible ones, and passing, when possible, from two or more discordant viewpoints to a higher which shall somehow include and transmute them'.[77] That account – of jarring and discordancy, and the afflictive, imperfect effort to make sense of incompatible perspectives – is a fine annotation of the style as well as the substance of Eliot's verse. But Eliot's aim to realize a 'higher' viewpoint in poetry is specially incited in his later poems that engage his religious faith. He viewed his entire life as an ongoing journey towards faith, and his biographers have agreed with this assessment.[78] Nonetheless, his conversion in 1927 did at the same time signal a point of departure; it was an inevitable next step for him rather than a Pauline break, but it was still an important progression, scandalizing many of his contemporaries who had not seen it coming. Virginia Woolf was 'shocked' by the news, which she found 'shameful and distressing', perhaps because it suggested that human character hadn't changed as much as she had imagined after 1910. Her private incredulity and disdain – her sense that there was 'something obscene in a living person sitting by the fire and believing in God'[79] – was in any event widely shared by the self-styled revolutionaries of her artistic and literary milieu.

Eliot reserved his own sense of shock and despair for the fact that 'the majority of people live below the level of belief or doubt'.[80] He saw this dominant world view reflected in 'modern literature' that is 'corrupted' by 'secularism', such that it is 'simply unaware of, simply cannot understand the meaning of, the primacy of the supernatural over the natural life'.[81] He did not imagine his own poetry or anyone else's could do much to re-enchant the world. I. A. Richards's rehearsal of Arnold's hope that 'poetry "is capable of saving us"' was, he thought, 'like saying that the wall-paper will save us when the walls have crumbled'.[82] But he did not therefore believe (to borrow W. H. Auden's glum line) that 'poetry makes nothing happen'.[83] Eliot was capable of such defeatism himself, but one should be careful in reading lines like 'poetry does not matter' (*CP* 187.21) as if they were axioms: that particular line's fuller contexts, for instance, do not suggest resignation but struggle, by meta-poetical ironies, to express something sincerely and truly, by acknowledging the thwartings that come with trying to do so. His poetry could not, he thought, give us 'the sense of confidence' in his poetic endeavour that he identifies in Tennyson; it is certainly nervier. But in granting that such confidence is 'one of the major pleasures of poetry',[84] he overestimates Tennyson's faith in his own poetry (examined in Chapter 2), and perhaps underestimates that which his own elliptical style might elicit, not least for the honesty with which he, like Tennyson, worked through his doubts in verse.

Eliot's faith in poetry was not a bulwark against unbelief, then, but it was bullish nonetheless, and became increasingly so in the years and decades after he formally affirmed his Anglicanism. In 'Religion and Literature' (1935), he underscored his conviction that works of imagination 'affect us wholly, as human beings': 'everything we eat has some other effect on us than merely the pleasure of taste and mastication; it affects us during the process of assimilation and digestion; and I believe that exactly the same is true of anything we read'.[85] Eliot's phrasing – *exactly* the same, *anything* we read – entreats us to take seriously his metaphor that might otherwise slide into the vaguer associations of simile. Assimilation and digestion was on Eliot's mind again when, just three years before his death, and some thirty-three years after he first advanced his theory of 'poetic assent' versus 'philosophical belief', he argued (in a pamphlet on George Herbert) that religious poetry 'should touch the feeling, and enlarge the understanding of those readers who hold no religious belief and find themselves unmoved by religious emotion'.[86] That is a notable departure from the credo that readers best engage with poetry's beliefs by disinterested appraisal. Eliot seems to have moved the ideal category of 'poetic assent' away from what, in delineating the nature of religious faith, John Henry Newman called 'notional assent', to the personally, imaginatively invested phenomena of 'real assent'.[87]

While it is therefore too crude to set Eliot's earlier poetry as incommensurable with his latter verses, his later poems do register a meaningful change. Barry Spurr makes a valuable observation but goes too far with it – reading too much for theme and too little for atmosphere and mood – when he contends that the pre-conversion *Waste Land*, with its dependence on the myth of the Holy Grail and the Passion Story, is 'at least as much a Christian poem as *Four Quartets*, which is an extended philosophical meditation on time and timelessness only intermittently specifically Christian in reference'. Spurr's cognate claim that 'the wasteland experience' 'pointedly persists' in Eliot's post-conversion poems is likewise incisive but overstated.[88] Allowing the general point that Eliot is a poet of 'faith' from the beginning to the end of his career, it is germane also to notice that his latter poems shed the acid mistrust of religion Robert Crawford detects in some of his earlier verses ('Mr Eliot's Sunday Morning Service', 'The Hippopotamus', 'Whispers of Immortality', 'Gerontion').[89] Eliot's fresh sympathy for religion never ripens into dogmatism, but it does admit a freshly invigorated possibility of redemption, with a Marian accent on the restorative female.[90]

What's changed for Eliot is subtle but profound. 'The trouble of the modern age is not merely the inability to believe certain things about God and man which our forefathers believed, but the inability to *feel* towards God and man as they did':[91] Eliot's general cultural diagnosis offers a key to unlocking the particular valency of belief in his poems, which makes itself felt as a shifting metaphysical atmosphere or mood, rather than by explicit doctrinal allegiances. In 1932, Eliot reported that 'Marina' was the poem he liked best of all he had written (*CP* 775), and whatever one makes of such a claim as an aesthetic judgement, it seems plausible that it arises from his awareness that he simply could not have written such a poem of renewal even a decade earlier (when he published *The Waste Land*).

The supernatural music that animates 'Marina' is, as Jason Harding has suggested, not only an analogue of the silent but harmonious 'music of the spheres' that moves Pericles to tears (after long years of silence, when he is reunited with the daughter supposed dead: *Pericles, Prince of Tyre* V. i. 232), it also marks a development in Eliot's poetics that culminates in 'the exquisite music of *Four Quartets* ("music heard so deeply, / That it is not heard at all")'.[92] More than this: 'Marina' is an essential bridging poem, recalling the interweaving sounds, rhythms and phrasings of Eliot's earliest verses, especially the euphonic countermelodies of 'La Figlia Che Piange', but tuning that verse music to the more overtly metaphysical purpose that finds its fullest expression in *Four Quartets*.

But before he gets to *Four Quartets*, Eliot of course writes other poems that constitute their own kinds of progression, stylistic and thematic, and which implicate verse styles at least as rebarbatively 'difficult' as anything he had written to this point. Reflecting on what his conversion meant for him as writer and a reader, he was keen to establish a new perspective implicitly opposed to what he took to be the corrupting influence of 'secularism', but which is not perforce a kind of unquestioning religious 'propaganda'.[93] 'Between the usual suspects of poetry and "devotional" verse there is an important field still unexplored by modern poets – the experience of a man in search of God, and trying to explain to himself his intenser human feelings in terms of the divine goal': so he explained to W. F. Stead on 9 August 1930, before fixing his claim to the first long poem he had written after his conversion: 'I have tried to do something of that in "Ash Wednesday"' (*CP* 731). That poem carries through much of the negative imagery of *The Hollow Men*; it proceeds by a similar sort of 'gesture without motion' (*CP* 81.12), and Eliot was certainly impatient to resist the poem being read as religious testimony. It was 'merely an attempt to put down in words a certain *stage* of the journey, a journey of which I insist that all my previous verse represents previous stages' (*CP* 730). Yet the *stage* of faith the poem represents is a notable advance. He also said of *Ash-Wednesday* that 'the whole thing aims to be a modern *Vita Nuova*'.[94] *The Hollow Men* operates out of the despair of stasis (an earlier draft had a more hopeful ending, but was revised into the crimping bathos that ends his published poem with a 'whimper').[95] By contrast, there is movement in *Ash-Wednesday*, and it is persistently trained on hope, even if it never reaches its destination. Locally, but also across the poem as a whole, words and phrases, images and ideas, wash into each other, meld and memorate. Proximate lines speak to each other, but this also occurs across the poem's length, between the first and the final sections that fumble to construe the relations of words and the Word. Section I opens:

> Because I do not hope to turn again
> Because I do not hope
> Because I do not hope to turn

Pound achieved his rhythmical effects at the level of the line unit,[96] and so he made little use of enjambement or suspended syntax across the verse-paragraph. But in each line here, Eliot re-limns his meanings, following more in the style of Hopkins. Differently from Hopkins, though, who (as noted in Chapter 4) uses the 'turn' of the verse-line to activate the unfolding syntax (especially through effects of *rejet* and *contre-rejet*), Eliot's line-ends here cut the syntax clean off, yet without cutting the strain of thought. While each new line in this section is a new beginning, it bears the weight of the lines before it.

The second 'Because' thus feels more pressure than the first; and the third, more than the second. The effect is cumulative, repeating as well as running on. Reprising and renegotiating; stuttering but never styptic. Each expression of 'hope', though repetitious and cast in the negative, is inaugurative, positively recuperated by the fact that it is not linear but cyclical – centripetal. The passage nicely illustrates Eliot's conception of 'music' in poetry as operating 'at a point of intersection':[97] 'the music of verse is not a line by line matter', Eliot advises us, 'but a question of the whole poem'.[98] Poetry happens on the move, in time, through consistent disruption that fashions new possibilities out of old, each occasion affirming a faith in poetry which is constitutively provisional and subjunctive, through a prosody that is correspondingly optative. His faith in poetry is predicated on the possibility of failing better, but with more 'hope' in the struggle than is to be found in Beckett's notorious deployment of that phrase (*Worstward Ho*). Section VI closes by remembering the same incomplete attempt to clarify the poem's restless preoccupation, but with a key-change from 'Because' to 'Although':

> Although I do not hope to turn again
> Although I do not hope
> Although I do not hope to turn

In labelling *Ash-Wednesday* Eliot's 'most difficult poem', Craig Raine conjectures that Eliot conceded as much and more when he noted that if the poem made it into a second edition, he would consider adding an epigraph from Byron's *Don Juan*: 'I don't pretend I quite understand / My own meaning when I would be *very* fine.'[99] But we need to handle such comments with care. It would be easy to take Eliot's suggestion as droll admission that his poetic refinements of language were, like Swinburne's, the mere 'hallucination of meaning'. But this would be to coarsen Eliot's faith, as Raine surely does when he declares that 'Eliot's despair compels him to God'.[100] 'Consequently I rejoice, having to construct something / Upon which to rejoice': those riddling lines from *Ash-Wednesday* are adduced by Raine as supporting proof; as is Eliot's essay on F. H. Bradley (1927), in which he articulates the purportedly 'related notion' that 'scepticism and disillusion are a useful equipment for religious understanding'.[101] But it is a mistake to jump from these uncontextualized quotations on why Eliot turned to God, to QED. Better, as a first step, to consult the OED, which offers a rich survey of the positive theological charge for the word 'turn' (that Eliot works so hard in *Ash-Wednesday*); or to survey the associations of that same word – from Cavalcanti, Lancelot Andrewes, *Othello*, Emerson and others – that Ricks and McCue harvest for the reader (*CP* 734).

Ash-Wednesday certainly forges its faith within the context of doubt; faith is not so much expressed as explored, and part of it rests on the efficacy of exploration itself. Eliot's philosophical training taught him early to view the acerbic rigour of doubting as productive rather than threatening; and as indicated in the epigraph quotation for this chapter, he imagined the highest goal of civilized intelligence to be one that does not overcome scepticism so much as unite its 'profoundest' expression with 'the deepest faith'.[102] But it is wrong to deduce that Eliot's religious faith was therefore itself negatively conceived as a last resort against despair. His attempts to articulate his faith drive him into strategies of indirection. Doubt is not unfaith or unbelief: it is not the dull negation of faith, it is its snatched reflection, glimpsing, however partially, a possibility it can recognize but cannot itself resolve. To live in doubt is, Eliot once remarked, to live 'parasitically', but such a condition is surely 'better than not living at all', for defining itself in relation to the minds of those who have believed something.[103] Even the seemingly blackest episodes in his journeying through faith, going into the 'dark dark dark' (*CP* 188.1), are better glossed as apophatic rather than sceptical. Indeed, he directly sets himself apart from Valéry, whom he judged 'too sceptical to hold convictions'.[104]

Eliot's religious faith is not therefore negative in the sense of despairing or disillusioned, nor are his poems that engage his faith negative in the sense of obscure for the sake of being stylishly 'very fine'. They are difficult, and they fail in a specific sense, not as an end in itself but as a way of opening up the possibilities of communication on this subject in the first place. Doubt may itself endow faith, as kinds of failure are indirectly successful, because he is not attempting to ferment devotion into verse, but instead (as already noted) to express 'the experience of a man in *search* of God'. More than two years after his baptism he described it as 'rather trying to be supposed to have settled oneself in an easy chair when one has just begun a long journey on foot'.[105] This is well to remember if his post-conversion poems are to be read, as they should be, for their faith that is both dynamically conceived – it is an ongoing 'search', a 'long journey' – and at the same time resistant to being tamed into the economy of language. It is in this sense that Rowan Williams describes the interaction of the poetic with the religious imagination as a 'return to language' that itself 'requires an act of faith; and an acceptance of the probability of failure'.[106] Failure, like doubt, is a matter of degree but also of pragmatic necessity, when 'the truths of religion' themselves cannot be treated as 'a question of something absolutely true (or false) in so many words', but only 'more nearly true than is the contradiction of them'.[107]

Throughout his career, Eliot's faith in poetry operates in the doubled divide between being unable to grasp absolutely what is absolutely true, and being unable to express that truth absolutely truly in verse. But where Wittgenstein closes his *Tractatus Logico-Philosophicus* with the lonely imperative, 'Whereof one cannot speak, thereof one must be silent', Eliot opens *The Waste Land* in the same year with a countervailing commitment to make noisy work out of what resists propositional discipline. 'You have to say the thing the difficult way', he later reflected on his subject matter, and also on the stage in his development as a poet: 'The only alternative is not saying it at all.'[108] What allows Eliot to seek communication where Wittgenstein falls into silence is explicable as a difference of genre: the poet intimates through gesture what the philosopher cannot capture into proposition. But there is something else going on as well; something changes as Eliot's writing tips towards religious themes. While there are surely connections of style and indeed sentiment between *The Hollow Men* and *Ash-Wednesday*, the former's broodings are coloured by the hollowed-out humanism of *The Waste Land*, whereas the latter takes the form of the *via negativa*: a willed asceticism, in a long tradition by which, Eliot understood, 'the Christian thinker ... proceeds by rejection and elimination'.[109] Both poems probe and scout painful failure; but if *Ash-Wednesday* fails to realize perfect faith, it does at least succeed in endeavouring towards it, overcoming the stymied resignations that characterize Eliot's earlier poem.

But perhaps the binary conception of success and failure in verse is unhelpful from the outset. Ben Lerner has argued inventively that all poems always fail, insofar as individual verse instances must fall short of what we imagine to be the unrealized potential of 'Poetry' as an art form. Yet Lerner also claims that insofar as we imagine that individual poems are, by whatever degree, failing, we also implicitly re-affirm the idea and possibility of 'Poetry', which is the reason poets carry on writing poems, and readers reading them.[110] In the terms of this chapter and book as a whole, Lerner's thesis implies that poetic failure constitutes the very kind of faith in poetry it would at first appear to undermine. The necessity of poetic failure becomes ennobling and indeed enabling, especially in the case of a poet like Eliot who so openly recognizes and courts communicative deficiencies within his verse. But it would be over-simple to leave things at that, as if all kinds of failure were to all intents and purposes the same. The success of Eliot's imperfections, so to speak, are singular, and intimately connected not only to his uniquely adroit repertoires of obliquity, but also to his imperfect struggles with faith that demanded commensurate indirectness for their faithful expression. 'One realises that one never arrives at anything, but must just go on fighting every day as long as the strength lasts':[111] so for Eliot's religious faith, so for his faith in poetry, so for his individual poems, which each separately and perpetually stage the fight to arrive.

Finally, taking up the burden of failure (and of fighting to fail better) more fully than any of his other poems, *Four Quartets* is Eliot's most substantial work on religious faith. In it he expressed 'much more of Christian hope' than in any of his previous poems (*CP* 899), and he ultimately came to see it as his 'best work',[112] being at once his most musical poem, in the ways already adumbrated in 'Marina', but at the same time his work most explicitly and meta-poetically concerned with how 'Words strain, / Crack and sometimes break, under the burden, / Under the tension, slip, slide, perish, / Decay with imprecision, will not stay in place, / Will not stay still' (*CP* 183–4.13–17). *Four Quartets* iterates and inspects not merely the challenge, in principle, of commissioning its subject, it is unsteady also about its own practice:

> You say I am repeating
> Something I have said before. I shall say it again.
> Shall I say it again?
>
> (*CP* 189.33–35)

Most starkly, the poem even turns against the medium of verse itself, by switching into the consciously contradistinctive mode of prose:

> That was a way of putting it – not very satisfactory:
> A periphrastic study in a worn-out poetical fashion,
> Leaving one still with the intolerable wrestle
> With words and meanings…
>
> (*CP* 187.18–21)

Such passages pick over the factitiousness of fixing thoughts and feelings into verse; they confess a shaken faith in poetry itself. Shaken, but not lost; being told, in the bluntest terms, that the worn-out poetical fashion is not very satisfactory, we are encouraged to scratch around for what 'meanings' might have fallen between the words. Drawing attention to the wrestle with words and meanings – which is 'intolerable' precisely because it cannot be won – draws us into the poetic 'wrestle' too. 'And so each venture', Eliot writes – performatively prising his suggestion against the line-ending – 'Is a new beginning'; and his figure of inauguration recalls the sense of 'penetrating' the other-country of our unconscious that he associated with the 'auditory imagination'. He announces 'a raid on the inarticulate', but, discouragingly: 'With shabby equipment always deteriorating / In the general mess of imprecision of feeling, / Undisciplined squads of emotion' (*CP* 191.8–11).

The poem's title has already conceded the essential imponderability of its subject. Eliot was 'very anxious to establish the *Four Quartets* as one poem' (881), for the reason that it was – as he said of Tennyson's *In Memoriam* – 'designed with great care', 'to form a continuous meditation' (*CP* 882). Calling his poems 'quartets' seemed 'to start people on the right track for understanding them', in the sense that the poem weaves together three or four superficially unrelated themes: 'the "poem" being the degree of success in making a new whole out of them' (*CP* 893). Each of the quartets is related to each other, as well as cyclically organized by seasons and elements; and individual images and rhythms (from earlier poems too) are abundantly requited and repurposed throughout. The central, enigmatic motif of ceaseless exploration – which may only end by arriving back at the beginning – impels the whole collection's meditative intention, but deliquesces only in the very last line, when 'the fire and the rose are one' (*CP* 209.46).

But if *Four Quartets* might, on the face of it, seem like the culmination of Symbolist poetics in its recourse to music as the supremely non-referential mode (and the poem has often been interpreted in that way), it might be better read as the culmination of Eliot's resistance to poetic self-reflexiveness. F. R. Leavis was right when he concluded that 'Eliot has no intellectually statable answer in his mind for us to elicit from the "music"'. But he was wrong to conclude that we have therefore been led to take this music 'with a mistaken kind of seriousness'.[113] *Four Quartets* operates in a different mode from philosophy or Christian apologetics, and so the criterion for taking it seriously or otherwise is different too. Its poetry makes profit from the fact that words may have meanings even where they have no referents. But his verse 'music' also essays to express beyond its own repertoire, as 'a form grows out of the attempt of somebody to say something.'[114] If Eliot's early verses feel the influence of Symbolist strategies, his later writings tend also, perhaps more so, towards Tractarianism. Not that he refashioned himself as some modernist John Keble; even after his conversion, he continued to criticize what he took to be the self-limitations of devotional verse.[115] But in the ways described above, his later poetics evolve and increasingly invite comparison with Newman's, as they also latterly edge closer to those of Rossetti and Hopkins, considered in earlier chapters.[116] 'I have long aimed', he explained in 1933 (without specifying exactly how long), 'to write poetry which should be ... so transparent that we should not see the poetry ... that in reading it we are intent on what the poem points at, and not on the poetry' (*CP* 894).

Later again, he explained that he was able to achieve a somewhat simpler, more immediate appeal in *Four Quartets* than in *The Waste Land* because of his intervening experience of writing plays, and also because he was in general terms more experienced and mature as a person and a poet.[117] To these influences might be added his more developed theological allegiance to truths beyond poetry itself. 'By the time of the *Four Quartets*, I couldn't have written in the style of *The Waste Land*', he told Donald Hall in 1959, before adding the sardonic disavowal: 'In *The Waste Land*, I wasn't even bothering whether I understood what I was saying.'[118] That's pretty arch, even for Eliot; his obiter dicta seems overstated, of a piece with his hand-waving claim to have written 'Journey of the Magi', one of his most overtly Christian poems, 'in three quarters of an hour after church time and before lunch one Sunday morning, with the assistance of half a bottle of Booth's gin'.[119] But there might yet be an honest admission buried within both his bantering admissions: that 'Journey of the Magi' was written quickly, and that *Four Quartets* differs from *The Waste Land* for being less forbidding in its style (relying less heavily on allusion, for instance).[120] The stylistic shift in Eliot that makes *Four Quartets* could hardly be said to make his verses 'transparent'; although they may in some ways seem comparatively simpler than other, earlier poems, they hardly give themselves up lightly. But that was not anyway what Eliot meant by his desired turn towards greater transparency or simplicity. The change in emphasis in his writing surely does have something do with his development as a writer and as a person, for the reasons he suggested; but it may also be read as a function of his maturing faith, which made him more pressingly 'bothered' that he and his readers 'understood' what his verses sought to 'communicate'.

Dante was the greatest of poets for Eliot on account of his 'peculiar lucidity', which is 'a *poetic* as distinguished from an *intellectual* lucidity'; where, the 'thought may be obscure, but the word is lucid, or rather translucent'. Dante's achievement in this respect was, Eliot judged, partly explicable in terms of the language in which he was working ('English poetry words have', by contrast, 'a kind of opacity which is part of their beauty'), and partly in respect of the age and culture in which Dante lived, where it was possible to be '*universal*', both as a language and also as a system of thought.[121] But Eliot also intuited a gift for verse style that was entirely Dante's own. After all, it was reading his poetry in Italian, when Eliot's grasp of that language was still limited, that first inspired his conviction that 'genuine poetry' can 'communicate before it is understood'.[122] Bothering about poetry being understood need not mean conceding to what's most readily parsed or paraphrased; Dante above all poets had proved this. Obscure thoughts, as matters of faith are wont to be, might yet be engaged with translucence, which can in turn entail its own conditions of difficulty. Delaying or even preventing cognitive closure may force a kind of narrative failure that itself constitutes and agitates its own kind of eloquence.

What's admirable in Dante's poetic 'music', Eliot thus found emulable – though he knew he could never replicate the achievement; though he knew that (writing in a different language, time and culture) he might only work towards it indirectly, by invoking and assaying the impediments to translucency. But in this he was implicitly aligned with Dante too, perhaps more than he knew. Even the last canto of *Paradiso*, which Eliot called 'the highest point that poetry has ever reached or ever can reach',[123] works through its vision by apophatic denial as well as cataphatic affirmation; specifically, through the interplay between the two, while at the same time beckoning beyond what this merely conceptual interplay might imply.[124] Dante abjures instrumental directness himself, that is, but his indirections, which include an appeal to the mind through the ear, are themselves not only needful but uniquely suggestive. Between philosophical proposition and verse style, as indeed between devotional poetry and Symbolism, there are, Eliot believed and demonstrated, degrees and strategies of communicability outside of those travestied by the impatience of readers who either want to know what the poem 'means' in prose, or relegate it to realms of pure sound or image. 'Any attempt on my part to explain would merely be saying something else', Eliot remarked of *Four Quartets* (*CP* 899). But that is not to shut us out, it is to draw us into his poem, which catalyses thoughts and feelings that point beyond signification, through the music of verse, to what only occurs within the event of poetry itself:

> Trying to use words, and every attempt
> Is a wholly new start, and a different kind of failure
>
> (*CP* 191.3–4)

Notes

Introduction

1. W. B. Yeats, *The Letters of W. B. Yeats*, ed. Allen Wade (New York: Macmillan, 1955), 922.
2. In the literary-historical period covered by this book, ardent attention is paid to the special nature of poetry: see G. E. Lessing's *Laocoön* (1766), described as the first modern attempt to define the distinctive spheres of art and poetry, and G. W. F. Hegel's *Lectures on Aesthetics* (1835), which asks after 'the general difference between the prosaic and poetic modes of conception, granted a possible similarity of the subject-matter in both cases' (*Aesthetics: Lectures on Fine Art* vol. II, trans T. M. Knox (Oxford: Clarendon Press, 1998, c1975), 973).
3. For Homeric hedging and the calculated equivocality of Plato's view of poetry, see Stephen Halliwell, *Between Ecstasy and Truth: Interpretations of Greek Poetics from Homer to Longinus* (Oxford: Oxford University Press, 2011).
4. Alfred North Whitehead, *Process and Reality* (New York: Free Press, 1979), 39.
5. Jacques Maritain, *Art and Scholasticism and The Frontiers of Poetry*. Translated by Joseph W. Evans (New York: Charles Scribner's Sons, 1962), 128.
6. Dana Gioia, *The Catholic Writer Today* (Wiseblood Books, 2014), 33. Gioia's witty remark is a useful starting point but it will be complicated in the very first chapter of this book, in the context of Blake's testimony that his poems were the product of divine dictation.
7. Introduction to *The Consolation of Philosophy* (Oxford: Oxford World's Classics, 2000).
8. Stephen Blackwood, *The Consolation of Boethius as Poetic Liturgy* (Oxford: Oxford University Press, 2015).
9. Michael D. Hurley, 'Interpreting Dante's *Terza Rima*', *Forum for Modern Language Studies* 43, no. 3 (2005), 320–31.
10. John Milton, *'Paradise Lost': Authoritative Text, Sources and Backgrounds, Criticism*, ed. Gordon Teskey (New York: Norton, 2005),

2. On the theo-poetics of rhyme, see Simon Jarvis, 'Why Rhyme Pleases', *Thinking Verse* 1 (2011), 17–43, repr. in Virginia Jackson and Yopie Prins, ed., *The Lyric Theory Reader: A Critical Anthology* (Baltimore, MD: The Johns Hopkins University Press, 2014), 434–50.

11 On Milton's expressive style, see Gordon Teskey, *The Poetry of John Milton* (2015) and (more trained on the relation of divine and human poetic creativity) *Delirious Milton: The Fate of the Poet in Modernity* (2006), both Harvard University Press. See also Christopher Ricks, *Milton's Grand Style* (Oxford: Oxford University Press, 1963).

12 See Geoffrey Hill's observation that 'it is a characteristic of the best English writing in the early sixteenth to late seventeenth centuries' that 'style *is* faith' – but that in 'later periods', the same 'equation' is only generally achieved in ways that are 'more isolated and beleaguered': 'In most instances style and faith remain obdurately apart. In some cases, despite the presence of well-intentioned labour, style betrays a fundamental idleness which is impossible to reconcile with the workings of good faith' ('Preface' to *Style and Faith*, in Geoffrey Hill, *Collected Critical Writings*, ed. Kenneth Haynes (Oxford: Oxford University Press, 2008), 263–4).

13 David Jones, *The Anathemata* (London: Faber & Faber, 1972), 15–16. Gabriel Josipovici argues that 'modernism' is more helpfully understood to emerge out of the Reformation, whereby the sacramental religion of the Middle Ages was transformed into a transcendental and intellectual religion (*Whatever Happened to Modernism?* (New Haven and London: Yale University Press, 2010), Ch. 2). See also Theodore Adorno, 'Theses upon Art and Religion Today,' *Kenyon Review* 7, no. 4 (1945): challenging 'the notion that art has broken away from religion only during the late stage of enlightenment and secularisation': 'art can keep faith to its true affinity with religion, the relationship with truth, only by an almost ascetic abstinence from any religious claim or any touching upon religious subject matter' (677).

14 J. Hillis Miller begins his important study of faith and literature by echoing Matthew Arnold's famous figure of 'the melancholy, long, withdrawing roar' of the sea of faith, following Arnold's assumption that religious faith made a progressive retreat: 'Post-medieval literature records, among other things, the withdrawal of God from the world' (*The Disappearance of God: Five Nineteenth-Century Writers* (London: Oxford University Press, 1963), 1). By contrast, where Miller examines five writers who purportedly represent 'the culmination of a long process' of secularization, this book evaluates five writers who complicate and in some respects confute our understanding of that 'process'.

15 Daniel Headrick, *The Tools of Empire* (Oxford: Oxford University Press, 1981), 130.

16 On intimations of poetry as 'an event with a performative force', see Charles Taylor, *A Secular Age* (Cambridge, MA: Harvard University Press, 2007), 755–65. On the diverse, urgent and sometimes fraught ways in which prosody was conceived and debated, see Meredith Martin, *The Rise and Fall of Meter: Poetry and English National Culture, 1860–1930* (Princeton and Oxford: Princeton University Press, 2012). On continuities of prosodical practice and the appetite for innovation, see Joseph Phelan, *The Music of Verse: Metrical Experiment in Nineteenth-Century Poetry* (Basingstoke: Palgrave Macmillan, 2011).

17 See Taylor, *A Secular Age*; also, Doreen Rosman, *The Evolution of the English Churches, 1500–2000* (Cambridge: Cambridge University Press, 2003); Callum Brown, *The Death of Christian Britain: Understanding Secularisation, 1800–2000* (London: Routledge, 2001); Hugh McLeod, *Religion and Society in England, 1850–1914* (Basingstoke: Macmillan, 1996); *Secularisation in Western Europe, 1848–1914* (New York: St Martin's, 2000); Jeffrey Cox, *English Churches in a Secular Society: Lambeth, 1870–1930* (Oxford: Oxford University Press, 1982). On the implications for literary criticism of this newly revised account of religion in the nineteenth century, see Charles LaPorte, 'Victorian Literature, Religion, and Secularization', *Literature Compass* 10, no. 3 (2013), 277–87.

18 To cite only a few important books published in the last decade: Joshua King, *Imagined Spiritual Communities in Britain's Age of Print* (Columbus: The Ohio State University Press, 2015); Kirstie Blair, *Form and Faith in Victorian Poetry and Religion* (Oxford: Oxford University Press, 2012); Charles LaPorte, *Victorian Poets and the Changing Bible* (Charlottesville and London: University of Virginia Press, 2011); Jason Hall ed., *Meter Matters: Verse Cultures of the Long Nineteenth Century* (Athens: Ohio University Press, 2011); William R. McKelvy, *The Cult of Literature: Devoted Readers, 1774–1880* (Charlottesville: University of Virginia Press, 2007); Emma Mason and Mark Knight, *Nineteenth-Century Religion and Literature* (Oxford: Oxford University Press, 2006).

19 See Philip Rieff on how Europe's 'long period of deconversion' 'first broke the surface of political history at the time of the French Revolution' (*The Triumph of the Therapeutic: Uses of Faith after Freud* (London: Chatto and Windus, 1966), 2). On 1914 as the high tide of secularism, see Theodore Ziolkowski, *Modes of Faith: Secular Surrogates for Lost Religious Belief* (Chicago and London: University of Chicago Press, 2007), 4, 423; also, Nikki R. Keddie, 'Secularism and Its Discontents', *Deadalus* (Summer 2003), 14–30.

20 For a comparative account of Blake and Hopkins that draws upon and extends some of the material in this book: see Michael D. Hurley, 'Theologies of Inspiration and Verse Craft', in *Constructing*

Nineteenth-Century Religion: Literary, Historical, and Religious Studies in Dialogue, ed. Joshua King and Winter Jade Werner (Ohio State University Press, forthcoming).

21 Most readers draw on Coleridge's formula to emphasize 'poetic faith' as Richard C. McCoy does in his study of Shakespeare; that is, as something 'more … poetic than spiritual', having 'little to do with religious beliefs or experiences'; as something that affirms instead an entirely secular faith in 'literature's intrinsic powers' (McCoy, *Faith in Shakespeare* (Oxford: Oxford University Press, 2013), ix, xi–xii. xiii). But Michael Tomko argues convincingly for Coleridge's theological investment in the 'suspension of disbelief' implied by 'poetic faith': see Tomko, *Beyond the Willing Suspension of Disbelief* (London: Bloomsbury, 2016). For another reading of Coleridge's poetic vision as a theology of imagination, explored through selected English poetry from Anglo-Saxon to the present century, see Malcolm Guite, *Faith, Hope and Poetry: Theology and the Poetic Imagination* (Farnham: Ashgate, 2012).

22 For fuller contexts, see Ziolkowski, *Modes of Faith.*

23 See Donald Davie, 'On Sincerity, from Wordsworth to Ginsberg', *Encounter* 31, no. 4 (1968), 61–6.

24 Bernard Richards, *English poetry of the Victorian Period, 1830–1890,* 2nd ed. (1988, 2001), 182. It is telling, for instance, that one of the most important studies of faith and literature in the period, Miller's *The Disappearance of God,* ignores Rossetti entirely in favour of writers who are seemingly more conflicted. On how and why 'the secularization narrative clearly has favored the literary study of figures who are irreligious, anti-religious, or only ambivalently religious', which often means men rather than women, see LaPorte, 'Victorian Literature, Religion, and Secularization', 279.

25 Richards, *English poetry of the Victorian Period,* 182. Richards is not picked on as an egregious but as a representative example; indeed, Richards strains to avoid privileging 'modern attitudes' (86). Such is the depth of the critical bias he represents, however, that he cannot escape the assumption that 'modern attitudes' will necessarily be secular. When he comes to Robert Browning and Tennyson, he notes that, 'Like many Victorians they clung to a consoling sense that God might be there' (187) – where 'clung' and 'consoling' presume that all such faith must thrive only as an act of desperation and fear, rather than as anything authentically and positively imagined or experienced.

26 See Joshua King, 'Hopkins' Affective Rhythm: Grace and Intention in Tension', *Victorian Poetry* 45, no. 3 (Fall 2007), 209–37.

27 Alexander Pope, *An Essay on Man, Epistle III,* l. 305 (*Alexander Pope: A Critical Edition of the Major Works*, ed. Pat Rogers (Oxford: Oxford university Press, 1993), 298).

28 Pope, *An Essay On Criticism*, l. 364–5 (*Pope: A Critical Edition*, 29).

29 Maritain, *Art and Scholasticism and The Frontiers of Poetry*, 13.
30 *The Poems of Tennyson*, ed. Christopher Ricks, 2nd ed., 3 vols. (London: Longmans, 1987), II. 390. 1.
31 See Timothy Steele, *Missing Measures: The Modernist Revolt Against Meter* (Fayetteville: University of Arkansas Press, 1990).
32 'Matthew Arnold', *The Use of Poetry and the Use of Criticism* (1933; repr. London: Faber & Faber, 1964), 118–19.
33 David Jones, *Epoch and Artist*, 2nd ed. (London: Faber & Faber, 1959), 113.

Chapter 1

1 David V. Erdman, *The Complete Poetry and Prose of William Blake* (2nd ed.), 416 (l. 19–20). All quotations from Blake's writings are from this edition, cited as 'E', with page numbers; where appropriate, plate and line numbers are also given.
2 George Saintsbury, *A History of English Prosody, from the Twelfth Century to the Present Day*, 3 vols. (London: Macmillan, 1906–10), vol. 3, 9–10 (hereafter *History*). While Saintsbury recognizes the common prejudice of Blake as 'mad', a footnote reveals that this is for Saintsbury a positive recommendation: 'What is man – especially a poet – good for if he is not a little mad?'
3 'The Word "mystic" has never brought anything but confusion into the study of Blake': Northrop Frye, *Fearful Symmetry* (Princeton, NJ: Princeton University Press 1969), 431. With the notable exception of Kathleen Raine (and a few others), scholars following Frye's efforts to delineate Blake's mythology (notably, Harold Bloom) have characteristically argued the same.
4 *Lord Byron, The Complete Poetical Works*, ed. Jerome J. McGann (Oxford: Clarendon Press, 1986), vol. 5, 116. For a fuller account of 'inspiration' in the period, see Timothy Clark, *The Theory of Inspiration: Composition as a Crisis of Subjectivity in Romantic and post-Romantic Writing* (Manchester: Manchester University Press, 1997), which shows (among other things) how the term moves fluidly between 'secular' and 'divine' senses, meaning at some points 'inspired vision or passion' (e.g., sublimity), and at others, 'God given'.
5 Charles Lamb, 'Oxford in the Vacation', *London Magazine* (October 1820), 367 (n).
6 Ibid.
7 Percy Bysshe Shelley, from *A Defence of Poetry*, in *Shelley's Poetry and Prose*, ed. Donald H. Reiman and Neil Fraistat (New York and London: W. W. Norton and Co., 2002), 532.
8 S. T. Coleridge, *The Poetical Works of S. T. Coleridge*, 3 vols (London: William Pickering, 1829), vol. 1, 333. Other accounts of

inspiration circulate in the period, including by Coleridge, in his figure of the poet as an Eolian harp – but even this cosier image presents the poet as able to 'tremble into thought' only through external stimulation, such that the poet channels rather than, with careful deliberation, controls or creates. Whether Plato ever allows that poetry is the product of *technê* is a matter of debate: for an argument against, see Penelope Murray, *Plato on Poetry* (Cambridge: Cambridge University Press, 1996), 10; for arguments in favour, see Stephen Halliwell, *Between Ecstasy and Truth: Interpretations of Greek Poetics from Homer to Longinus* (Oxford: Oxford University Press, 2012), 163, 178. However much Plato might concede the role of craft in the act of poetic creation, he fixes on inspiration as poetry's primary source, and for this reason indicts poetry as irredeemably irrational.

9 G. E. Bentley, *Blake Records*, 2nd ed. (New Haven; London: Paul Mellon Centre for Studies in British Art by Yale University Press, 2004), 399.

10 Ibid., 381.

11 Sarah Haggarty, *Blake's Gifts: Poetry and the Politics of Exchange* (Cambridge: Cambridge University Press, 2010), Ch. 4 (112).

12 George Dyer, 'On Poetical Genus and its Subjection to Rules,' *Poetics* (1812): II, 29. A fuller passage from this article is quoted as an epigraph to Stuart Curran's, *Poetic Form and British Romanticism* (Oxford: Oxford University Press, 1986), 3. Curran establishes the centrality of form and genre for Romantic poetry, and for the very reason that it comes under such pressure to innovate according to Romantic notions of 'genius'.

13 See Jacques Maritain, *The Dream of Descartes* (New York: Philosophical Library, 1944); also, Theodore Roszak, *The Cult of Information: The Folklore of Computers and the True Art of Thinking* (New York: Pantheon Book, 1986), Ch. 10.

14 Susan Fox makes this argument well in her study of *Poetic Form in Blake's Milton* (Princeton, NJ: Princeton University Press, 1976), one of the few works to examine Blake's rhetorical designs. Fox's complaint that Blake's 'verbal structures have been considered too esoteric or too confused to yield any systematic rhetorical criticism' (xi) is now four decades old but remains relevant insofar as studies of Blake's vision or thought continue to far outnumber those on his style or execution.

15 This is Mackenzie's gloss on Hopkins's confessional poem 'To seem the stranger' (*The Poetical Works of Gerard Manley Hopkins*, ed. Norman H. Mackenzie (Oxford: Clarendon, 1990), 445–7 (446)).

16 Andrew Lincoln notes that if Blake thought of *America* as an intervention in the political debate stimulated by the French Revolution, the price of 10s. 6d (*E* 693) would have put it 'well out of the reach of a popular audience': 'From *America* to *The Four Zoas*', in *The Cambridge Companion to William Blake*, ed. Morris Eaves (Cambridge: Cambridge University Press, 2003), 210 (hereafter *CC*).

17 Robert Ryan. 'Blake and Religion', in *CC*, 166.

18 For a fuller account of Blake's belief in art's capacity to affect the national character by altering its religious vision, following the example of Milton, see Ryan, 'Blake and Religion', 154.

19 Christopher Rowlands, *Radical Christianity: a Reading of Recovery* (Cambridge: Polity Press, 1988), 113–14. For fuller contexts, see also Rowlands, *Blake and the Bible* (New Haven and London: Yale University Press, 2010).

20 Sarah Haggarty made the valuable point to me that, while recognizing Blake's originality, there are suggestive connections to be made with what Flaxman in practice, and Cumberland in theory, is doing with the 'chaste' outline of Greek art; and that Blake's reaction against Rubens and Reynolds might also be seen as part of the wider, systematic opposition of Venetian to Flemish artists that he adopts and adapts rather than innovates from scratch.

21 See Derek Attridge, 'Rhythm and Metre in Blake's Verse', in *William Blake in Context*, ed. Sarah Haggarty (Cambridge: Cambridge University Press, forthcoming): Attridge argues that all the poems within *The Songs of Innocence and Experience* assume the ballad beat (or what Attridge identifies as an English approximation of the Russian 'dolnik' form), with the exception only of 'The Little Black Boy', and the lines that end the stanzas of Experience's 'Little Girl Lost'.

22 John Milton, *Complete Poems and Major Prose*, ed. Merritt Y. Hughes (Indianapolis: Hackett Pub., 2003), 210.

23 See S. Foster Damon, *A Blake Dictionary: The Ideas and Symbols of William Blake* (Boulder: Shambhala, 1979). Damon draws parallels between Milton's *L'Allegro and Il Penseroso* and Blake's *Songs of Innocence and of Experience*; *Comus* and *The Book of Thel*; Milton's divorce pamphlets and *Visions of the Daughters of Albion*; Milton's political works and *America*; *The Four Zoas* and *Paradise Lost*; *The Christian Doctrine* (pamphlet) and *The Marriage of Heaven and Hell*. He calls Blake's *Milton* 'a study of Milton's spiritual development, an analysis of his errors, and an account of his relationship to Blake' (274–5).

24 'Who protects minute particulars, every one in their own identity' (pl. 38.23; *E* 185); 'Instead of the Mutual Forgivenesses, the Minute Particulars, I see' (pl. 38.61; *E* 185); 'But saw not by whom; they were hidden within in the minute particulars' (pl. 45.8; *E* 194); 'Albion I cannot be thy Wife. thine own Minute Particulars' (pl. 45.44; *E* 195); 'You shall want all the Minute Particulars of Life' (pl. 88.43; *E* 247); 'Minute Particulars in slavery I behold among the brick-kilns' (pl. 89.17; *E* 248); 'Must see it in its Minute Particulars; Organized & not as thou' (pl. 91.21; *E* 251); 'You accumulate Particulars, & murder by analyzing, that you' (pl. 91.26; *E* 251); 'But General Forms have their vitality in Particulars: & every' (pl. 91.29; *E* 251).

25 Leslie Tannenbaum, 'Prophetic Form: The "Still Better Order" of Blake's Rhetoric', in *Rhetorical Traditions and British Romantic Literature*, ed. Don H. Bialostosky and Lawrence D. Needham (Bloomington and Indianapolis: Indiana University Press, 1995), Ch. XII (185). For further contexts, see M. H. Abrams, *The Mirror and the Lamp* (New York: Oxford University Press, 1953), 184–95.

26 'Clearness and precision have been the chief objects in painting these Pictures. Clear colours unmuddied by oil, and form and determinate lineaments unbroken by shadows'; 'colours unsullied with oil or with cloggy vehicle' (*E* 530).

27 See Bindman, 'Blake as a Painter', in *CC*, 102.

28 I am grateful to David Bindman for corresponding with me on this question: fuller evaluation of Blake's later style may be found in Bindman, *Blake as an Artist* (Oxford; New York: E. P. Dutton, 1977).

29 Saintsbury, *History*, 9.

30 Ibid.

31 John Beer, *Blake's Visionary Universe* (Manchester: Manchester University Press, 1969), 14.

32 Saintsbury, *A History of English Prose Rhythm* (London: Macmillan and Co. Ltd, 1912), Appendix I, 469.

33 William Wordsworth, *Poems, including Lyrical Ballads,* 2 Vols (London: Longman, Hurst, Rees, Orme, and Brown, 1815), II, 374.

34 Alicia Ostriker, *Vision and Verse in William Blake* (Madison: University of Wisconsin Press, 1965), 102, 103, 103–4.

35 Ostriker, *Vision and Verse,* viii.

36 See Derek Attridge, 'The Case for the English Dolnik, or, How Not to Introduce Prosody', *Poetics Today* 33, no. 1 (2012), 1–26.

37 Representative comments can be found in: Arthur Symons, *William Blake* (1907); S. Foster Damon, *William Blake* (1924); Laurence Binyon, *Poems of Blake* (1931); Frye, *Fearful Symmetry* (1947); Ostriker, *Vision and Verse* (1965); Hollander, 'Blake and the Metrical Contract' (1965); Kathleen Raine, 'A Note on Blake's "Unfettered Verse"' (1969); M. H. Abrams, 'English Romanticism: The Spirit of the Age' (1970); William Kumbier, 'Blake's Epic Verse' (1978); Harvey Gross, *Sound and Form in Modern Poetry* (1984); Timothy Steele, *Missing Measures* (1990); Attridge, 'Rhythm and Metre in Blake's Verse' (forthcoming).

38 Susan Wolfson, *Formal Charges: the Shaping of Poetry in British Romanticism* (Stanford, CA: Stanford University Press, 1999), 62.

39 For a fuller account, see Ryan, 'Blake and Religion', 150–68.

40 G. K. Chesterton, *G. F. Watts* (London: Duckworth & Co., 1920), 168.

41 See Michael D. Hurley, *G. K. Chesterton* (Tavistock: Northcote House/British Council, 2012).

42 'There are two things, and two things only, for the human mind', Chesterton thought: 'a dogma and a prejudice'; a dogma is 'a definite point', a prejudice is only 'a direction' ('That an ox may be eaten, while a man should not be eaten, is a doctrine. That as little as possible of anything should be eaten is a prejudice; which is also sometimes called an ideal': *The Collected Works of G. K. Chesterton* (San Francisco: Ignatius Press, 1987), vol. 4, 48.

43 For a fuller account, including Blake's sense that amelioration might best or only come through 'an apocalyptic transformation', see Ryan, 'Blake and Religion', 150–68 (153).

44 E. P. Thompson, *Witness Against the Beast: William Blake and the Moral Law* (Cambridge: Cambridge University Press, 1994), 10.

45 *In Memoriam*, and Tennyson's notion of poetic 'drift', will be taken up in Chapter 2.

46 Henri de Lubac, *Further Paradoxes*, trans. Ernest Beaumont (London: Longmans, Green; Westminster, MD: Newman Press, 1958), 14. For further discussion of this passage, and further connections between Blake's and Chesterton's modes of thinking and writing, see Hurley, *G. K. Chesterton*, 60–1; 84, 95, 102–3 (n.17).

47 Ibid., 9–10.

48 Ibid.

49 Blake's poems of 'Experience' were published several years after those of 'Innocence', and were not initially sold together: even after the two collections did appear together in 1794, Blake continued for more than two decades to make copies of the collections separately (the two sets were not consistently printed and sold together until as late as 1818). While printed editions routinely offer a settled order for the poems, Blake sought at different stages to re-order them. See David Fuller's account of Blake's publishing history, in *Blake's Heroic Argument* (London: Croom Helm, 1988), 75.

50 John Beer offers a deft reading of this wordplay: 'Blake's Poetry and Prophecies', in *The Cambridge History of English Poetry*, ed. Michael O'Neill (Cambridge: Cambridge University Press, 2010), 440–55 (446).

51 The section continues, 'So quickly, waiting for a hand', and then across the drama not merely of a line-break, but a break in stanza, comes the negation of expectation: 'A hand that can be clasped no more –' (*The Poems of Tennyson*, ed. Christopher Ricks, 2nd ed. 3 vols. (London: Longmans, 1987), II, 325–6 (l. l–5)).

52 Ibid., I. 206. 6.

53 See David V, Erdman, '*America*: New Expanses', in *Blake's Visionary Forms Dramatic*, ed. David V. Erdman and John E. Grant (Princeton: Princeton University Press, 1970), 92–114.

54 Susan J. Wolfson, 'Blake's Language in Poetic Form', in *CC*, 68, 81. For an early and excellent account of how we cannot 'respond appropriately to his art if we confine our attention to his words alone in interpreting a form that consists of words, designs, and borders, integrally combined', see Jean H. Hagstrum, *William Blake: Poet and Painter* (Chicago; London: University of Chicago Press, 1964), 3.

55 For a fuller discussion, see Tannenbaum, 'Prophetic Form: The "Still Better Order" of Blake's Rhetoric'.

56 S. T. Coleridge, *The Notebooks of Samuel Taylor Coleridge*, III, Entry 3970.

57 David Fuller notes that Blake was not always consistent or conventional in his use of upper versus lowercase characters; nor are his spacings for punctuation marks consistent: 'Modernizing Blake's Text: Syntax, Rhythm, Rhetoric', *Romantic Circles Praxis Series*, ed. Wayne C. Ripley and Justin Van Kleeck. 25 August 2015. https://www.rc.umd.edu/praxis/editing_blake/fuller/fuller.html.

58 Ibid. Fuller quotes Bogen's findings of one of the few texts for which a variorum of punctuation has been attempted, *The Book of Thel*: of its hundred and twenty-five lines (only two of which are unpunctuated), as few as thirty-nine are punctuated identically in the seventeen extant copies. See *The Book of Thel: A Facsimile and a Critical Text*, ed. Nancy Bogen (Providence, RI: Brown University Press, 1971), 10.

59 Nelson Hilton, 'Blake's Early Works', in *CC*, 203.

60 Fuller, 'Modernizing Blake's Text: Syntax, Rhythm, Rhetoric'.

61 E. D. Hirsch Jr. claims that 'of all the Romantic poets, Blake had the most fully developed sense of humor', *Innocence and Experience: an Introduction to Blake* (New Haven: Yale University Press, 1964), 75.

62 See Andrew Lincoln, *Spiritual History: A Reading of William Blake's* Vala *or* The Four Zoas (Oxford and New York: Oxford University Press, 1995).

63 Lorraine Clark, *Blake, Kierkegaard, and the Spectre of Dialectic* (Cambridge: Cambridge University Press, 1991).

64 Jonathan Roberts lucidly observes that Blake's poetry 'is not (primarily) about the assertion of propositions; nor is it (primarily) a record of religious belief; rather it is the linguistic enactment of a religious sensibility': *Blake. Wordsworth. Religion* (London and NY: Continuum Books, 2010), 95. Roberts demonstrates how, for instance, *Songs of Innocence and Experience* is noteworthy for the diversity of its engagements (with children, the outcast, the mentally ill, the enslaved, the city, the country, warfare and peace), such that the poems collectively perform a religious faith of radical tolerance, in the way 'they are inclusive and open-hearted' (97). *Jerusalem*, likewise, while being an outspokenly religious text, also implicitly performs its religious vision through its ethic of inclusivity, in featuring Blake's home, whales, beetles, the Congo; and so on.

65 *Falling Upward: A Spirituality or the two Halves of Life* (London: John Wiley & Sons, 2011), xxxi. See also Rohr's *The Naked Now: Learning to See as the Mystics See* (New York: Crossroad, 2009).
66 Saintsbury, *History*, 19–20.
67 Even his early poems bear diverse influences, from (among others) Shakespeare, Milton, Spenser, Thomson, Chatterton, Collins, Gray, Macpherson's Ossian, the Authorized Version of the Bible, Elizabethan lyric and the ballad. Many are imitative; but they are rich in experiment too, prefiguring the intricate triumphs of sound in his *Songs of Innocence and Experience*, as well as his strong enjambments that occur throughout his later writing, especially in his long lines. On his strong enjambments, see Northrop Frye, *Fearful Symmetry: A Study of William Blake* (Princeton: Princeton University Press, 1947), 183; also Derek Attridge, 'Rhythm and Metre in Blake's Verse'.
68 Robert Lowth, *Lectures on the Sacred Poetry of the Hebrews*, Translated by G. Gregory. 2nd ed. 2 vols. (London, 1816), II, 69.
69 Howes, 'Doubts Concerning the Translation and Notes of the Bishop of London to Isaiah, vindicating Ezekiel, Isaiah, and other Jewish Prophets from Disorder in Arrangement', in *Critical Observations on Books, Antient and Modern* Vol. 2. 1776–1813 (New York: Garland, 1972), 109–449 (139). Quoted by Leslie Tannenbaum, who offers an excellent commentary on how contemporary studies of biblical poetics relate to Blake ('Prophetic Form: The "Still Better Order" of Blake's Rhetoric'). Tannenbaum notes that even if Blake had not read Howes's treatise himself, he would certainly have been familiar with his ideas, or at the very least his principles on the essential 'order' of prophetic form.
70 On the debt of Blake's long lines to the Bible and Macpherson's Ossian poems, see Derek Attridge, 'Rhythm and Metre in Blake's Verse'; on Blake's echoing broadsides, Leveller verses and other popular and sub-literary verse, see John Hollander, 'Blake and the Metrical Contract', in *From Sensibility to Romanticism*, ed. Harold Bloom and F. W. Hilles (New York: Oxford University Press), 293–310.

Chapter 2

1 'Doubt and Prayer', *The Poems of Tennyson*, ed. Christopher Ricks, 2nd edn, 3 vols. (London: Longmans, 1987), III, 249 (l. 10). All quotations from Tennyson's poetry come from this edition and are hereafter given by volume, page number and line numbers.
2 Hallam Tennyson, *Alfred, Lord Tennyson: A Memoir by his Son* (2 vols., London: Macmillan, 1897), ii, 416 (hereafter *M*).

3 John D. Jump, ed., *Lord Alfred Tennyson: The Critical Heritage* (London: Routledge & Kegan Paul, 1967), 155 (hereafter *CH*).

4 Norman Page, ed., *Tennyson: Interviews and Recollections* (London: Macmillan, 1983), 114 (hereafter *IR*).

5 Ibid., 93.

6 Ian Jack, *The Poet and his Audience* (Cambridge: Cambridge University Press, 1984), 117.

7 Observed by William Allingham (*IR* 58). For a fuller account of Tennyson's audible readings and their effects on his audiences, see Phyllis Weliver, *Mary Gladstone and the Victorian Salon: Music, Literature, Liberalism* (Cambridge: Cambridge University Press, 2017), Ch. 6.

8 'What can be done to get away from the perpetually recurring discussions of Browning's theology?' was, it seems, a familiar refrain: see F. J. Furnivall, *A Grammatical Analysis of 'O Lyric Love'* (read before the London Browning Society, 1887).

9 *The Letters of Alfred Lord Tennyson*, ed. Cecil Y. Lang and Edgar F. Shannon, Jr. (3 vols.; Oxford: Clarendon Press, 1982–90), iii. 328. In the same letter to his friend William Allingham, Tennyson bemoans that there is no 'fixed way of indicating a poet's intention as to the pronunciation of his verses'. It is instructive to notice also that in heaping his complaints about the ignorance of Churchmen over 'modern criticism' of the Bible and comparative religions, he complains also that when it comes to the rites of the mass and sharing scripture, 'they certainly cannot read aloud' (*M.* ii. 401). For incisive discussion on this last point, which has wider ramifications for Tennyson's attitude to form and faith, see Kirstie Blair, *Form and Faith in Victorian Poetry and Religion* (Oxford: Oxford University Press, 2012), 164.

10 W. H. Auden, *Forewords and Afterwords*, selected by Edwards Mendelson (London: Faber and Faber, 1973), 222.

11 Letter to Eric R. Dodds, 3 May 1947, quoted in Richard Davenport-Hines, *Auden* (London: Heinemann, 1955), 231.

12 T. S. Eliot anticipated Auden, when he claimed Tennyson had 'the finest ear of any English poet since Milton' (*T. S. Eliot, Selected Prose*, ed. Frank Kermode (London: Faber and Faber, 1975), 239); and while Eliot does not qualify his judgement, his reservations on the intellectual substance of Tennyson's verses clearly come through (see, notably, his essay 'In Memoriam'). Horne, quoted earlier, is keen to clarify that his judgement on Tennyson's mere 'music' is no outright slur: 'Be this said not in reproach, – but in honour of him and of the English language, for his learned sweetness': *CH* 155.

13 See Seamus Perry's exemplary account of Tennyson's style and the suspicions that attend it: *Alfred Tennyson* (Tavistock, Devon: Northcote House Publishers, 2005). See also Eric Griffiths on how

'Tennyson thought *in* melody' (*The Printed Voice of Victorian Poetry* (Oxford: Clarendon Press, 1989), 107).

14 *Nineteenth-Century Minor Poets*, ed. W. H. Auden (London: Faber and Faber, 1966), 22.

15 Ibid., 23.

16 James I. Wimsatt, *Hopkins's Poetics of Speech Sound: Sprung Rhythm, Lettering, Inscape* (Toronto, Buffalo, London: University of Toronto Press, 2006), 12.

17 For a fuller account of Auden's complicated relationship with Tennyson, including Auden's sense that Tennyson evaded his responsibility 'to discover a living religious faith', see John Fuller, 'Tennyson and Auden', *Tennyson Among the Poets: Bicentenary Essays*, ed. Robert Douglas-Fairhurst and Seamus Perry (Oxford: Oxford University Press, 2009), 390–408 (404).

18 Perry, *Alfred Tennyson*, 14. On Tennyson's conflicted relationship with aestheticism, see also Angela Leighton, 'Touching Forms: Tennyson and Aestheticism', in *On Form: Poetry, Aestheticism and the Legacy of a Word* (Oxford: Oxford University Press, 2007), Ch. 3.

19 Kirstie Blair, *Form and Faith*, Ch. 5 (166).

20 Quoted in *Tennyson, In Memoriam: A Casebook*, ed. John Dixon Hunt (London Macmillan, 1970), 111.

21 See, notably, J. F. A. Pyre, *The Formation of Tennyson's Style* (Madison, 1921); W. David Shaw, *Tennyson's Style* (Ithaca and London: Cornell University Press, 1976); Perry, *Alfred Tennyson*, Ch. 1.

22 *Maud* and 'The Lotus-Eaters', for instance, two of his favourite pieces to read aloud, demanded very different performances, and witnesses testify that he rendered each with high drama, but quite distinctly. For an account of Tennyson's range as a reader, see Weliver, *Mary Gladstone and the Victorian Salon*, Ch. 6.

23 *IR* 94.

24 For a fuller account of Tennyson's ideas on poetic 'drift', see Matthew Campbell, *Rhythm and Will and Victorian Poetry* (Cambridge: Cambridge University Press, 1999), who quotes these instances (167) and contextualizes them (Ch. 6).

25 Edmund Gosse, *Father and Son: a Study of Two Temperaments* (New York: Scribner's, 1907), 246.

26 On religious restlessness, see 'Wages' (1867, 1869), 'Vastness' (1885); 'A Voice Spoke Out of the Skies' (1865, 1892); 'Despair' (1881); 'Faith (1892). On interfaith truths, see 'Akbar's Dream' (1892) and 'The Higher Pantheism' (1867, 1869); also, 'The Ancient Sage' (1885), and 'Kapiolani' (1892). Ricks quotes these poems and more in his fuller account of the religious explorations of Tennyson's later verse: *Tennyson* (London and New York: Macmillan, 1972), 296–7.

27 Richard C. McCoy, *Faith in Shakespeare* (Oxford: Oxford University Press, 2013), 4; McCoy's study is predicated on this dubiously polarized distinction between kinds of faith, poetic versus religious, citing as authoritative support Anthony Kenny's reductive claim that religious faith cannot be 'true' if it is held 'tentatively': that it must indeed be held 'with the same degree of certainty as knowledge' (4). For further travesties of the status of religious faith and its relation to 'certainty' and 'knowledge', see Franco Moretti's 'Conjectures on World Literature' (*New Left Review* 1, January–February 2000, 54–68), which figures theology and its attendant faith as a fixed and arbitrary matter of total and blind allegiance. A more subtle account will be offered later in this chapter, in respect of John Henry Newman's categories of faith by 'notional' versus 'real assent'.

28 Charles Kingsley, 'Tennyson', *Fraser's Magazine* 42 (September 1850), 245–55, 245, 255. See Blair's discussion of Kingsley's account of *In Memoriam* as establishing him as a 'deliberate champion of vital Christianity' (*Form and Faith*, 176).

29 *In Memoriam* was 'what he had to say on religion', according to Benjamin Jowett (*M* i. 325); but for another great poem negotiating faith (but the faith of the nation rather more than the poet's own travails), see *The Idylls of the King*, which Charles LaPorte delineates as 'Tennyson's most arduous intervention into the Victorians' changing understanding of scripture', and as a poem that 'aims at a more profound and comprehensive engagement with the Bible than is to be found in the better-known religious vacillations of *In Memoriam*' (*Victorian Poets and the Changing Bible* (Charlottesville and London: University of Virginia Press, 2011), Ch. 2 (68).

30 T. S. Eliot, 'In Memoriam', *Selected Essays by T. S. Eliot* (London: Faber & Faber, 1933), 336.

31 Ricks, *Tennyson*, 13; William Empson, *Seven Types of Ambiguity* (London: Penguin [1930] 3rd edn. 1995), 29.

32 *IR* 58.

33 Ricks, *Tennyson*, 238.

34 Ibid., 239.

35 Shaw, *Tennyson's Style*, 226–7.

36 H. F. Lowry, A. L. P. Norrington and F. L Malhauser, eds, *The Poems of Arthur Hugh Clough* (London: Clarendon Press, 1951), 409.

37 Quoted in Ricks, *Tennyson*, 108.

38 Auditing only the opening few short stanzas by way of illustration: the 'Great Duke' ending of the very first line is repeated in the third; 'Duke' returns as an end-rhyme later too (l. 189). In the same stanza, 'fall' returns as the end-rhyme 'befall' (l. 138), and 'hall' as 'council-hall' (l. 174). From the second stanza, 'deplore' returns in line forty, and 'evermore' at line two hundred and sixty; 'for', already an auto-rhyme within its stanza, echoes widely through the rest of the poem, including in the prominent first position of the line, no less than thirteen times. In the third short stanza quoted above, 'blow' and 'low' also return as end-rhymes (l. 111; l. 182).

39 Quoted in Hugh I'Anson Fausset, *Tennyson: a Modern Portrait* (*London, Selwyn* & *Blount*, 1923), 302.

40 *CH* 349–50.

41 For a fuller account of the workings of Tennyson's stanza, see Sarah Gates, 'Poetics, Metaphysics, Genre: The Stanza Form of *In Memoriam*', *Victorian Poetry* 37 (1999), 507–19.

42 Blair, *Form and Faith*, 163. Blair's claim here helpfully directs the reader to further argument by her on this subject: 'Alfred Tennyson', in Rebecca Lemon, Emma Mason, Jonathan Roberts and Christopher Rowlands, eds, *The Blackwell Companion to the Bible in English Literature* (Oxford: Blackwell, 2009), 496–511. On Tennyson's wider relation to higher criticism, see also LaPorte, *Victorian Poets and the Changing Bible*.

43 For excellent studies of the particular tussle with faith in the poem, with special reference to science, see Eleanor Buston Mattes, *In Memoriam: The Way of the Soul* (New York: Exposition Press, 1951), 55–63; Basil Wiley, *More Nineteenth Century Studies* (London: Chatto & Widnus, 1956), 79–105.

44 A number of scholars have advanced this position, but I am indebted here to Donald Hair's lucid overview, in his 'Tennyson's Faith: A Re-Examination', *University of Toronto Quarterly* 55, no. 2 (1985–6), 185–203.

45 Perry, *Alfred Tennyson*, 10.

46 Herbert F. Tucker, *Tennyson and the Doom of Romanticism* (Cambridge, MA: Harvard University Press, 1988), 25.

47 *The Lives of the Poets*, 3 vols. ed. John H. Middendorf (New Haven and London: Yale University Press, 2010) vol.1, 175–6.

48 The 'confusion' Lewis identifies is between 'the organization of a response and the pretence of a response', and it is abetted by 'Romantic Primitivism … which prefers the merely natural to the elaborated, the un-willed to the willed': C. S. Lewis, *A Preface to 'Paradise Lost'* (New York: Oxford University Press, 1965), 55.

49 Sigmund Freud, 'Mourning and Melancholia' (1917), trans. Joan Riviere, in *General Psychological Theory*, ed. Philip Rieff (New York: Macmillan, Collier Books, 1963), 164–79.

50 Wallace Stevens, *Opus Posthumous*, ed. Samuel French Morse (New York: Alfred A. Knopf, 1957), 206.

51 *Lyrical Ballads, and Other Poems*, 1797–1800, ed. James Butler and Karen Green (Ithaca and New York: Cornell University Press, 1992), 755: 'there can be little doubt but that more pathetic situations and sentiments, that is, those which have a greater proportion of pain connected with them, may be endured in metrical composition, especially in rhyme, than in prose'.

52 Harold Nicholson, *Tennyson: Aspects of his Life, Character and Poetry* (London: Constable, 1923), 252.
53 Arthur Sidgwick and Eleanor M. Sidgwick, *Henry Sidgwick, A Memoir* (London: Macmillan, 1906), 468–9.
54 J. Hillis Miller, *The Disappearance of God: Five Nineteenth Century Writers* (Champaign: University of Illinois Press, 1963), 13.
55 Isobel Armstrong, *Language as Living Form in Nineteenth-Century Poetry* (Brighton: Harvester, 1982), 186.
56 Matthew Arnold, *On the Classical Tradition*, ed. R. H. Super (Ann Arbor: University of Michigan Press, 1960), 204.
57 See Tucker on how and why *In Memoriam* 'trades in clichés, at great and local levels': *Tennyson and the Doom of Romanticism*, 378ff.
58 Perry, *Alfred Tennyson*, 139.
59 See Marion Shaw, '*In Memoriam* and Popular Religious Poetry', *Victorian Poetry*, 15 (1977), 1–8.
60 Although Hallam Tennyson denied that his father ever expressed such a quandary (see Philip L. Elliot, The Making of a Memoir (2nd edn, Lincoln, 1995), 20, n.), the poem itself does, insistently and repeatedly.
61 See Helen Small, 'Tennyson and Late Style', *Tennyson Research Bulletin*, 8 (2005), 226–59 (232).
62 LaPorte, *Victorian Poets and the Changing Bible*, Ch. 2.
63 See Gordon D. Hirsch, 'Tennyson's Commedia', *Victorian Poetry* 8, no. 2 (1970), 93–106.
64 For further discussion of the theo-poetics animating *terza rima*, see Michael D. Hurley, 'Interpreting Dante's Terza Rima', *Forum for Modern Language Studies* 43, no. 3 (2005), 320–31.
65 For an ingenious argument on the sonnet-like halo of the *In Memoriam* stanza, see Denise Gigante, 'Forming Desire: On the Eponymous *In Memoriam* Stanza', *Nineteenth-Century Literature* 53, no. 4 (1999), 480–504.
66 Quoted in Laurence W Mazzeno, *Alfred Tennyson: The Critical Legacy* (New York: Camden House, 2004), 16.
67 Quoted in Ricks, *Tennyson*, 296 n.
68 Walter E. Houghton, *The Victorian Frame of Mind*, 1830–1870 (New Haven, CT: Yale University Press, 1957).
69 Campbell notes that Tennyson's poem entitled 'Will' was written in association with his Wellington Ode, which further establishes the connection between it and *In Memoriam*, as poems of willed word music: *Rhythm and Will*, 26.
70 See R. Keith Miller, 'Swinburne: the Will to Believe', *ARIEL: A Review of International English Literature* 8, no. 4 (October 1977).
71 'Fascinated as everybody must be by the music of his verse, it is doubtful whether part of the effect may not be traced to something like a trick of words and letters' (John Morely, quoted in, *Swinburne:*

The Critical Heritage, ed. Clyde K. Hyder (London: Routledge & Kegan Paul, 1970), 26).

72 *IR* 93.

73 Ibid.

74 *Great English Painters: Selected Biographies from Allan Cunningham's Lives of Eminent British Painters*, ed. and Introduced by William Sharp (London: Walter Scott, 1886), xxii.

75 Michael D. Hurley, 'How Philosophers Trivialize Art: Bleak House, Oedipus Rex, "Leda and the Swan"', *Philosophy and Literature* 33, no. 1 (2009), 107–25.

76 For a fuller account, see Michael Tomko, *Beyond the Willing Suspension of Disbelief* (London: Bloomsbury, 2016), 4–5. See also Frederick Burwick, whose study of *Illusion and Drama* (University Park: Pennsylvania State University Press, 1991) further elaborates the importance and ubiquity of the idea of the 'waking dream' in this period.

77 Tomko, *Suspension of Disbelief*, 1.

78 Hair, 'Tennyson's Faith: A Re-Examination', 185–203.

79 *Grammar of Assent* (New York: Image Books, 1955), 91.

80 Ibid., 245; *Idea of a University* (London: Longmans, Green, and Co, London, 1907), 275; Newman, *Grammar*, 245.

81 For a sustained comparison of the differences between the men when it came to religious authority, see 'Tennyson, Newman and the Question of Authority', *Newsletter* (National Conference on Literature and Religion), No. 6 (1 April 1985), 14–21.

82 See Joseph J. Collins, 'Tennyson and Kierkegaard', *Victorian Poetry* 11, no. 4 (1973), 345–50: 'The speaker in *In Memoriam* invokes man's free will, "O living will that shalt endure" (CXXXI, 1), as a power ostensibly coequal with the divine will; that this may indeed have been Tennyson's belief is suggested by his declaration that free will is "apparently an act of self-limitation by the Infinite, and yet a revelation by Himself of Himself"' (*M.* i. 316–17). A. C. Bradley acknowledges that since the will 'is regarded by him as "Heaven-descended"', apparently, 'in the region of these final poems and of the Prologue, "human" and "divine" are not regarded as mutually exclusive terms'. Such 'aesthetic-metaphysical' floundering in 'the fantasy-medium of possibility' Kierkegaard consistently disparaged (347).

83 Newman, 'Implicit and Explicit Reason', Sermon 13 in *Fifteen Sermons Preached Before the University of Oxford* (London: Longmans, Green, and Co., 1909), 251–77; 257.

84 Newman, *Grammar*, 245.

85 Newman draws on Locke's earlier account of 'assent', but differs by insisting that 'real assent' is all or nothing, where Locke figures it by degrees; also, while Locke recognizes the importance of rhetorical style in eliciting assent, he figures inference and assent as identical modes, whereas Newman sees them as different in kind, and therefore invests far more fully in the importance of the language through which assent might be elicited. For fuller contexts, see Michael D. Hurley, 'John Henry Newman, Thinking out into language', in *Thinking Through Style: Non-Fiction Prose of the Long Nineteenth Century*, ed. Michael D. Hurley and Marcus Waithe (Oxford: Oxford University Press, 2018), Ch. 6. Also: Edward P. J. Corbett, 'A Comparison of John Locke and John Henry Newman on the Rhetoric of Assent', *Rhetoric Review* 1, no. 1 (1982), 40–9.

86 Quoted in Ricks, *Tennyson*, 214.

87 Peter Sacks among others has complained that whereas shorter and therefore more 'intense' elegies 'leave the reader invigorated as well as comforted', the great length of *In Memoriam* 'robs it of the energetic processional drive that is so important to elegy'. Sacks, *The English Elegy: Studies in the Genre from Spenser to Yeats* (Baltimore: Johns Hopkins Press, 1985), 202.

88 See John D Rosenberg, *Elegy for an Age: The Presence of the Past in Victorian Literature* (London: Anthem Press, 2005), 51.

89 *Westminster Review*, October 1855, 191. On Tennyson's theology of idealized and universalized 'love', see his 'Doubt and Prayer', which affirms, by proper nouns, that 'Love' 'is, and was, / My Father, and my Brother, and my God!' (III. 249. 7–8)

Chapter 3

1 William Michael Rossetti, 'Memoir', in *The Poetical Works of Christina Georgina Rossetti* (London: Macmillan and Co., Ltd., 1904), liv. (hereafter *PW*).

2 Jan Marsh, *Christina Rossetti: a Literary Biography* (London: Jonathan Cape, 1994), 23, 5.

3 *PW*, lxvi.

4 The diagnosis came from Dr Charles Hare. Marsh offers the most notorious alternative explanation: that Rossetti might have been abused by her father (Marsh, *Rossetti*, 52–3). Other speculations include the suggestion that she had had a love affair, and that she was affecting her condition to avoid domestic and social duties.

5 Marsh, *Rossetti*, 50.

6 Germaine Greer, *Goblin Market by Christina Rossetti* (New York: Stonehill Publishing Co., 1975), xvi.

7 *Letters of Dante Gabriel Rossetti*, ed. Oswald Doughty and John Robert Wahl, vol. 2 (Oxford: The Clarendon Press, 1965), 391.

8 F. A Rudd, 'Christina Rossetti', *Catholic World* 4 (March 1867), 839. Quoted in Edna Kotin Charles, *Critical Perspectives* 1862–1982 (London and Toronto: Associated University Press, 1985), 32 (hereafter *CP*).
9 *Athenaeum*, 26 April 1862, 557–8; quoted in *Poems and Prose: Christina Rossetti*, ed. Jan Marsh (London: Dent, 1994), 460 (hereafter *PP*).
10 *Fraser's Magazine*, July 1864, 204; quoted in *PP* 460–1.
11 *Saturday Review*, 23 June 1866, 761–2; quoted in *PP* 461.
12 *The Examiner*, 18 December 1875, 1418; quoted in *PP* 462.
13 Harry Baxton Foreman, 'Criticism on Contemporaries. N. VI. The Rossettis. Part 1. Christina Rossetti', *Tinsley's Magazine* 5 (August 1869), 63–4; quoted in *CP*, 36.
14 Arthur Christopher Benson, 'Christina Rossetti', *National Review* 26 (February 1895), 757; quoted in *CP*, 36.
15 Ibid., 756; quoted in *CP*, 49.
16 'Christina Rossetti', *Saturday Review*, 5 January 1895, 5; quoted in *CP*, 62.
17 Foreman, 'Criticism', 62–5; quoted in *CP*, 45.
18 George Saintsbury, *A History of English Prosody, from the Twelfth Century to the Present Day* (London: Macmillan, 1910), vol. 3, 357.
19 *Literary World* (Boston) 6 (May 1876), 181–2; quoted in *CP*, 57.
20 'The Rossetti's', *Literary World*, 5 November 1881, 396; quoted in *CP*, 39.
21 Benson, 'Christina Rossetti', 758; quoted in *CP*, 40.
22 Ibid, 754–5; quoted in *CP*, 56.
23 *Literature*, 22 January 1898, pp. 66–8; quoted in *CP*, 59.
24 Edmund Gosse, 'Christina Rossetti', *Century Magazine* 46 (June 1893): 21117. For a flavour of Gosse's prosodical stringency, see 'A Plea for Certain Exotic Forms of Verse', *Cornhill Magazine* (July 1877), where he lambasts that 'vague "poetical licence" which incompetent workmen are so fond of falling back upon', but which 'in reality does not exist'. For fuller contexts, see Michael D. Hurley, 'On or about July 1877', in *Victorian Transformations: Genre, Nationalism, and Desire in Nineteenth-Century Literature ed. Bianca Tredennick* (Farnham: Ashgate, 2011), 61–78.
25 Quotations from *The Letters of Christina Rossetti*, ed. Anthony H. Harrison (London: University Press of Virginia, 1997-2004), 4 vols. Respectively, 4.377; 3.125; 1.93; 3.68; 3.185; 2.310. (hereafter *L*).
26 Saintsbury, *History*, 357–8.
27 Ibid., 353. Where Ruskin is fixated on the purported calamity of 'modern poetry', Saintsbury estimates Rossetti having studied 'nearly all the printed stock of verse before 1600', 'every poet of the slightest repute since that date, and a great many poets who

neither have nor deserve any' (I.14). Still, he cannot resist the predictable comparison with Barrett Browning, and it serves him poorly, as he lambasts Browning's 'fatal want of form' (242), and her 'horrible and heartrending cacophonies', in direct opposition to Rossetti's style (301). Yet he wishes principally to press the case for Rossetti's stylistic surety 'on her own record, without "rascally comparison"', and here, his argument is compelling (301).

28 Saintsbury, *History*, 359.

29 Gosse, 'Christina Rossetti'.

30 William Michael Rossetti, ed., *Dante Gabriel Rossetti: His Family Letters, with a Memoir* (London: Ellis, 1895), 2:323.

31 In granting that her verse offers 'felicitous music', for instance, Stuart Curran complains that she 'falls back on pretty language, the bane of so many women poets': Curran, 'The Lyric Voice of Christina Rossetti', *Victorian Poetry* 9, no. 3 (Autumn 1971), 298.

32 See Eric Griffiths on how well-meaning critics have distorted Rossetti by emphasizing her expressive agency as a female rather than a male poet: 'The Disappointment of Christina G. Rossetti', *Essays in Criticism* XLVII, no. 2 (1997), 107–42.

33 Notably, Diane D'Amico, *Christina Rossetti: Faith, Gender, and Time* (Baton Rouge: Louisiana State University Press, 1999); Mary Arseneau, *Recovering Christina Rossetti: Female Community and Incarnational Poetics* (Basingstoke: Palgrave Macmillan, 2004); Karen Dieleman, *Religious Imaginaries: The Liturgical and Poetic Practices of Elizabeth Barrett Browning, Christina Rossetti, and Adelaide Procter* (Athens: Ohio University Press, 2012); Elizabeth Ludlow, *Christina Rossetti and the Bible: Waiting with the Saints* (London: Bloomsbury, 2014); Dina Roe, *Christina Rossetti's Faithful Imagination: The Devotional Poetry and Prose* (Basingstoke: Palgrave Macmillan, 2006).

34 For right-minded complaints in this vein, see Joshua Taft, 'The Forms of Discipline: Christina Rossetti's Religious Verse', *Victorian Poetry* 51, no. 3 (Fall 2013), 311–30; Joel Westernholm, 'In Defence of *Verses*: The Aesthetic Reputation of Christina Rossetti's Late Poetry', *Renascence* 51, no. 3 (Spring 1999), 191–203. For an exemplary re-reading of Rossetti's 'faith' as it operates in her late *Verses*, however, see Joshua King, *Imagined Spiritual Communities in Britain's Age of Print* (Columbus: The Ohio State University Press, 2015), Ch. 7.

35 Algernon Charles Swinburne, 'The Poems of Dante Gabriel Rossetti', *The Fortnightly Review* (1 May, 1870), 551–79 (552).

36 Ibid., 552–3.

37 *Letters of Matthew Arnold*, ed. George W. E. Russell (London: Macmillan, 1901), I, 84.

38 'We would ask Mr. Arnold to consider whether the acceptance this poem is sure to win, does not prove to him that it is better to forget all his poetic theories, ay, and Homer and Sophocles, Milton and Goethe too, and speak straight out of things which he has felt and tested on his own pulses.' (*The North British Review* – unsigned, August 1854)

39 *Letters of Matthew Arnold to Arthur Hugh Clough*, ed. H. F. Lowry (London: Oxford University Press, 1932), 146.

40 *Matthew Arnold, The Poetry: the Critical Heritage*, ed. Carl Dawson (London: Routledge and Kegan Paul, 1973), 282.

41 It is ironic that Ruskin should have been the first scourge of her poem's apparent formal imperfections, given his thoughtful discussion of the virtues of imperfection (e.g. 'The Nature of Gothic' in the second volume of *The Stones of Venice*). But that perhaps suggests not only the difference of competence that Ruskin brought to bear on art and architecture as against poetry, but also the difference between what might count as the virtues of perfection within these distinctive modes.

42 *Christina Rossetti: The Complete Poems*, ed. R.W. Crump; notes and intro. by Betty S. Flowers (London: Penguin, 2005), 1111. (hereafter *Penguin*).

43 R. W. Crump, ed., *The Complete Poems of Christina Rossetti: A Variorum Edition*, 3 vols (Baton Rouge and London: Louisiana State University Press, 1979–90), III, 164. All quotations from Rossetti's poems are taken from this edition, cited in text by volume, page and (unless the complete poem is given) line number.

44 *The Prose Works of William Wordsworth*, ed. W. J. B. Owen and Jane Worthington Smyser (Oxford: Clarendon Press, 1974), vol. 1, 148.

45 *Penguin*, 1111. Also: R. W. Crump, 'Eighteen Moments' Monuments: Christina Rossetti's *Bouts-Rimés* Sonnets in the Troxell Collection', *The Princeton University Library Chronicle* 33, no. 3 (1972), 222–3.

46 See Crump, 'Eighteen Moments' Monuments', 210–29.

47 *PW*, lxviii.

48 See Constance W. Hassett, *Christina Rossetti: The Patience of Style* (Charlottesville and London: University of Virginia Press, 2005), and *The Achievement of Christina Rossetti*, ed. David A. Kent (Ithaca: Cornell University Press, 1987).

49 *PW*, lxix.

50 Matthew Arnold, in *The English Poets*, ed. Thomas Humphry Ward (London: Macmillan and Co., 1880), vol. 1, 6.

51 Alice Law, 'The Poetry of Christina G. Rossetti', *Westminster Review* 143 (April 1895), 444–5; quoted in *CP*, 55.

52 The quotation comes from Newman's *Apologia*, and is cited by G. B. Tennyson in the context of his useful account of the Tractarian anxiety that a concern for literary technique was 'indecorous':

'almost certainly because it did not seem fitting for exponents of Reserve to parade a concern for apparent superficialities': see *Victorian Devotional Poetry: The Tractarian Mode* (Cambridge, MA: Harvard University Press, 1981), 41.

53 For fuller contexts on the Tractarian's imaginative investment in poetry, see G. B. Tennyson, *Victorian Devotional Poetry*; Kirstie Blair, *Form and Faith in Victorian Poetry and Religion* (Oxford: Oxford University Press, 2012).

54 John Keble, *De Poetica Praelectiones acadendcae Oxonii habitae, annis MDCCCXYXII-MDCCCXLI* (London: J. H. Parker, 1844), in *The Mind of the Oxford Movement*, ed. Owen Chadwick (London: A. & C. Black, 1963), 70.

55 *PW*, 481.

56 This letter is not collected in Harrison's four-volume edition of her letters; but it can be viewed on the digital database for that edition: number 206A. Recipient Unknown, 1864.

57 Christina G. Rossetti. *Time Flies: A Reading Diary* (London, 1885), 79.

58 Quoted in J. C. Reid, *The Mind and Art of Coventry Patmore* (London: Routledge & Paul, 1957), 31.

59 *PP*, 432.

60 Hallam Tennyson, Alfred, *Lord Tennyson: A Memoir by his Son* 2 vols. (London: Macmillan, 1897), I, 11.

61 For her childhood and life-long love of linguistic play, see Marsh, *Rossetti*, 7–8.

62 *PP*, 400.

63 Ibid.

64 Oscar Wilde describes Pater's *Studies in the History of the Renaissance* in these terms (a partial quotation from a sonnet by Swinburne), in a letter to Ernest Radford: *The Letters of Oscar Wilde*, ed. Rupert Hart-Davis (New York: Harcourt, Brace & World, 1962), 471.

65 Walter Pater, *Appreciations: with an Essay on Style* (London: Macmillan, [1889] 1901), 17.

66 Ibid.

67 William Empson, *Seven Types of Ambiguity* (London: Penguin [1930] 3rd edn. 1995), 39. Empson's magisterial sweep through English literary history does not make a single reference to Rossetti.

68 F. R. Leavis, *The Common Pursuit* (London: Chatto and Windus, 1952), 30. Even where Victorian poetry is (as it often is) designed to be a 'vehicle' for 'explicit intellectual and moral intentions', in practice, Leavis argues, it is 'unable to be in essence anything but relaxed, relaxing and anodyne'.

69 For a discussion of this remark, and fuller contexts, see J. Mordaunt Crook, *Brasenose: The Biography of an Oxford College*

(Oxford: Oxford University Press, 2008), 275–6; Gordon Mckenzie, *The Literary Character of Walter Pater* (Berkeley: University of California Press, 1967), 10.

70 Matthew Arnold, 'The Study of Poetry', in *The Last Word: The Complete Prose Works of Matthew Arnold*, ed. R. H. Super (Ann Arbor: University of Michigan Press, 1977), vol 9, 161.

71 *The Poems of Matthew Arnold*, ed. Kenneth Allott, 2nd edn ed. Miriam Allott (London: Longman, 1979), 252–77 (l. 25, 29–30).

72 For an astute discussion of this quotation from Newman, see T. R. Wright, 'Newman on Literature: "Thinking out into language"', *Literature and Theology* 5, no. 2 (1991), 181–97.

73 John Henry Newman, *Essays Critical and Historical* (London: Longmans, Green and Co., 1907), Vol. II, 442.

74 Emma Mason, *Religious Intellectuals: The Poetic Gravity of Emily Brontë and Christina Rossetti* (Unpublished PhD: Warwick, 2000), 194: 'Embraced by a mysterious ritual atmosphere, the reader of Rossetti's poetry, I think, is invited to enter a reflective state wherein she might think deeply about what she purports to believe. This is important to Rossetti, not only due to her conviction that thought was the basis of faith, but because without believers qualified to analyse and so defend religion, Christianity as a system would be unarmed against secular attack.'

75 For an extended account of Newman's ideas on style, and his own practice of it in respect of his faith, see Michael D. Hurley, 'John Henry Newman, Thinking out into Language', in *Thinking Through Style: Non-Fiction Prose of the Long Nineteenth Century*, ed. Michael D. Hurley and Marcus Waithe (Oxford: Oxford University Press, 2018), Ch. 6.

76 Saintsbury, *History*, 356.

77 For fuller contexts on soul sleep, see Linda E. Marshall, 'What the Dead Are Doing Underground: Hades and Heaven in the Writings of Christina Rossetti', *Victorian Newsletter*, Fall (1987), 55–60.

78 *Penguin*, 888–9.

79 See G. B. Tennyson, *Victorian Devotional Poetry: The Tractarian Mode* (1981), which builds on Chapman, *Faith and Revolt: Studies in the Literary Influence of the Oxford Movement* (1970), to argue that Rossetti is 'the true inheritor of the Tractarian mode in poetry' (198). Emma Mason shows how Reserve extends to her 'reticent diction': 'Christina Rossetti and the Doctrine of Reserve,' *Journal of Victorian Culture* 7, no. 2 (2002), 196–219.

80 In addition to Mason's 'Christina Rossetti and the Doctrine of Reserve' cited above, as well as books previously cited by D'Amico (1999) and Arseneau (2004), see Kevin A. Morrison, 'Christina Rossetti's Secrets', *Philological Quarterly* 90, no. 1 (2011), 97–116; Krista Lysack, 'The Productions of Time: Keble, Rossetti, and

Victorian Devotional Reading', *Victorian Studies* 55, no. 3 (2013), 451–70.

81 Adam Mazel, 'You, Guess': The Enigmas of Christina Rossetti', *Victorian Literature and Culture* (2016), 44, 511–33 (527).

82 This quotation, widely attributed to Arnold, was advice he gave in the last year of his life to his friend G. W. E. Russell, recorded in Russell's book *Matthew Arnold* (New York: Haskell House Publishers Ltd, 1904), 9. For a fuller account of arguments on style and their relations with thought, see *Thinking Through Style*, ed. Michael D. Hurley and Marcus Waithe.

83 G. W. F. Hegel, *Aesthetics*, trans. T. M. Knox (Oxford: Clarendon Press, 1975), vol. II, 1012–13.

84 On the religious depths she reaches through the apparently simple idea of community, for instance, see King, *Imagined Spiritual Communities in Britain's Age of Print*, Ch. 7; on how Rossetti incorporates the Church Fathers into her poetics, see Ludlow, *Christina Rossetti and the Bible*.

85 Rowan Williams, *The Edge of Words: God and the Habits of Language* (London: Bloomsbury, 2014), 146.

86 Ibid., 136.

87 Ibid., 134.

88 *The Letters of Robert Browning and Elizabeth Barrett*, ed. Elvan Kintner (Cambridge, MA: Belknap, 1969), vol. 1, 464.

89 Even Robert Browning, in his first correspondence with Barrett Browning, commends her verse by describing it with the ambivalent phrase, 'fresh strange music': *The Brownings' Correspondence*, ed. Philip Kelley and Ronald Hudson (Winfield, KS: Wedgestone Press, 1992), vol. X, 17.

90 W. K. Wimsatt, 'One Relation of Rhyme to Reason', *Modern Language Quarterly* 5 (1944), 323–38.

91 *Penguin* 1113.

92 Crump, 'Eighteen Moments' Monuments: Christina Rossetti's *Bouts-Rimés* Sonnets in the Troxell Collection', *The Princeton University Library Chronicle* 33, no. 3 (1972), 222–3.

93 Some years later she tries to draw him out again, asking him if he can muster the 'energy' to complete (i.e. compete in) a *bout-rimés* sonnet, for which she provides the rhymes (*L* 1.93).

94 See Geoffrey Hill's insightful account of the creative unruliness of rhyme patterning in Henry Vaughan, for which he coins the term 'metaphysical phonetics': 'A Pharisee to Pharisees', in *Collected Critical Writings* ed. Kenneth Haynes (Oxford: Oxford University Press, 2008), 316–27 (326).

95 Arnold's reference to prosody as the 'mechanical part' in poetry comes from the Preface to *Poetical Works*, 1853, where he asserts that if poets and nations must only have one part of poetry, the mechanical or 'spirituality and feeling', that it 'does most harm to

Art' to have only the latter. Yet even this account that privileges the importance of prosody as literary inheritance for which poets have a duty of care presupposes a clean cut between form and content that Rossetti's practice of perfection implicitly disputes.

96 *Seek and Find* (London: SPCK, 1879), 24–5.

97 F. L. Lucas, 'Christina Rossetti', *Ten Victorian Poets*, 3rd edn (Cambridge: Cambridge University Press, 1940), 130.

98 Empson, *Seven Types of Ambiguity*, 39.

99 This quotation comes from Thomas Campion (*Observations in the Art of English Poesie* (Edinburgh: Edinburgh University Press, 1966), 4), which helpfully reminds us that rhyme-hating had a long history, but that it is also – as Simon Jarvis shows – often inflected by theological grudging: see Jarvis, 'Why Rhyme Pleases', in *The Lyric Theory Reader: A Critical Anthology*, ed. Virginia Jackson and Yopie Prins (Baltimore, MD: The Johns Hopkins University Press, 2014), 434–50.

100 *PW*, lxvii. It is striking to notice that Rossetti actually wrote two other poems entitled 'Yet a Little While'; but the broader point is that she restlessly re-worked a similar kind of impatient spiritual yearning, in poems that otherwise might look quite different as well as similar to the one that is the spur for the analysis here.

101 Chesterton, 'The Romance of Rhyme', *The Living Age*, 13 March 1920, 656–64 (657).

102 Ibid.

103 For a valuable account of how Rossetti's 'lighthearted' verse is 'wiser, less conventional, and more engaging than the uninitiated reader might suppose', see Hassett, *Patience of Style*, Ch. 3 (118).

104 Saintsbury, *History*, 356.

Chapter 4

1 *The Collected Works of Gerard Manley Hopkins: Vols. I and II: Correspondence*, ed. R. K. R. Thornton and Catherine Phillips (Oxford: Oxford University Press, 2013), II, 544 (hereafter *C* I or II).

2 *The Collected Works of Gerard Manley Hopkins: Volume III: Diaries, Journals, and Notebooks*, ed. Leslie Higgins (Oxford: Oxford University Press, 2013), 423 (hereafter *C* III)

3 Ibid. See W. H. Gardner, *Gerard Manley Hopkins* (II, 144), Sheila Deane *Bardic Style*, 27); Gardner's entry in *Gerard Manley Hopkins as a Cywyddwr* [from the Transactions of the Honourable Society of Cymmrodorion, 1940] (London: The Honourable Society of Cymmrodorion, 1941), 184–8.

4 Sonnets written soon afterwards were also influenced by the same example: 'The chiming of consonants I got in part from the Welsh, which is very rich in sound' (*C* I.267).

5 'I do not of course claim to have invented sprung rhythms but only sprung rhythm; I mean that single lines and single instances of it are not uncommon in English ... but what I do ... is to enfranchise them as a regular and permanent principle of scansion.' (*C* I.281); 'no one has professedly used it and made it the principle throughout' (*C* I.317). Although sprung rhythm bears influences of previous styles, then, it is a mistake to imagine that any single poet or tradition anticipates sprung rhythm as such. See Michael D. Hurley, 'What Sprung Rhythm Really Is NOT', *Hopkins Quarterly* 33, no. 3 (2006), 71–94.

6 Hopkins suggests that the 'peculiar beat' of sprung rhythm is evident in 'St Dorothea' (*C* I.187), but while that poem edges away from the tentative orthodoxy of his earlier rhythms, it is yet far closer to them than to his poems in sprung rhythm that begin with 'The Wreck'. See Paul Kiparsky, 'Sprung Rhythm', in *Phonetics and Phonology, vol.* 1: *Rhythm and Meter*, ed. Paul Kiparsky and Gilbert Youmans (San Diego: Academic Press, 1989), 305–40.

7 Graham Storey suggests: 'It is important to realize that the stimulus to formulate his thoughts about metre came directly from the teaching he was officially given to do' (*The Journals and Papers of Gerard Manley Hopkins*, ed. Humphry House and Graham Storey, 2nd edn (London: Oxford University Press, 1959), xxvii). Lecturing may well have helped Hopkins to clarify his ideas: but although he draws upon examples from his notes to explicate sprung rhythm for Bridges and Dixon, the notes contain nothing that specifically relates to how he would employ sprung rhythm in practice – which is far more intense, variegated and complex than parallel metrical structures he gleans from Shakespeare, Milton, nursery rhymes and other sources.

8 Robert Martin, *Gerard Manley Hopkins*: *A Very Private Life* (London: Harper Collins, 1991), 204.

9 Elsewhere: 'I cannot think of altering anything. Why shd. I? I do not write for the public' (*C* I.282). Only his 'occasional' pieces admit to being 'partly a compromise with popular taste' (*C* II.576).

10 Walter Ong, 'Hopkins' Sprung Rhythm and the Life of English Poetry', in *Immortal Diamond*: *Studies in Gerard Manley Hopkins*, ed. Norman Weyand and Raymond V. Schoder (London: Sheed and Ward, 1949). For an overview of this critical tradition as well as a valuable development of it (arguing that sprung rhythm 'was largely inspired by and a response to the aspiration of Roman Catholics to create a space for voicing their own ambiguous situation within Victorian culture'), see Joseph Pizza, 'Hopkins's Counter Stress', *Literature and Theology* 25, no. 1 (March 2011), 47–63 (49). For yet more recent studies, see Kirstie Blair, *Form and Faith in Victorian Poetry and Religion* (Oxford: Oxford University Press, 2012), Ch. 6; also, Meredith Martin's reading of Hopkins's prosody as 'a crucial site for resolving his spiritual dilemmas, as well as dilemmas about what he perceived, as an "exiled" Catholic, to be England's wavering Christianity': *The Rise and Fall of Meter Poetry and English National Culture*, 1860–1930 (Princeton, NJ: Princeton University Press, 2012), 52.

11 Eric Griffiths, *The Printed Voice of Victorian Poetry* (Oxford: Clarendon Press, 1989), 261–359 (267). See also Geoffrey Hill's richly insightful essay, 'Redeeming the Time', to which Griffiths is in part responding (*The Lords of Limit: Essays on Literature and Ideas* (London: André Deutsch, 1984), 84–103).

12 *C* III.489. Also *C* III.592: 'As we drove home the stars came out thick: I leant back to look at them and my heart opening more than usual praised our Lord to and in whom all beauty comes home'.

13 *The Poems of Gerard Manley Hopkins*, 4th edn. ed W. H. Gardner and N. H. Mackenzie (Oxford: Oxford University Press, 1967), 70, 66. (hereafter *P*).

14 See Martin, *The Rise and Fall*; Blair, *Form and Faith*; Yopie Prins, 'Victorian Meters', in Joseph Bristow, ed., *The Cambridge Companion to Victorian Poetry* (Cambridge: Cambridge University Press, 2000), 110–11.

15 The quotation is parenthetically glossed by Hopkins: '(that is, acknowledge that they have an absolute excellence in them and are steps in a scale of infinite and inexhaustible excellence)'.

16 'On the question of his inability to see that his poems might serve his religion, one should remember', Catherine Phillips and R. K. R. Thornton suggest (*C* I.47, n.20), 'that *The Month*, published by his own Jesuit province, rejected "The Wreck of the Deutschland" and "The Loss of the Eurydice", and that his local Superiors refused permission for two of his Marian pieces to be displayed; D. G. Rossetti, Hall Caine, and Patmore rejected his poems, so it is perhaps not so surprising that he felt the way he did.'

17 Although it cannot be the whole story, some anxiety of influence seems plausible, given his later admission that: 'The effect of studying masterpieces is to make me admire and do otherwise', and that even 'an echo' of other writers in one's work as 'a disease, an evil': *C* II.963, 712.

18 *C* I.70. Hopkins's injunction here reads rather like the episode in Flann O'Brien's *The Third Policeman*, when the bemused protagonist is invited to witness 'a medium fair example of supreme art': *The Third Policeman* (London: Flamingo, 1967), 72.

19 *The Collected Poems of Wallace Stevens* (New York: Alfred A. Knopf, 1975), 392.

20 *The Art of Poetry* (II. 386–9).

21 *The Collected Works of Gerard Manley Hopkins. Volume IV: Oxford Essays and Notes*, ed. Leslie Higgins (Oxford: Oxford University

Press, 2006), 161 (hereafter *C* IV). The ideal state for art is thus 'regularity of likeness tempered by irregularity or difference' (*C* IV.152).

22 See also his essay on 'The Origin of Our Moral Ideas': 'In art we strive to realise not only unity, permanence of law, likeness, but also, with it, difference, variety, contrast: it is rhyme we like, not echo, and not unison but harmony' (*C* IV.221).

23 Of certain rhymes, for instance, he writes of 'the ordinary licence of rhyming s's proper or sharp to s's flat or z's, th proper to th = dh and so on' (*C* II.594).

24 *C* I.281. He happily identifies 'outriding feet' as a licence, but yet wishes to distinguish his usage from similar effects in Shakespeare's later plays, where they are employed as mere 'licence', 'whereas', Hopkins calls his 'calculated effects' (*C* I.318). But he also concedes where his experiments founder: 'Some of my rhymes I regret' (*C* II.576); the run-over rhymes were 'experimental, perhaps a mistake' (*C* II.747).

25 For a fuller account of the moral and theological as well as aesthetic investment in artistic and poetic form by Hopkins and his contemporaries, see Michael D. Hurley, 'On or about July 1877', in *Victorian Transformations: Genre, Nationalism, and Desire in Nineteenth-Century Literature*, ed. Bianca Tredennick (Farnham: Ashgate, 2011), 61–77.

26 For a fuller account of these differences, see Michael D. Hurley, 'Rhythm', in *The Oxford Handbook of Victorian Poetry*, ed. Matthew Bevis (Oxford: Oxford University Press, 2013), 19–35.

27 Paul Kiparsky, 'Sprung Rhythm', in *Phonetics and Phonology, Vol. 1: Rhythm and Meter* (San Diego: Academic Press, 1989), 305–40.

28 Quoted in *Digby Mackworth Dolben, Richard W. Dixon, Henry Bradley, Three Friends* (Oxford: Oxford University Press, 1932), 104.

29 See Hurley, 'On or about July 1877'.

30 Norman H. MacKenzie, *A Readers' Guide to Gerard Manley Hopkins* (London: Thames and Hudson, 1981), 209, 207.

31 Quoted in J. W. Mackail, *The Life of William Morris*, 2 vols. (London: Longmans, Green, & Co., 1899), I, 186.

32 *C* I.437. A similar, seemingly pagan but actually Christian account of inspiration may be found in his account of Wales as his 'mother of Muses', or indeed 'England … wife / To my creating thought': it is the 'charge' of God in his experience of the world there that moves him, rather than the place itself: *C* II.804; *P* 101.

33 *The Sermons and Devotional Writings of Gerard Manley Hopkins*, ed. Christopher Devlin, S.J. (London: Oxford University Press, 1959), 156.

34 Ibid., 158.

35 Ibid.

36 Hans Urs von Balthasar, *The Glory of the Lord: a Theological Aesthetics*, Vol. 3, trans. Andrew Louth … [et al.]; ed. John Riches (Edinburgh: T. & T. Clark, 1986), 386. Perhaps he has Newman and his *Grammar of Assent* in mind, too, the instructive importance of which text is touched on in the chapters on Tennyson and Eliot in this book.

37 Bernadette Watermann Ward, *World as Word, Philosophical Theology in Gerard Manley Hopkins* (Washington DC: The Catholic University Press, 2002), 235.

38 The fullest and most sophisticated account of Hopkins's poetry as prayer may be found in Martin Dubois, *Gerard Manley Hopkins and the Poetry of Religious Experience* (Cambridge: Cambridge University Press, 2017), Ch. 2. I am grateful to Robin Kirkpatrick for encouraging me to see how, in Dante, 'praise style' is absolutely central from the *Vita nuova* onwards, and points to the characteristically apo/cataphatic understanding of language that guides Dante throughout. See also Vittorio Montemaggi, *Reading Dante's* Commedia *as Theology* (Oxford: Oxford University Press, 2016).

39 See Joshua King, 'Hopkins' Affective Rhythm: Grace and Intention in Tension', *Victorian Poetry* 45, no. 3 (2007), 209–37.

40 Hopkins, *Sermons*, 262.

41 See Michael D. Hurley, 'Passion and Playfulness in the Letters of G. M. Hopkins', in *Letter Writing Among Poets: from William Wordsworth to Elizabeth Bishop*, ed. Jonathan Ellis (Edinburgh: Edinburgh University Press, 2015), 141–54.

42 Ibid.

43 For instance: *C* I, 476.309 (n. 3); *C* II.903.

44 Blair, *Form and Faith*, 220–32 (222); see also Jennifer A. Wagner, *A Moment's Monument: Revisionary Poetics and the Nineteenth-Century English Sonnet* (London: Associated University Presses, 1996); Joseph Phelan, *The Nineteenth-Century Sonnet* (Houndsmills: Palgrave, 2005); Daniel A. Harris, *Inspirations Unbidden: The 'Terrible Sonnets' of Gerard Manley Hopkins* (Berkeley and Los Angeles: University of California Press, 1982).

45 *P* 101. Perhaps there is more than mere circularity going on in this poem, as Anna Nickerson has suggested to me (if 'began' provokes us to hear a subdued pun with 'begat'); but even if so, there remains a significant contrast, if only in explicitness, between the movement and redemptive promise of this poem and what occurs in the 'terrible sonnets'.

46 Graham Storey, *A Preface to Hopkins* (Harlow: Longman, 1981), 35.

47 Hopkins rightly said of sprung rhythm that it is employed to especially 'good effect' in 'passionate passages' (*C* II.705).

48 John Keeble, *Keble's Lectures on Poetry*, 1832–1841, trans. E. K. Francis, 2 vols. (Oxford: Clarendon Press, 1912), vol. II, 101.

49 Charles Taylor, *A Secular Age* (Cambridge, MA: Harvard University Press, 2007), 757–8.

50 Paul Fussell, *Poetic Meter and Poetic Form* (New York: McGraw-Hill, 1979), 127–8.

51 See Joseph Phelan's analysis of 'Spring' and Hopkins's curtal sonnets in, *Nineteenth-Century Sonnet*, 102.

52 This comment was collected from one of his undergraduates by I. A. Richards for his study of literary judgement, *Practical Criticism* (Routledge: London [1929] reprinted 1991), 87.

53 Of the three extant drafts, 'will' is underlined in line nine in one copy; in another from the same month and year (September 1880), the entire line is omitted and later added in the margin; and in another copy from the following year, 'will' is also stressed: see *The Later Poetic Manuscripts of Gerard Manley Hopkins in Facsimile*, ed. Norman H. MacKenzie (New York; London: Garland, 1991), 214, 216–17.

54 Michael D. Hurley, 'The Audible Reading of Poetry Revisited', *British Journal of Aesthetics* 44, no. 4 (2004), 393–407.

55 See Chapter 3 on Rossetti for an example of a contradistinctive verse style of symmetries rather than abruptness, in which chapter there is also mention of Rowan William's notion of language put under 'pressure' to mean more than it might, perhaps more than it intends, through the characteristically Hopkinsian technique of 'carefully calculated shocks' (Williams, *The Edge of Words: God and the Habits of Language* (London: Bloomsbury, 2014), 146).

56 J. Hillis Miller, *The Disappearance of God: Five Nineteenth-Century Writers* (Cambridge, MA: Harvard University Press, 1963), 355–6. The letter Miller quotes dates from 1 to 2 April 1885 (*C* II.722)

57 Ibid., 356.

58 Hopkins, *Later Poetic Manuscripts*, 122–5.

59 The most comprehensive and sophisticated account of Hopkins's theory of poetry is James I. Wimsatt's, *Hopkins's Poetics of Speech Sound: Sprung Rhythm, Lettering, Inscape* (Toronto, Buffalo and London: University of Toronto Press, 2006), though see my caveats on his thesis: *Modern Philology* 107, no. 4 (May 2010), 126–30.

60 Hopkins, *Journals*, 267.

61 *C* II.782 Correspondingly: 'Want of earnest' is, he thinks, 'the deepest fault a work of art can have' (*C* II.724).

62 Some pre-conversion writings appear to hint that 'Truth is not absolutely necessary for Art', and that 'the pursuit of deliberate Beauty alone is enough to constitute and employ in art'. But he only finds this to hold in the 'lower arts', and the wider context of the essay suggests an identification of truth with beauty ('Truth and Beauty then are the ends of Art: but when this is said it may be added that Truth itself is reducible probably to the head of Beauty' (*C* IV.107)).

63 Hopkins, *Journals*, 289.

64 Manuscript, D.vi.2, Campion Hall. For an astute analysis of this passage, see Tom Zaniello, *Hopkins in the Age of Darwin* (Iowa City: University of Iowa Press, 1988), 33–4.

65 *T. S. Eliot: Selected Prose*, ed. John Hayward (London: Penguin Books, 1953), 118.

66 *Wordsworth & Coleridge: Lyrical Ballads*, ed. R. L. Brett and A. R. Jones, 2nd edn (London and New York: Routledge, 1991), 266. Walter Pater, *Appreciations: with an Essay on Style* (London: Macmillan, [1889] 1901), 17. For further discussion of 'difficulty overcome', see Chapter 3 of this book, where Pater's articulation of this idea is explored in respect of Christina Rossetti.

67 Manuscript, D.vi.2, Campion Hall.

68 Hopkins, *Journals*, 276.

69 *C* II.918: 'I laughed outright and often, but very sardonically, to think you [Bridges] and the Canon could not construe my last sonnet; that he had to write to you for a crib. It is plain that I must go no farther on this road: if you and he [Dixon] cannot understand me who will?'

70 See also Martin's argument that Hopkins's habit of diacritical annotation is 'not limited to the performance or pronunciation of the poem; it is also a commentary on the perception of and connection to the realms of the natural and spiritual': *The Rise and Fall*, 57.

Chapter 5

1 T. S. Eliot, 'Leçon de Valéry', *Paul Valéry Vivant* (Marseilles, 1946), 76. See also *The Listener*, 9 January 1947.

2 *The Poems of T. S. Eliot. Volume I, Collected and Uncollected Poems*, ed. Christopher Ricks and Jim McCue (London: Faber & Faber, 2015), 53. All references to Eliot's poems are from this edition, cited hereafter as *CP*, with page and line numbers; unless otherwise stated, letters and other prose writings by Eliot that are quoted from this edition are also given with this same abbreviation.

3 Ezra Pound to Felix E. Schelling, July 1922, ed. D. D. Paige, *The Letters of Ezra Pound 1907–1941* (New York: Harcourt, Brace, 1950), 180.

4 'The Art of Poetry I: T. S. Eliot', *Paris Review*, 21 (Spring–Summer 1929), 54.

5 Ezra Pound, Canto 81; T. S. Eliot, 'The Music of Poetry', in *On Poetry and Poets* 2nd edn (London: Faber & Faber, 1957), 37 (hereafter *OPP*).

6 'The Music of Poetry', *OPP*, 37.

7 Timothy Steele challenges Eliot's rationale, arguing that he and his contemporaries mis-identify diction with metre, and metrical composition with scansion, and thus depose metre itself – which none of the previous revolutions in poetry to which Eliot refers had previously sought to do. See Steele, *Missing Measures: Modern Poetry and the Revolt Against Meter* (Fayetteville and London: The University of Arkansas Press, 1990).

8 'Reflections on *Vers Libre*', *New Statesman*, vol. VIII 204 (3 March 1917), 518–19. On the connotations of 'vers libre' as against 'free verse', see Steele, *Missing Measures*, 16–18.

9 'Reflections on *Vers Libre*', 518–19.

10 'The Music of Poetry', *OPP*, 37.

11 Ibid. He goes on to say: 'only a bad poet could welcome free verse as a liberation from form'.

12 'Reflections on *Vers Libre*', 518–19; T. S. Eliot, 'Introduction: 1928', *Selected Poems of Ezra Pound* (London: Faber & Faber, 1948), 16.

13 'Hamlet and His Problems', *The Sacred Wood* 2nd edn (London: Methuen, 1928), 100.

14 'Four Elizabethan Dramatists', *SE*, 114.

15 'Professionalism in Art', *Times Literary Supplement* [London, England] 31 January 1918, 49–50 (49).

16 For an astute discussion of these comments by Pound, and Eliot's other emendations to the poem's rhythm, see Robert B. Shaw, *Blank Verse: A Guide to Its History and Use* (Athens, Ohio: Ohio University Press), 124–8.

17 'Reflections on *Vers Libre*', 518–19.

18 Winters articulates this fallacy in his 1937 essay 'Poetic Convention', reprinted in *In Defense of Reason* (New York: Swallow Press, 1947) 64. See also Terry Eagleton's 'Incarnational Fallacy' in *How to Read a Poem* (Malden, MA: Blackwell, 2007), 59–64.

19 'The Frontiers of Criticism', *OPP*, 110.

20 Pericles Lewis, *The Cambridge Introduction to Modernism* (Cambridge: Cambridge University Press, 2007), 129–51.

21 William Empson, *Using Biography* (London: Chatto and Widnus, 1984), 189.

22 'Pound and Eliot: a Distinction', in *Donald Davie: Modernist Essays: Yeats, Pound, Eliot*, ed. Clive Wilmer (Manchester: Carcanet, 2004), 96.

23 'T. S. Eliot: The End of an Era', in *Davie: Modernist Essays*, 21, 16.

24 Ibid., 15, 20.

25 '"The Dry Salvages": A Reconsideration', in *Davie: Modernist Essays*, 226.

26 See James Longenbach, '"Mature Poets Steal": Eliot's Allusive Practice', in *The Cambridge Companion to T. S. Eliot*, ed. David

A. Moody (Cambridge; NY: Cambridge University Press, 1994), 176–88.

27 Robert Graves and Laura Riding, *A Survey of Modernist Poetry* (New York: Doubleday, 1928), 236. See James Longebach's '"Mature poets steal": Eliot's allusive practice' (cited above), for an astute discussion of this quotation (and that by Ricks on 'rufflement' quoted later in this chapter) in respect of Eliot's use of allusion in particular.

28 Writing towards the end of the twentieth century, Maud Ellmann still felt it necessary to admonish critics who have 'overlooked' *The Waste Land's* 'broken images in search of the totality it might have been'): *The Poetics of Impersonality: T. S. Eliot and Ezra Pound* (Cambridge, MA: Harvard University Press, 1987), 92.

29 Christopher Ricks, *Eliot and Prejudice* (London: Faber & Faber, 1988), 7.

30 'The Frontiers of Criticism', *OPP*, 109.

31 Ibid., 106.

32 For Eliot's changing uses of allusion, see James Longenbach, '"Mature Poets Steal": Eliot's Allusive Practice', in *Cambridge Companion*, 176–88; for his changing critical assumptions on the status of 'facts' and 'analysis', see Richard Shusterman, 'Eliot as philosopher', in *Cambridge Companion*, 31–47.

33 See, for instance, his prefaces: to the second edition of *The Sacred Wood, and* to the 1964 edition of *The Use of Poetry* & *The Use of Criticism*; also, his essay, 'To Criticize the Critic'.

34 'The Art of Poetry I: T. S. Eliot', *Paris Review* 21 (spring–summer 1929), 54.

35 'What Dante Means to Me', *To Criticise the Critic and Other Writings* (Lincoln and London: University of Nebraska Press, 1965).

36 See Eliot, 'Introduction: 1928', *Selected Poems of Ezra Pound*, 16: 'it may be only once in five or ten years that experience accumulates to form a new whole and finds its appropriate expression'.

37 A poem 'may tend to realize itself first as a peculiar rhythm before it reaches expression in words, and that this rhythm may bring to birth the idea and the image' ('The Music of Poetry', *OPP*, 38); but he also cautions: 'About such things one can only say that different poets' minds work differently and that one poet's mind works differently at different times' (*Vassar Miscellany News*, 10 May 1933 (451)).

38 'The Music of Poetry', *OPP*, 27.

39 Ibid.

40 'The Social Function of Poetry', *OPP*, 24.

41 Ibid.

42 *The Use of Poetry and the Use of Criticism* (1933; repr. London: Faber & Faber, 1964), 115 (hereafter *UPUC*).

43 'Dante' (1929), in *Selected Essays by T. S. Eliot* (London: Faber & Faber, 1933), 238 (hereafter *SE*).

44 Eliot uses these terms loosely across his writings, and sometimes in unhelpfully enigmatic ways; such as when he suggests: 'Understanding poetry seems to me largely to consist of coming to see that it is not necessary to "understand"'. (*SE*, 730).

45 'Dante', *SE*, 261.

46 'A Note of Introduction', to *In Parenthesis*, ed. David Jones (London: Faber & Faber, 1963), viii.

47 Ibid.

48 'The Metaphysical Poets', *SE*, 289.

49 *UPUC*, 152. Quoting this, Robert Crawford offers an illuminating discussion of the divisions and connections between the conception of the modern poet and poetry as both 'primitive' and 'civilized' (*The Modern Poet* (Oxford: Oxford University Press, 2001), 8; 58; *passim*).

50 T. S. Eliot, 'Tarr', *Egoist*, September 1918, 106. Eliot goes on to say: although the poet must use only 'the phenomena of civilization in expressing it', the poet's experience must be 'deeper than civilization'. For a fuller discussion, see Crawford, *The Modern Poet*, 58ff.

51 'Matthew Arnold', *UPUC*, 118–19.

52 'Yeats', *OPP*, 252.

53 Paul Valéry, *The Art of Poetry*, trans. Denise Folliot (London: Routledge and Kegan Paul, 1958), 42. Eliot recollects in 1928: 'the form in which I began to write, in 1908 or 1909, was directly drawn from the study of Laforgue together with the later Elizabethan drama; and I do not know anyone who started from exactly that point': *The Complete Prose of T. S. Eliot: The Critical Edition, Vol.* 3: *Literature, Politics, Belief*, 1927–1929, ed. Frances Dickey, Jennifer Formichelli and Ronald Schuchard (Baltimore: Johns Hopkins University Press & London: Faber & Faber, 2015), 518.

54 'The Music of Poetry', *OPP*, 36, 38.

55 Ibid., 30, 29.

56 'The Music of Poetry', *OPP*, 31.

57 Ibid.

58 From a letter by Yeats to Margot Ruddock, early April 1936. For an illuminating discussion of Yeats's remarks, and fuller contexts for poetic 'difficulty', see Geoffrey Hill, 'A Postscript on Modernist Poetics', *Geoffrey Hill, Collected Critical Writings*, ed. Kenneth Haynes (Oxford: Oxford University Press, 2008), 565–80 (567–8).

59 'Matthew Arnold', *UPUC*, 118–19.

60 John Carey, *The Intellectuals and the Masses* (London: Faber & Faber, 1992), 17.

61 Geoffrey Hill, 'The Art of Poetry', *The Paris Review*, No. 80.
62 'The Music of Poetry', *OPP*, 30. Emphasis mine.
63 'Poetry and Verse', *The Chapbook* (April 1921), 9.
64 'The Social Function of Poetry', *OPP*, 18.
65 'Swinburne as Poet', *SE*, 325.
66 'The Music of Poetry', *OPP*, 29.
67 'Swinburne as Poet', *SE*, 327.
68 Ibid. 324, 327.
69 Ibid. *SE*, 327.
70 'In Memoriam', *SE*, 337.
71 Ibid., 333.
72 Ibid., 331.
73 'Religion and Literature', *SE*, 388. Eliot offers similar sentiments in 'The Function of Criticism' and *After Strange Gods*.
74 'Dante', *SE*, 257, 258. Emphasis mine.
75 I. A. Richards, *Science and Poetry* (London: K. Paul, Trench, Trubner & Co. ltd, 1926.), 64.
76 'A Note on Poetry and Belief', *The Enemy: a Review of Art and Literature* (1 January 1927), 16–17.
77 *Knowledge and Experience in the Philosophy of F. H. Bradley* (London: Faber & Faber, 1964), 147–8.
78 See Barry Spurr, 'Anglo-Catholicism and the "Religious Turn" in Eliot's Poetry', *Religion and Literature* 44 (Spring 2012), 136–43. Spurr argues for Eliot's conversion as 'the culmination of many years of searching, both within Christianity and well beyond it' (137); and that 'he was moving towards this position for many years (arguably, from infancy)' (138).
79 *The Letters of Virginia Woolf. Vol.* 3, 1923-1928, ed. Nigel Nicolson (London: Hogarth Press, 1977), 475–8. On the ways in which Eliot's religious faith was seen to be at odds with his modernist moment, at the time and since, see Craig Woelfel, 'T. S. Eliot and our Beliefs about Belief', *Religion and Literature* 44 (Spring 2012), 128–36.
80 'A Note on Poetry and Belief', *Enemy*, 1, 16–17.
81 'Religion and Literature', *SE*, 352.
82 *The Dial* (March 1927), 243. For a fuller discussion of Eliot's reaction to Richards, see Peter McDonald, *Serious Poetry: From Yeats to Hill* (Oxford: Clarendon Press, 2002), 103–4.
83 From 'In Memory of W. B. Yeats' (section II, l. 5). Geoffrey Hill suggests that Auden's line might have been a negative riposte to Eliot, or at least that he was addressing his 'audience and its immense expectations, anticipating the immense audience Raymond Williams would have, audiences who certainly expected something to happen as a result of poetry being written by and talked about by famous people with seemingly well-worked out social programmes' ('A Postscript on Modernist Poetics', 565–80 (568–9)).

84 'In Memoriam', *SE*, 328.

85 'Religion and Literature', *SE*, 394.

86 T. S. Eliot, *George Herbert* (London: Longmans Green, 1962), 19.

87 For a fuller account of Newman's thesis on 'notional' versus 'real assent', see Michael D. Hurley, 'John Henry Newman: Thinking out into language', in *Thinking Through Style*, ed. Michael D. Hurley and Marcus Waithe (Oxford: Oxford University Press, 2018), Ch.6.

88 Barry Spurr, '"Anglo-Catholic in Religion": T. S. Eliot and Christianity', *The New Cambridge Companion to T. S. Eliot*, ed. Jason Harding (Cambridge: Cambridge University Press, 2016), 188.

89 Crawford, *Savage and the City in the Work of T. S. Eliot* (Oxford: Clarendon Press, 1988), 116–20.

90 Barry Spurr, quoted above for arguing for the continuities in Eliot's faith and practice across his career, usefully observes that 'Eliot's Marianism' is one of those places where 'we do find a sharp contrast between his earlier and his later poetry': '"Anglo-Catholic in Religion": T. S. Eliot and Christianity', 198.

91 'The Social Function of Poetry', *OPP*, 24.

92 Jason Harding, 'T. S. Eliot's Shakespeare', *Essays in Criticism* 62, no. 2 (2012), 160–77 (169).

93 'Religion and Literature', *SE*, 292.

94 Letter to George Bell, 20 July 1930. *The Letters of T. S. Eliot: Volume* 5: 1930–1931 ed. John Haffenden and Valerie Eliot (Yale University Press, 2015), 258.

95 Christopher Ricks, *Decisions and Revisions in T. S. Eliot* (London: The British Library, 2003), 96. For an astute reading of this change in the context of Eliot's conversion, see Spurr, '"Anglo-Catholic in Religion": T. S. Eliot and Christianity', 198.

96 See Donald Davie, *Ezra Pound: Poet as Sculptor* (London: Routledge & Kegan Paul, 1965).

97 'The Music of Poetry', *OPP*, 32.

98 Ibid., 36.

99 Craig Raine, *T. S. Eliot* (Oxford: Oxford University Press, 2006), 22.

100 Ibid., 24. On the same page, Raine also flatly misreads Hopkins's conversion as being motivated only by negative reasons too (fear of God and dread of Hell): see Chapter 4 of this book for a contrary account of Hopkins's positive, incarnational theology.

101 Ibid.

102 For a fuller discussion of Eliot's scepticism, see Jeffrey M. Perl, *Skepticism and Modern Enmity: Before and After Eliot* (Baltimore and London: Johns Hopkins University Press, 1989).

103 *The Letters of T. S. Eliot Volume* 3: 1926-1927, ed. John Haffenden (London: Faber & Faber, 2012), 476–7. See both the letter and the footnotes.

104 *To Criticise the Critic and Other Writings*, 40. Valéry himself claimed that 'Skilled verse is the art of a profound sceptic': See Paul Valéry, 'Concerning Adonis', in *The Art of Poetry*, trans. Denise Folliot with an introduction by T. S. Eliot (London, 1958), 8–34; 18.

105 Quoted in Manju Jain, *T. S. Eliot and American Philosophy: The Harvard Years* (Cambridge: Cambridge University Press, 1992), 250.

106 Rowan Williams, 'Poetic and Religious Imagination', *Theology* 80, no. 675 (1977), 80–178 (182).

107 *Letters of T. S. Eliot Volume* 3, 648.

108 'T. S. Eliot, The Art of Poetry No. 1' (Interviewed by Donald Hall), *The Paris Review*, Issue 21, Spring–Summer 1959.

109 'The "Pensées" of Pascal', *SE*, 408.

110 Ben Lerner, *The Hatred of Poetry* (New York: Farrar, Straus and Giroux, 2016).

111 *Letters of T. S. Eliot Volume* 3, 229.

112 See 'T. S. Eliot, The Art of Poetry No. 1'.

113 F. R. Leavis, *The Living Principle: 'English' as a Discipline of Thought* (London 1975), 174.

114 'The Music of Poetry', *OPP*, 37.

115 'To be a "devotional poet" is a limitation: a saint limits himself by writing poetry, and a poet who confines himself to even this subject matter is limiting himself too': T. S. Eliot, *After Strange Gods: A Primer of Modern Heresy* (London: Faber & Faber, 1934), 48.

116 On Tractarian poetics, see Chapter 3 in this book; also, Kirstie Blair, *Form and Faith in Victorian Poetry and Religion* (Oxford: Oxford University Press, 2012), Ch. 1; G. B. Tennyson, *Victorian Devotional Poetry: The Tractarian Mode* (Cambridge, MA: Harvard University Press, 1981), Ch. II.

117 See 'T. S. Eliot, The Art of Poetry No. 1'

118 Ibid.

119 *The Letters of T. S. Eliot Volume* 3, 700.

120 Longenbach, '"Mature Poets Steal": Eliot's Allusive Practice', in *Cambridge Companion*, 176–88.

121 'Dante', *SE*, 239, 238.

122 Ibid., 239, 238.

123 Ibid., 251.

124 I am indebted here to Vittorio Montemaggi's argument on the apophatic–cataphatic interplay in Dante's theological poetics: *Reading Dante's Commedia as Theology* (Oxford: Oxford University Press, 2016), 166.

Index

www.ingramcontent.com/pod-product-compliance
Lightning Source LLC
Chambersburg PA
CBHW071408100726
47908CB00004B/1105

9781350111639